APPLICATIONS FOR ENROLLMENT OF SEMINOLE NEWBORN FREEDMEN ACT OF 1905

TRANSCRIBED BY

JEFF BOWEN

NATIVE STUDY
Gallipolis, Ohio
USA

Other Books and Series by Jeff Bowen

1901-1907 Native American Census Seneca, Eastern Shawnee, Miami, Modoc, Ottawa, Peoria, Quapaw, and Wyandotte Indians (Under Seneca School, Indian Territory)

1932 Census of The Standing Rock Sioux Reservation with Births And Deaths 1924-1932

Census of The Blackfeet, Montana, 1897- 1901 Expanded Edition

Eastern Cherokee by Blood, 1906-1910, Volumes I thru XIII

Choctaw of Mississippi Indian Census 1929-1932 with Births and Deaths 1924-1931 Volume I

Choctaw of Mississippi Indian Census 1933, 1934 & 1937, Supplemental Rolls to 1934 & 1935 with Births and Deaths 1932-1938, and Marriages 1936-1938 Volume II

Eastern Cherokee Census Cherokee, North Carolina 1930-1939 Census 1930-1931 with Births And Deaths 1924-1931 Taken By Agent L. W. Page Volume I

Eastern Cherokee Census Cherokee, North Carolina 1930-1939 Census 1932-1933 with Births And Deaths 1930-1932 Taken By Agent R. L. Spalsbury Volume II

Eastern Cherokee Census Cherokee, North Carolina 1930-1939 Census 1934-1937 with Births and Deaths 1925-1938 and Marriages 1936 & 1938 Taken by Agents R. L. Spalsbury And Harold W. Foght Volume III

Seminole of Florida Indian Census, 1930-1940 with Birth and Death Records, 1930-1938

Texas Cherokees 1820-1839 A Document For Litigation 1921

Choctaw By Blood Enrollment Cards 1898-1914 Volumes I thru XVII

Starr Roll 1894 (Cherokee Payment Rolls) Districts: Canadian, Cooweescoowee, and Delaware Volume One

Starr Roll 1894 (Cherokee Payment Rolls) Districts: Flint, Going Snake, and Illinois Volume Two

Starr Roll 1894 (Cherokee Payment Rolls) Districts: Saline, Sequoyah, and Tahlequah; Including Orphan Roll Volume Three

Other Books and Series by Jeff Bowen

Cherokee Intruder Cases Dockets of Hearings 1901-1909 Volumes I & II

Indian Wills, 1911-1921 Records of the Bureau of Indian Affairs
Books One thru Seven;

Native American Wills & Probate Records 1911-1921

Turtle Mountain Reservation Chippewa Indians 1932 Census with Births & Deaths, 1924-1932

Chickasaw By Blood Enrollment Cards 1898-1914 Volume I thru V

Cherokee Descendants East An Index to the Guion Miller Applications Volume I
Cherokee Descendants West An Index to the Guion Miller Applications Volume II (A-M)
Cherokee Descendants West An Index to the Guion Miller Applications Volume III (N-Z)

Visit our website at **www.nativestudy.com** to learn more about these
and other books and series by Jeff Bowen

Originally published:
Baltimore, Maryland
2012

Reprinted by:

Native Study LLC
Gallipolis, OH
www.nativestudy.com
2020

Library of Congress Control Number: 2020915851

ISBN: 978-1-64968-038-9

Credit for cover image is given to the Florida Memory State Library
and Archives website. Image titled "Seminole Indian and Papoose, Miami, Fla."

Made in the United States of America.

This series is dedicated to the descendants of the
Seminole Newborn Freedmen listed in these applications
and
The best librarian, ever, Randall Fulks.

Commissioner to the Five Civilized Tribes.

NOTICE.

Opening of Land Office at Wewoka,

IN THE SEMINOLE NATION, INDIAN TERRITORY.

Notice is hereby given that on Monday, September 4, 1905, the Commissioner to the Five Civilized Tribes will establish a land office at Wewoka, in the Seminole Nation, Indian Territory, for the purpose of allowing citizens and freedmen of the Seminole Nation to select allotments of land for their minor children enrolled under the Act of Congress approved March 3, 1905 (33 Stat. L 1060), and for the further purpose of allowing citizens and freedmen of the Seminole Nation, whose allotments are incomplete, to select additional land in order to bring the value of their allotments up to the standard of $309.09, as nearly as may be practicable.

Each child whose enrollment in accordance with the Act of March 3, 1905, has been duly approved by the Secretary of the Interior, is entitled to receive an alllotment of forty acres without regard to the character or value of the land selected.

Selection of allotments for minor children must be made by their citizen or freedmen parents or by a duly appointed guardian, or curator, or by a duly appointed administrator.

TAMS BIXBY,
Commissioner.

Muskogee, Indian Territory,
July 29, 1905.

This particular notice makes mention of the Act of 1905. The Creek and Seminole were closely related tribes. Both tribes' notices were like similar in nature.

v

Seminole Newborn Freedman (Sem.Fr.NB.41) had eight pictures included with case stating that the pictures were placed in the file for safekeeping. Only four of the images were of the quality for reproduction. It was felt that the pictures needed to be reproduced with the hope that maybe someone might be able to connect the images with their family history.

The image above isn't clear enough for any form of identification but the genealogical significance from the label in the upper left hand corner, "Blanton School" may help any family members research. This photo was also included with Seminole Newborn Freedman (Sem.Fr.NB.41)

INTRODUCTION

The *Applications for Enrollment of Seminole Newborn Freedmen Act of 1905,* National Archive film M-1301, Roll 402 are found under the heading of Applications for Enrollment of the Commission to the Five Civilized Tribes. For this book, I have transcribed the application forms filled out by individuals applying for enrollment in the Five Civilized Tribes under the Dawes Commission. These applications contain considerably more information than stated on the census cards found in series M-1186. M-1301 (Seminole Newborn Freedmen by Birth) possesses its own numerical sequence, separate from M-1186. To find each party's roll number you would have to reference M-1186.

Interestingly enough, it seems as if the Seminole Freedmen, as they were called, were the only African-Americans that legitimately had a right to any tribal allotments within the tribes. Unlike the other Five Civilized Tribes, which held African-Americans as slaves, the Seminole adopted blacks into their tribe as Seminoles. The other tribes, such as the Chickasaw, fought very hard for the right to not share their lands while the other three tribes reluctantly gave in to pressure from the government. These tribes felt as though they were the owners of their lands, not their former slaves. Most members of the four other tribes felt this way because they had lost their lands in the East and they had signed new treaties with the United States, although a few disagreed. "The Cherokees, Creeks, Chickasaws and Choctaws all had taken from the Euro-Americans the practice of black slavery, while the Seminoles chose to adopt blacks into their bands."[1]

The freedmen from all tribes faced problems when it came to trying to find a home because they were so unpopular. According to the Dawes Commission, "There was opposition to freedmen in all tribes, but the commission had met less of it when it tried to enroll Creeks and Seminoles because intermarriage with them was much more common and accepted in those tribes than it was among the Choctaws and Chickasaws. A Choctaw law of 1883 specified that intermarriage with 'freedmen of African descent' did not confer rights of citizenship, and the Chickasaws had similar laws to discourage intermarriage. If the commission followed 'tribal laws, customs, and usages' as required in the Curtis Act, then it would have to consider any children of a mixed marriage freedmen rather than citizens by blood. That, of course, was common custom not only among the Five Civilized Tribes but throughout the South in this period. The rights of children of mixed marriages became one of the most bitter and long running controversies of the entire enrollment period."[2]

The applicants in this series for the most part make mention of their tribal adoption status. While many give an approximate age, some are more precise, including a fifty-two year-old who filed an application for their newborn. It is hard to believe that

---

[1] The WPA Oklahoma Slave Narratives, Baker, pg. 5.

[2] The Dawes Commission and the Allotment of the Five Civilized Tribes, 1893-1914, p. 71

in 1905 there was a separation of only forty years from the end of the Civil War and slavery itself.

As was found previously in my Seminole Newborn series there are some application numbers with more than one applicant's name included. The film's title stated that there were 92 applications, but during transcription it was found that many applicants were able to use the same claim numbers multiple times with different children's names, resulting in 56 additional applications.

The explanation of what it took to qualify as a Newborn Seminole can be found within the following statute:

"That the Commission to the Five Civilized Tribes is authorized for ninety days after the date of the approval of this act to receive and consider applications for enrollment of infant children born prior to March fourth, nineteen hundred and five, and living on said latter date, to citizens of the Seminole tribe whose enrollment has been approved by the Secretary of the Interior; and to enroll and make allotments to such children, giving to each an equal number of acres of land and such children shall also share equally with other citizens of the Seminole tribe in the distribution of all other tribal property and funds."[3]

Besides the applications themselves, researchers will find the identities of other individuals within these applications—doctors, lawyers, mid-wives, and other relatives— that may help with your genealogical research. Since the Creek and Seminole tribes were so closely related, this volume will complement my recent fourteen-volume Creek newborn series and two-volume Seminole newborn series.

Jeff Bowen
Gallipolis, Ohio
NativeStudy.com

---

[3] Annual Reports of the Department of the Interior For the Fiscal Year Ended June 30, 1905, p. 607.

Applications for Enrollment of Seminole Newborn Freedmen
Act of 1905

Sem. Freed.
N B 1

Muskogee, Indian Territory, June 29, 1905.

Amey,
Wewoka, Indian Territory.

Dear Madam:

On May 3, 1905 you appeared before the Commission and made application for the enrollment of your son Cleveland Add as a Seminole freedman and at that time submitted your affidavit only as to the birth of said child. It will be necessary, before the rights of said child can be finally determined, for you to supply the Commission with the affidavit of the attending physician or midwife at the birth of said child, or in case no midwife or physician attended you at the birth it will be necessary for you to furnish the Commission with the affidavits of two disinterested persons who know the circumstances attending the birth of said Cleveland Add, when he was born and whether or not he was living March 4, 1905.

Respectfully,

Chairman.

CD-1

Sem. Freed.
NB-1.

Muskogee, Indian Territory, June 29, 1905.

Commission to the Five Civilized Tribes,
Creek Enrollment Division.

Gentlemen:

On May 3, 1905 there were filed with this Commission applications for the enrollment of Cleveland Add, born December 30, 1901, and Leroy Add, born October 5, 1903, as Seminole freedmen. It is stated in said applications that the father of said children is Albert Add, a citizen by adoption of the Creek Nation, and that their mother is Amey, a citizen by adoption of the Seminole Nation.

You are requested to inform the Seminole Enrollment Division as to whether application has been made to the Commission for the enrollment of Cleveland Add and Leroy Add as citizens of the Creek Nation and if so what disposition, if any, has been made of such application.

Applications for Enrollment of Seminole Newborn Freedmen
Act of 1905

Respectfully,

Chairman.

DEPARTMENT OF THE INTERIOR.
COMMISSION TO THE FIVE CIVILIZED TRIBES.

Muskogee, Indian Territory, July 13, 1905.

Commissioner to the Five Civilized Tribes,
    Seminole Enrollment Division,
        Muskogee, Indian Territory.

Gentlemen:

    Receipt is acknowledged of your communication of June 29, 1905 (Sem.Fr.NB.1), in which you ask if application for the enrollment as a citizen of the Creek Nation has been made for Cleveland and Leroy Add, children of Albert Add, a citizen of the Creek Nation and Amey, a citizen by adoption of the Seminole Nation.

    In reply you are advised that the records of this office have been examined and it does not appear that application has been made for the enrollment of said children as citizens of the Creek Nation.

                Respectfully,

                        Tams Bixby
                        Commissioner.

W.O.B.

REFER IN REPLY TO THE FOLLOWING:
Sem N B F 1

DEPARTMENT OF THE INTERIOR,
COMMISSIONER TO THE FIVE CIVILIZED TRIBES.

Muskogee, Indian Territory, December 29, 1905.

McKennon & Willmott,
    Attorneys for the Seminoles,
        Wewoka, Indian Territory.

Gentlemen:

    On May 3, 1905, application was made to the Commission to the Five Civilized Tribes for the enrollment of Cleveland Add as a new born Seminole freedman under the provisions of the act of Congress approved March 3, 1905.

2

Applications for Enrollment of Seminole Newborn Freedmen
Act of 1905

It appears that this child was born December 30, 19C1, and is the son of Amey whose name appears upon the final roll of citizens of the Seminole Nation opposite Number 1906.

There is on file with the records of this office the affidavit of Amey to the birth of Cleveland Add December 30, 1901. It is desired that there be supplied at the earliest practicable date the affidavits of the attending physician or midwife at the birth of said child or the affidavits of two disinterested parties who have actual knowledge of the birth of the child and that he is the son of Amey and was living on March 4, 1905. Please give this matter your early attention.

Respectfully,

Tams Bixby
B C
Commissioner.

Sem. Fr. NB 1

Muskogee, Indian Territory, June 19, 1906.

McKennon & Wilmot[sic],
Attorneys for Seminoles,
Wewoka, Indian Territory.

Gentlemen:

Receipt is hereby acknowledged of the affidavit of Betsy Johnson to the birth of Cleveland Add and the same has been filed in the matter of the enrollment of said child.

Respectfully,

Commissioner.

REFER IN REPLY TO THE FOLLOWING:

DEPARTMENT OF THE INTERIOR,
COMMISSIONER TO THE FIVE CIVILIZED TRIBES.

Muskogee, Indian Territory, December 22, 1906.

Chief Clerk,
Seminole Enrollment Division.

Dear Sir:

Receipt is hereby acknowledged of your letter under date of December 15, 1906 requesting information as to whether application has been made for the enrollment of

3

Applications for Enrollment of Seminole Newborn Freedmen
Act of 1905

Cleveland Add child of Albert Add, a citizen of the Creek Nation, and Amey Add, a citizen of the Seminole Nation, as a citizen of the Creek Nation under the Act of Congress approved April 26, 1906.

In reply you are advised that it does not appear from the records of this office that application has been made for the enrollment of said Cleveland Add as a citizen of the Creek Nation.

Respectfully,

Wm O. Beall,
Acting Commissioner.

Department of the Interior.
Commissioner to the Five Civilized Tribes,
MUSKOGEE, IND. TER,

Amey,
Wewoka, Indian Territory.

AP

REFER IN REPLY TO THE FOLLOWING:
Sem Fr NB-1

DEPARTMENT OF THE INTERIOR,
COMMISSIONER TO THE FIVE CIVILIZED TRIBES.

Muskogee, Indian Territory, March 4, 1907.

Amey,
Wewoka, Indian Territory.

Dear Madam:

You are hereby advised that on February 12, 1907, the Secretary of the Interior approved the enrollment of your child, Cleveland Add as a Seminole freedman, under the Act of Congress approved March 3, 1905, and his name appears upon the roll of such freedmen enrolled under said Act, opposite No. 123.

Respectfully,

Tams Bixby   Commissioner.

4

Applications for Enrollment of Seminole Newborn Freedmen
Act of 1905

Department of the Interior.
Commissioner to the Five Civilized Tribes,
MUSKOGEE, IND. TER,

Amey,
      Wewoka, Indian Territory.

AP

REFER IN REPLY TO THE FOLLOWING:
Sem-Fr-NB-1.

DEPARTMENT OF THE INTERIOR,
COMMISSIONER TO THE FIVE CIVILIZED TRIBES.

Muskogee, Indian Territory, April 15, 1907.

Amey,
      Wewoka, Indian Territory.

Dear Madam:

You are hereby advised that on February 12, 1907, the Secretary of the Interior approved the enrollment of your minor child, Cleveland Add, as a new born Seminole freedman, and his name appears on the final roll of such citizens of the Seminole Nation opposite No. 123.

Respectfully,

Tams Bixby   Commissioner.

Sem NB F 1
BIRTH AFFIDAVIT.
DEPARTMENT OF THE INTERIOR.
COMMISSION TO THE FIVE CIVILIZED TRIBES.

IN RE APPLICATION FOR ENROLLMENT, as a citizen of the   Seminole   Nation, of
Cleveland Add   , born on the 30 day of December , 1901

Name of Father:	Albert Add	a citizen of the Creek	Nation.
Name of Mother:	Amey (Add)	a citizen of the Seminole	Nation.

Postoffice   Wewoka I.T.

5

Applications for Enrollment of Seminole Newborn Freedmen
Act of 1905

UNITED STATES OF AMERICA, Indian Territory, ⎫
Western   DISTRICT.   ⎭

I, Betsey Johnson   , a   Midwife   , on oath state that I attended on Mrs. Amey (Add)   , wife of   Albert Add   on the   30 day of   December , 1901; that there was born to her on said date a   male   child; that said child was living March 4, 1905, and is said to have been named   Cleveland Add   is still living

Witnesses To Mark:
⎰ John W. Willmott
⎱ J.G. Mayhill

Betsey Johnson x

her

mark

Subscribed and sworn to before me   26   day of   May   , 1906.

John W. Willmott
Notary Public.

My com exp's
Oct. 5-1906

Sem NB F 1

IN RE APPLICATION FOR ENROLLMENT, as a citizen of the   Seminole   Nation, of Cleveland Add   , born on the 30   day of Dec   , 1901

Name of Father: Albert Add   a citizen of the   Creek   Nation.
Name of Mother: Amey   (1906)   a citizen of the   Seminole   Nation.

Postoffice   Wewoka

Child present

UNITED STATES OF AMERICA, Indian Territory, ⎫
Western   DISTRICT.   ⎭

I,   Amey   , on oath state that I am   21   years of age and a citizen by adoption   , of the   Seminole   Nation; that I am not the lawful wife of   Albert Add, who is a citizen, by adoption   of the   Creek   Nation; that a   male

6

Applications for Enrollment of Seminole Newborn Freedmen
Act of 1905

child was born to me on 30   day of   Dec.   , 1901; that said child has been named
Cleveland Add   , and was living March 4, 1905.

her

Witnesses To Mark: Amey x
  { Chas E Webster   mark
  { Frank C. Sabourin

    Subscribed and sworn to before me this 3rd day of   May   , 1905.

Chas E Webster
Notary Public.

Sem NB F 1
BIRTH AFFIDAVIT.

DEPARTMENT OF THE INTERIOR.
COMMISSION TO THE FIVE CIVILIZED TRIBES.

    IN RE APPLICATION FOR ENROLLMENT, as a citizen of the   Seminole   Nation, of
Leroy Add   , born on the 5 day of Octo , 1903

Name of Father: Albert Add   a citizen of the   Creek   Nation.
Name of Mother: Amey   (1906)   a citizen of the   Seminole   Nation.

Postoffice   Wewoka, I.T.

AFFIDAVIT OF MOTHER.

UNITED STATES OF AMERICA, Indian Territory,⎱
    Western   **DISTRICT.** ⎰

    I,   Amey   , on oath state that I am   21   years of age and a citizen by
adoption   , of the   Seminole   Nation; that I am not the lawful wife of   Albert
Add   , who is a citizen, by adoption   of the   Creek   Nation; that a
male   child was born to me on 5 day of Octo   , 1903; that said child has been
named   Leroy Add   , and was living March 4, 1905.

her

Witnesses To Mark: Amey x
  { Chas E Webster   mark
  { Frank C. Sabourin

7

Applications for Enrollment of Seminole Newborn Freedmen
Act of 1905

Subscribed and sworn to before me this 3 day of   May   , 1905.

Chas E Webster
Notary Public.

AFFIDAVIT OF ATTENDING PHYSICIAN OR MID-WIFE.

UNITED STATES OF AMERICA, Indian Territory,
Western   DISTRICT.

I,   Peggie Kelley   , a   midwife   , on oath state that I attended on
Mrs.   Amey   , ~~wife of~~   and that   on the 5 day of   Octo   , 1903; that there
was born to her on said date a   male   child; that said child was living March 4, 1905,
and is said to have been named Leroy Add

her
Peggie x Kelley
Witnesses To Mark: mark
  ⎰ Chas E Webster
  ⎱ Frank C. Sabourin

Subscribed and sworn to before me 3 day of   May   , 1905.

Chas E Webster
Notary Public.

Sem NB FR 2
BIRTH AFFIDAVIT.
DEPARTMENT OF THE INTERIOR.
COMMISSION TO THE FIVE CIVILIZED TRIBES.

IN RE APPLICATION FOR ENROLLMENT, as a citizen of the   Seminole   Nation, of
Lucy Noble   , born on the 2nd   day of   March , 1901

Name of Father: Nero Noble (870)   a citizen of the   Seminole   Nation.
                          (1939)
Name of Mother: Rachael Noble (nee Carter)   a citizen of the   Seminole   Nation.

Postoffice   Tidmore I.T.

8

Applications for Enrollment of Seminole Newborn Freedmen
Act of 1905

Child present

_____

AFFIDAVIT OF MOTHER.

UNITED STATES OF AMERICA, Indian Territory, ⎱
   Western   DISTRICT. ⎰

    I,   Rachael Noble   , on oath state that I am 22   years of age and a citizen by   adoption   , of the   Seminole   Nation; that I am the lawful wife of   Nero Noble   , who is a citizen, by blood   of the   Seminole   Nation; that a female   child was born to me on 2nd day of   March   , 1901; that said child has been named   Lucy Noble   , and was living March 4, 1905.

Rachel Noble

Witnesses To Mark:
⎰
⎱

    Subscribed and sworn to before me this 11th day of   May   , 1905.

Chas E Webster
Notary Public.

_____

AFFIDAVIT OF ATTENDING PHYSICIAN OR MID-WIFE.

UNITED STATES OF AMERICA, Indian Territory, ⎱
   Western   DISTRICT. ⎰

    I,   Becca Carter   , a midwife   , on oath state that I attended on Mrs. Rachael Noble   , wife of   Nero Noble   on the 2nd day of   March , 1901; that there was born to her on said date a   female   child; that said child was living March 4, 1905, and is said to have been named   Lucy Noble

her
Becca x Carter
mark

Witnesses To Mark:
⎰ Frank C. Sabourin
⎱ Chas E Webster

    Subscribed and sworn to before me 11th day of   May   , 1905.

Chas E Webster
Notary Public.

_____

Applications for Enrollment of Seminole Newborn Freedmen
Act of 1905

Sem NB FR 2
BIRTH AFFIDAVIT.

DEPARTMENT OF THE INTERIOR.
COMMISSION TO THE FIVE CIVILIZED TRIBES.

IN RE APPLICATION FOR ENROLLMENT, as a citizen of the   Seminole   Nation, of Albert Noble , born on the   29   day of   September , 1904

Name of Father: Nero Noble   (870)   a citizen of the   Seminole   Nation.
                                  (1939)
Name of Mother: Rachael Noble (nee Carter)   a citizen of the   Seminole   Nation.

               Postoffice   Tidmore I.T.

Child present

AFFIDAVIT OF MOTHER.

UNITED STATES OF AMERICA, Indian Territory, ⎱
   Western   DISTRICT. ⎰

     I,   Rachael Noble   , on oath state that I am   22   years of age and a citizen by adoption   , of the   Seminole   Nation; that I am the lawful wife of   Nero Noble , who is a citizen, by   blood   of the   Seminole   Nation; that a   male   child was born to me on   29   day of   September , 1904, that said child has been named Albert Noble   , and is now living.

                                Rachel Noble

Witnesses To Mark:
    {

     Subscribed and sworn to before me this   11th   day of   May   , 1905.

                      Chas E Webster
                      Notary Public.

AFFIDAVIT OF ATTENDING PHYSICIAN OR MID-WIFE.

UNITED STATES OF AMERICA, Indian Territory, ⎱
   Western   DISTRICT. ⎰

     I,   Lottie King   , a   midwife   , on oath state that I attended on Mrs.   Rachael Noble   , wife of   Nero Noble   on the   29   day of September , 1904; that there was born to her on said date a   male   child; that said child is now living and is said to have been named   Albert Noble

                           her
                   Lottie   x   King
                       mark

Applications for Enrollment of Seminole Newborn Freedmen
Act of 1905

Witnesses To Mark:
  { Frank C. Sabourin
  { Chas E Webster

Subscribed and sworn to before me this 11th day of   May   , 1905.

Chas E Webster
Notary Public.

Sem NB FR 2
BIRTH AFFIDAVIT.

DEPARTMENT OF THE INTERIOR.
COMMISSION TO THE FIVE CIVILIZED TRIBES.

IN RE APPLICATION FOR ENROLLMENT, as a citizen of the   Seminole   Nation, of
Cora Noble   , born on the 10   day of   January , 1903

Name of Father: Nero Noble   (870)   a citizen of the   Seminole   Nation.
Name of Mother: Rachael Noble (nee Carter)   a citizen of the   Seminole   Nation.

Postoffice   Tidmore I.T.

Child present

AFFIDAVIT OF MOTHER.

UNITED STATES OF AMERICA, Indian Territory, }
  Western   **DISTRICT.** }

  I,   Rachael Noble   , on oath state that I am   22   years of age and a citizen
by   adoption   , of the   Seminole   Nation; that I am the lawful wife of   Nero
Noble   , who is a citizen, by blood   of the   Seminole   Nation; that a
female   child was born to me on   10   day of   January   , 1903; that said child
has been named   Cora Noble   , and was living March 4, 1905.

Rachel Noble

Witnesses To Mark:
  {

Subscribed and sworn to before me this 11th   day of   May   , 1905.

Chas E Webster
Notary Public.

11

Applications for Enrollment of Seminole Newborn Freedmen
Act of 1905

UNITED STATES OF AMERICA, Indian Territory,
    Western   DISTRICT.

I,   Lizzie Moore   , a midwife   , on oath state that I attended on Mrs. Rachael Noble   , wife of   Nero Noble   on the 10 day of   January   , 1903; that there was born to her on said date a   female   child; that said child was living March 4, 1905, and is said to have been named Cora Noble

her

Lizzie x Moore

mark

Witnesses To Mark:
    Frank C. Sabourin
    Chas E Webster

Subscribed and sworn to before me 11th day of   May   , 1905.

Chas E Webster

Notary Public.

Sem NB FR 3
BIRTH AFFIDAVIT.

DEPARTMENT OF THE INTERIOR.
COMMISSION TO THE FIVE CIVILIZED TRIBES.

IN RE APPLICATION FOR ENROLLMENT, as a citizen of the   Seminole   Nation, of Edie Jackson   , born on the 30 day of Octo , 1904

Name of Father: Davis Jackson   1961   a citizen of the Seminole Nation.
Name of Mother: Emma Payne   2315   a citizen of the Seminole Nation.

Postoffice   Wewoka IT

Applications for Enrollment of Seminole Newborn Freedmen
Act of 1905

(Child present)

UNITED STATES OF AMERICA, Indian Territory, ⎱
Western   DISTRICT. ⎰

I,   Emma Payne   , on oath state that I am   21   years of age and a citizen by adoption   , of the   Seminole   Nation; that I am not the lawful wife of   Davis Jackson   , who is a citizen, by   adoption   of the   Seminole   Nation; that a   Female   child was born to me on   30   day of   Octo   , 1904; that said child has been named   Edie Jackson   , and was living March 4, 1905.

Emma Payne

Witnesses To Mark:
{

Subscribed and sworn to before me this 2 day of   May   , 1905.

Chas E Webster
Notary Public.

_____

AFFIDAVIT OF ATTENDING PHYSICIAN OR MID-WIFE.

UNITED STATES OF AMERICA, Indian Territory, ⎱
Western   DISTRICT. ⎰

I,   Lydia Fields   , a   midwife   , on oath state that I attended on Mrs.   Emma Payne   , ~~wife of~~ on the   30   day of   Octo   , 1904; that there was born to her on said date a   Female   child; that said child was living March 4, 1905, and is said to have been named   Edie Jackson

Lydia Fields

Witnesses To Mark:
{

Subscribed and sworn to before me 2 day of   May   , 1905.

Chas E Webster
Notary Public.

_____

13

Applications for Enrollment of Seminole Newborn Freedmen
Act of 1905

Sem NB FR 3
BIRTH AFFIDAVIT.

DEPARTMENT OF THE INTERIOR.
COMMISSION TO THE FIVE CIVILIZED TRIBES.

IN RE APPLICATION FOR ENROLLMENT, as a citizen of the   Seminole   Nation, of
Nettie Jackson   , born on the 1st day of   August   , 1902

Name of Father: Davis Jackson   (2315)   a citizen of the   Seminole   Nation.
Name of Mother: Emma Payne   (1961)   a citizen of the   Seminole   Nation.

Postoffice   Wewoka IT

(more evidence needed)   OK

AFFIDAVIT OF MOTHER.

UNITED STATES OF AMERICA, Indian Territory,
     Western   DISTRICT.

     I,   Emma Payne   , on oath state that I am   21   years of age and a citizen by
adoption   , of the   Seminole   Nation; that I am not the lawful wife of   Davis
Jackson   , who is a citizen, by adoption   of the   Seminole   Nation; that
a   Female   child was born to me on   1st day of   August   , 1902; that said child
has been named   Nettie Jackson   , and was living March 4, 1905.

                                   Emma Payne
Witnesses To Mark:

     Subscribed and sworn to before me this   2 day of   May   , 1905.

                                   Chas E Webster
                                        Notary Public.

AFFIDAVIT OF ATTENDING PHYSICIAN OR MID-WIFE.

UNITED STATES OF AMERICA, Indian Territory,
     Western   DISTRICT.

     I,   Affie Davis   , a   midwife   , on oath state that I attended on Mrs.
Emma Payne   , ~~wife of~~   on the   1st day of   August   , 1902; that there was
born to her on said date a   female   child; that said child was living March 4, 1905,
and is said to have been named   Nettie Jackson

                                        her
                                   Affie x Davis
                                        mark

14

Applications for Enrollment of Seminole Newborn Freedmen
Act of 1905

Witnesses To Mark:
{ Frank C. Sabourin
{ Edward Merrick

Subscribed and sworn to before me 6th day of   May   , 1905.

< Seal >   Edward Merrick
                                                Notary Public.
Midwife appeared before Commission May 6-1905.

B.A. #156

DEPARTMENT OF THE INTERIOR,
COMMISSION TO THE FIVE CIVILIZED TRIBES.
Wewoka, Indian Territory, May 3, 1905.

In the matter of the application for the enrollment of Jimmie Davis, as a freedman of the Seminole Nation.

John Davis, being duly sworn, testified as follows testifies as follows:

Q. What is your name? A. John Davis.
Q. What is your post office address? A. Wewoka.
Q. Do you now desire to make application for the enrollment of Jimmie Davis as a freedman of the Seminole Nation? A. Yes sir.
Q. Is Jimmie Davis your child? A. Yes sir.

John Davis, the witness, is identified on the records of the Commission on Seminole Freedman Card No. 807, Approved Roll No. 2615.

Q. Who is the mother of Jimmie Davis? A. Mariah Carter, she was before I married her.

Mariah Davis is identified on the records of the Commission as Mariah Carter, Seminole Freedman Card No. 634, Approved Roll No. 1962.

Q. Are you and Mariah Davis living together now? A. No sir, we have parted.

15

Applications for Enrollment of Seminole Newborn Freedmen
Act of 1905

Q. Is this child, Jimmie Davis, living? A. Yes sir.

Q. Where is he? A. He is at my place.

Q. With you? A. Yes sir.

Q. Why didn't you bring him in? A. I had him here yesterday, but you wanted his mother, and I went out to his mother's and didn't bring Jimmie back today.

Q. Why didn't his mother come in? A. She is in a delicate state and couldn't come.

Q. Who attended on Mariah Davis at the time this child was born? A. My Mother, Harriett Davis.

Q. Is she living? A. Yes sir.

Q. Where is she? A. She is at home.

Q. When was Jimmie born? A. October 11, 1902.

Q. Who does Jimmie live with now? A. With me, his father.

Frank C. Sabourin, being duly sworn, states that he is stenographer to the Commission to the Five Civilized Tribes, and that the above and foregoing is a true and correct copy of his stenographic notes taken in said case on said date.

Frank C. Sabourin

Subscribed and sworn to before me this 5th day of May, 1905.

⟨ Seal ⟩

Edward Merrick
Notary Public.

Harriett Davis appears at office same day and furnished midwife affidavit.

_____

Sem NB FR 4

BIRTH AFFIDAVIT.

DEPARTMENT OF THE INTERIOR.

COMMISSION TO THE FIVE CIVILIZED TRIBES.

_____

IN RE APPLICATION FOR ENROLLMENT, as a citizen of the　　　Seminole　　　Nation, of
Jimmie Davis　　, born on the　11th　day of　October　, 1902

Name of Father: John Davis　　　(2616)　a citizen of the　Seminole　Nation.
Name of Mother: Mariah Davis　　(1962)　a citizen of the　Seminole　Nation.
　　　　　　　　(Nee Carter)

Postoffice　　Wewoka IT

_____

16

Applications for Enrollment of Seminole Newborn Freedmen
Act of 1905

AFFIDAVIT OF MOTHER.

UNITED STATES OF AMERICA, Indian Territory, ⎱
.... DISTRICT. ⎰

I, ..., on oath state that I am ......years of age and a citizen by ...., of the .... Nation; that I am the lawful wife of ...., who is a citizen, by .... of the .... Nation; that a .... child was born to me on ..... day of..............., 1......, that said child has been named ...., and was living March 4, 1905.

Witnesses To Mark: *See testimony of*
⎰ .... *father taken*
⎱ .... *May 3, 1905.*

Subscribed and sworn to before me this .... day of..............., 1905.

....
Notary Public.

Child present

AFFIDAVIT OF ATTENDING PHYSICIAN OR MID-WIFE.

UNITED STATES OF AMERICA, Indian Territory, ⎱
    Western   DISTRICT. ⎰

I,   Harriett Davis   , a   midwife   , on oath state that I attended on Mrs.   Mariah Davis (nee Carter)   , wife of   Jchn Davis   on the 11 day of October   , 1902; that there was born to her on said date a   male   child; that said child was living March 4, 1905, and is said to have been named Jimmie Davis

her
Harriett x Davis
mark

Witnesses To Mark:
⎰ Frank C. Sabourin
⎱ Chas E Webster

Subscribed and sworn to before me 4 day of   May   , 1905.

Chas E Webster
Notary Public.

17

Applications for Enrollment of Seminole Newborn Freedmen
Act of 1905

Sem NB FR 5
BIRTH AFFIDAVIT.

DEPARTMENT OF THE INTERIOR.
COMMISSION TO THE FIVE CIVILIZED TRIBES.

_____

IN RE APPLICATION FOR ENROLLMENT, as a citizen of the   Seminole   Nation, of Rachael Grayson   , born on the   7   day of   Feby   , 1905

Name of Father: John Tyler   a citizen of the   U S   ~~Nation.~~
Name of Mother: Amanda Grayson   (1966) a citizen of the   Seminole   Nation.

Postoffice   Kanowa IT

_____

Child present

AFFIDAVIT OF MOTHER.

UNITED STATES OF AMERICA, Indian Territory, ⎱
   Western   DISTRICT. ⎰

I,   Amanda Grayson , on oath state that I am   18   years of age and a citizen by adoption   , of the   Seminole   Nation; that I am not the lawful wife of   John Tyler   , who is a citizen, by   of the   U.S.   Nation; that a   Female   child was born to me on   7   day of   Feby   , 1905, that said child has been named Rachael Grayson   , and is now living.

                                                            her
                                             Amanda x Grayson
Witnesses To Mark: mark
   ⎰ Chas E Webster
   ⎱ Frank C. Sabourin

Subscribed and sworn to before me this   6   day of   May   , 1905.

                                             Chas E Webster
                                             Notary Public.

_____

AFFIDAVIT OF ATTENDING PHYSICIAN OR MID-WIFE.

UNITED STATES OF AMERICA, Indian Territory, ⎱
   Western   DISTRICT. ⎰

I,   Julia Franklin   , a   midwife   , on oath state that I attended on Mrs. Amanda Grayson   , ~~wife of~~   on the   7   day of   Feby , 1905; that there was born to her on said date a   Female   child; that said child is now living and is said to have been named Rachael Grayson
                                             Julia Franklin

18

Applications for Enrollment of Seminole Newborn Freedmen
Act of 1905

Witnesses To Mark:

{

Subscribed and sworn to before me this 6 day of   May   , 1905.

Chas E Webster
Notary Public.

Sem NB FR 6
BIRTH AFFIDAVIT.
DEPARTMENT OF THE INTERIOR.
COMMISSION TO THE FIVE CIVILIZED TRIBES.

IN RE APPLICATION FOR ENROLLMENT, as a citizen of the   Seminole   Nation, of
Bond Noble   , born on the 30   day of   March   , 1903

Name of Father: Logan Noble   (785)   a citizen of the   Seminole   Nation.
Name of Mother: Susie Noble (nee Mills) (1977) a citizen of the   Seminole   Nation.

Postoffice   Wewoka

Child present
AFFIDAVIT OF MOTHER.

UNITED STATES OF AMERICA, Indian Territory,
   Western   **DISTRICT.**

I,   Susie Noble   , on oath state that I am   20   years of age and a citizen by
adoption   , of the   Seminole   Nation; that I am the lawful wife of   Logan Noble ,
who is a citizen, by blood   of the   Seminole   Nation; that a   male   child
was born to me on   30th   day of   March   , 1903; that said child has been named
Bond Noble   , and was living March 4, 1905.

her
Susie x Noble
mark

19

Applications for Enrollment of Seminole Newborn Freedmen
Act of 1905

Witnesses To Mark:
 { Frank C. Sabourin
 { Chas E Webster

  Subscribed and sworn to before me this 11th day of May , 1905.

Chas E Webster
Notary Public.

AFFIDAVIT OF ATTENDING PHYSICIAN OR MID-WIFE.

UNITED STATES OF AMERICA, Indian Territory, ⎫
  Western   **DISTRICT.** ⎬
          ⎭

  I, Tyra Mills , a mother of Susie Noble , on oath state that I attended on Mrs. Susie Noble , wife of Logan Noble on the 30 day of March, 1903; that there was born to her on said date a child; that said child was living March 4, 1905, and is said to have been named Bond Noble

her
Tyra x Mills
mark

Witnesses To Mark:
 { Frank C. Sabourin
 { Chas E Webster

  Subscribed and sworn to before me 11th day of May , 1905.

Chas E Webster
Notary Public.

Sem NB FR 6
BIRTH AFFIDAVIT.

DEPARTMENT OF THE INTERIOR.
COMMISSION TO THE FIVE CIVILIZED TRIBES.

  IN RE APPLICATION FOR ENROLLMENT, as a citizen of the Seminole Nation, of Leah Noble , born on the 16 day of January , 1905

Name of Father: Logan Noble (785) a citizen of the Seminole Nation.
Name of Mother: Susie Noble (nee Mills) (1977) a citizen of the Seminole Nation.

Postoffice Wewoka IT

20

Applications for Enrollment of Seminole Newborn Freedmen
Act of 1905

Child present

UNITED STATES OF AMERICA, Indian Territory,
    Western   DISTRICT.

I,   Susie Noble   , on oath state that I am   20   years of age and a citizen by adoption   , of the   Seminole   Nation; that I am the lawful wife of   Logan Noble , who is a citizen, by   blood   of the   Seminole   Nation; that a   female child was born to me on   16   day of   January   , 1905; that said child has been named   Leah Noble   , and was living March 4, 1905.

her
Susie x Noble
mark

Witnesses To Mark:
   Frank C. Sabourin
   Chas E Webster

Subscribed and sworn to before me this 11th   day of   May   , 1905.

Chas E Webster
Notary Public.

UNITED STATES OF AMERICA, Indian Territory,
    Western   DISTRICT.

I,   Tyra Mills   , a mother of Susie Noble   , on oath state that I attended on Mrs.   Susie Noble   , wife of   Logan Noble   on the 16 day of   January , 1905; that there was born to her on said date a   female   child; that said child was living March 4, 1905, and is said to have been named Leah Noble

her
Tyra x Mills
mark

Witnesses To Mark:
   Frank C. Sabourin
   Chas E Webster

Subscribed and sworn to before me 11th day of   May   , 1905.

Chas E Webster
Notary Public.

21

Applications for Enrollment of Seminole Newborn Freedmen
Act of 1905

Sem NB FR 7
BIRTH AFFIDAVIT.

DEPARTMENT OF THE INTERIOR.
COMMISSION TO THE FIVE CIVILIZED TRIBES.

IN RE APPLICATION FOR ENROLLMENT, as a citizen of the   Seminole   Nation, of
Parah Bruner   , born on the   31   day of   July   , 1901

Name of Father: Doran Bruner   1983   a citizen of the   Seminole   Nation.
Name of Mother: Mary Ann Bruner   1984   a citizen of the   Seminole   Nation.

Postoffice   Wolf IT

(Child present)

AFFIDAVIT OF MOTHER.

UNITED STATES OF AMERICA, Indian Territory,
Western   DISTRICT.

about

I,   Mary Ann Bruner   , on oath state that I am   52   years of age and a citizen by
adoption   , of the   Seminole   Nation; that I am the lawful wife of   Doran
Bruner   , who is a citizen, by   adoption   of the   Seminole   Nation; that a
male   child was born to me on   31   day of   July   , 1901, that said child has been
named   Parah Bruner   , and is now living.

her
Mary Ann   x   Bruner
Witnesses To Mark: mark
   Chas E Webster
   Frank C. Sabourin

Subscribed and sworn to before me this   17   day of   May   , 1905.

Chas E Webster
Notary Public.

AFFIDAVIT OF ATTENDING PHYSICIAN OR MID-WIFE.

UNITED STATES OF AMERICA, Indian Territory,
Western   DISTRICT.

I,   Minerva Wilson   , a   midwife   , on oath state that I attended on
Mrs.   Mary Ann Bruner   , wife of   Doran Bruner and my mother   on the   31
day of   July , 1901; that there was born to her on said date a   male   child; that said
child is now living and is said to have been named   Parah Bruner

22

Applications for Enrollment of Seminole Newborn Freedmen
Act of 1905

Witnesses To Mark:
    { Chas E Webster
    { Frank C. Sabourin

                   her
         Minerva x Wilson
                 mark

Subscribed and sworn to before me this 17 day of   May   , 1905.

                       Chas E Webster
                       Notary Public.

Sem NB FR 8
BIRTH AFFIDAVIT.
DEPARTMENT OF THE INTERIOR.
COMMISSION TO THE FIVE CIVILIZED TRIBES.

IN RE APPLICATION FOR ENROLLMENT, as a citizen of the   Seminole   Nation, of Ramsey M Bruner   , born on the 21 day of January , 1904

                           freedman
Name of Father: Mose Bruner   a ~~citizen~~ of the Chickasaw   Nation.
Name of Mother: Ellen Iona Bruner   (1986) a citizen of the   Seminole   Nation.

               Postoffice   Kanawa I.T.

Child present
AFFIDAVIT OF MOTHER.

UNITED STATES OF AMERICA, Indian Territory, }
    Western   **DISTRICT.**

    I,   Ellen Iona Bruner   , on oath state that I am 20 years of age and a citizen by   adoption   , of the   Seminole   Nation; that I am the lawful wife of Mose Bruner   , who is a ~~citizen, by~~ freedman   of the   Chickasaw   Nation; that a   male   child was born to me on 21   day of   January   , 1904; that said child has been named Ramsey M Bruner   , and was living March 4, 1905.

Applications for Enrollment of Seminole Newborn Freedmen
Act of 1905

Ellen Bruner

Witnesses To Mark:

{

Subscribed and sworn to before me this   17   day of   May   , 1905.

Chas E Webster
Notary Public.

AFFIDAVIT OF ATTENDING PHYSICIAN OR MID-WIFE.

UNITED STATES OF AMERICA, Indian Territory, ⎱
    Western   DISTRICT. ⎰

I, Mary Ann Bruner , a mother of Ellen Iona Bruner , on oath state that I attended on Mrs.   Ellen Iona Bruner   , wife of   Mose Bruner   on the 21   day of January   , 1904; that there was born to her on said date a   male   child; that said child was living March 4, 1905, and is said to have been named Ramsey M Bruner

her
Mary Ann x Bruner
mark

Witnesses To Mark:
   { Frank C. Sabourin
    Chas E Webster

Subscribed and sworn to before me 17   day of   May   , 1905.

Chas E Webster
Notary Public.

Applications for Enrollment of Seminole Newborn Freedmen
Act of 1905

Sem NB FR 9
BIRTH AFFIDAVIT.

DEPARTMENT OF THE INTERIOR.
COMMISSION TO THE FIVE CIVILIZED TRIBES.

IN RE APPLICATION FOR ENROLLMENT, as a citizen of the   Seminole   Nation, of
Leford Noble   , born on the   31   day of   May , 1902

Name of Father: George Noble   a citizen of the   Creek   Nation.
Name of Mother: Delia Noble   (2004)   a citizen of the   Seminole   Nation.

Postoffice   Wewoka, I.T.

Child at home

AFFIDAVIT OF MOTHER.

UNITED STATES OF AMERICA, Indian Territory, ⎤
      Western   DISTRICT. ⎦

I,   Delia Noble   , on oath state that I am   39   years of age and a citizen by
adoption   , of the   Seminole   Nation; that I am the lawful wife of   George
Noble, who is a citizen, by   adoption   of the   Creek   Nation; that a   male
child was born to me on   31st   day of   May   , 1902; that said child has been named
Leford Noble   , and was living March 4, 1905.

Delia Noble

Witnesses To Mark:
{

Subscribed and sworn to before me this 10th   day of   May   , 1905.

Chas E Webster
Notary Public.

AFFIDAVIT OF ATTENDING PHYSICIAN OR MID-WIFE.

UNITED STATES OF AMERICA, Indian Territory, ⎤
      Western   DISTRICT. ⎦

I,   Bessie Noble   , a   midwife   , on oath state that I attended on
Mrs.   Delia Noble   , wife of   George Noble   on the   31 day of   May   , 1902;
that there was born to her on said date a   male   child; that said child was living
March 4, 1905, and is said to have been named   Leford Noble
                                                               her
                                                Bessie   x   Noble
                                                              mark

25

Applications for Enrollment of Seminole Newborn Freedmen
Act of 1905

Witnesses To Mark:
    ⎰ Frank C. Sabourin
    ⎱ Chas E Webster

    Subscribed and sworn to before me 10th day of   May   , 1905.

                         Chas E Webster
                         Notary Public.

Sem NB FR 9
BIRTH AFFIDAVIT.

DEPARTMENT OF THE INTERIOR.
COMMISSION TO THE FIVE CIVILIZED TRIBES.

IN RE APPLICATION FOR ENROLLMENT, as a citizen of the   Seminole   Nation, of Rachael Noble   , born on the 9th day of January , 1905

Name of Father: George Noble   a citizen of the Creek   Nation.
Name of Mother: Delia Noble   (2004) a citizen of the Seminole Nation.

                  Postoffice   Wewoka, I.T.

Child Present

AFFIDAVIT OF MOTHER.

UNITED STATES OF AMERICA, Indian Territory, ⎱
    Western   **DISTRICT.** ⎰

    I, Delia Noble   , on oath state that I am 39 years of age and a citizen by adoption , of the Seminole Nation; that I am the lawful wife of   George Noble, who is a citizen, by adoption of the   Creek   Nation; that a female child was born to me on 9th day of January   , 1905; that said child has been named Rachael Noble , and was living March 4, 1905.

                    Delia Noble
Witnesses To Mark:
    ⎰

    Subscribed and sworn to before me this 10th day of   May   , 1905.

                  Chas E Webster
                  Notary Public.

Applications for Enrollment of Seminole Newborn Freedmen
Act of 1905

AFFIDAVIT OF ATTENDING PHYSICIAN OR MID-WIFE.

UNITED STATES OF AMERICA, Indian Territory,
Western   DISTRICT.

I,   Lydia Fields   , a   midwife   , on oath state that I attended on Mrs.   Delia Noble   , wife of   George Noble   on the   9th day of January , 1905; that there was born to her on said date a   female   child; that said child was living March 4, 1905, and is said to have been named   Rachael Noble

Lydia Fields

Witnesses To Mark:

{

Subscribed and sworn to before me   10   day of   May   , 1905.

Chas E Webster
Notary Public.

Sem NB FR 9
BIRTH AFFIDAVIT.

DEPARTMENT OF THE INTERIOR.
COMMISSION TO THE FIVE CIVILIZED TRIBES.

IN RE APPLICATION FOR ENROLLMENT, as a citizen of the   Seminole   Nation, of Stephan Noble   , born on the   15   day of   June , 1900

Name of Father: George Noble   a citizen of the   Creek   Nation.
Name of Mother: Delia Noble   (2004)   a citizen of the   Seminole   Nation.

Postoffice   Wewoka, I:T.

(Child at home)

AFFIDAVIT OF MOTHER.

UNITED STATES OF AMERICA, Indian Territory,
Western   DISTRICT.

I,   Delia Noble   , on oath state that I am   39   years of age and a citizen by adoption   , of the   Seminole   Nation; that I am the lawful wife of   George Noble, who is a citizen, by   adoption   of the   Creek   Nation; that a   male child was born to me on   15th   day of   June   , 1900; that said child has been named   Stephen Noble   , and was living March 4, 1905.

Delia Noble

27

Applications for Enrollment of Seminole Newborn Freedmen
Act of 1905

Witnesses To Mark:

{

Subscribed and sworn to before me this 10 day of May , 1905.

Chas. E. Webster
Notary Public.

AFFIDAVIT OF ~~ATTENDING PHYSICIAN OR MID-WIFE~~.
Midwife dead.

UNITED STATES OF AMERICA, Indian Territory, ⎤
Western   DISTRICT. ⎦

saw

I, Bessie Noble , a midwife , on oath state that I attended on
Mrs. Delia Noble , wife of George Noble on the 15th day of June ,
1900; that there was born to her on said date a male child; that said child was living
March 4, 1905, and is said to have been named Stephen Noble

Bessie (her x mark) Noble

Witnesses To Mark:
⌠ Frank C. Sabourin
⌡ Chas. E. Webster

Subscribed and sworn to before me 10 day of May , 1905.

Chas. E. Webster
Notary Public.

DEPARTMENT OF THE INTERIOR,
COMMISSION TO THE FIVE CIVILIZED TRIBES.
MUSKOGEE, I.T. AUGUST 12, 1904.

In the matter of the application for the enrollment of Stephen Noble as a Creek
Freedman.

APPEARANCE: M. L. Mott, attorney for Creek Nation.

George Noble being duly sworn testified as follows:

Q What is your name? A George Noble.
Q How old are you? A Forty two.
Q What is your post office address? A Wewoka.
Q Do you make application for the enrollment of Stephen Noble as a Creek Freedman?
A Yes sir.
Q Are you his father? A Yes sir.

28

Applications for Enrollment of Seminole Newborn Freedmen
Act of 1905

Q Are you a citizen of the Creek Nation? A Yes sir.

The records of the Commission show that George Noble is listed for enrollment on Creek Freedman card Field No. 1516 and that his name is contained in the partial list of Creek Freedmen approved by the Secretary of the Interior March 28, 1902, No. 4920.

Q Is Stephen Noble living? A Yes sir.
Q What is the name of his mother? A Delia Noble.
Q Is she a citizen of the Seminole Nation? A Yes sir.

The records of the Commission show that the name of Delia Noble appears on the approved Seminole roll, No. 2004.

Q When was Stephen Noble born? A I can see in a minute.
Q Have you a record of it? A Yes sir; I put it down what month it was born; I have got the names down in a book at home; I never could think of it, so I just put it down; 1900; born June.

The applicant presents for the inspection of the Commission pocket memorandum book in which is found what purports to be a record of the date of the birth of Stephen Noble.

Q Did you do this writing in this book? A Yes sir.
Q When did you write it in this book? A I don't remember exactly when; but I done that myself in the book; I don't remember when.
Q You say you did this yourself? A Yes sir.
Q Did you do it soon after this child was born? A Yes sir.
Q In this book? A Yes sir.
Q Have you got it written down in another? A Yes, down in a bible but I didn't bring it with me, I just had the day book here.
Q Did you copy this from the Bible? A Yes sir.
Q When did you make that entry in the Bible about the date of birth? A Just after he was born
Q Does this in this book give the same date that it does in the Bible? A Yes sir.
Q Have you a child named Leeford? A Yes sir.
Q When was that child born? A 1902.
Q What day and month? A I can't tell you, cause I never could keep track; I am short of recollection and the onliest[sic] way I can remember a thing is to put it down.
A Both of the children is right there.
Q Is Stephen older than Leeford? A Yes sir.
Q How much older? A He must be two years older than Leeford.
Q More than two or less than two? A About two years older.

The book which the applicant presents contains the following entries:
Stephen Noble born June the 15th 1900.
Leeford Noble born May the 31 1902.

29

Applications for Enrollment of Seminole Newborn Freedmen
Act of 1905

Q Did you wife make an affidavit about the birth of Stephen? A I believe she did.
Q Were you with her when she made it? A Yes sir: I was over there.
Q Are you positive that this date that you have here gives the correct date of the birth of Stephen? A Yes sir.
Q If your wife gives a different date, she is mistaken, is she? A She might be; that's the correct date from the one in the Bible cause I seed the one in the Bible when the child was born and then I went and got a copy.
Q The affidavit made by your wife states that the child was born on the 19th of June, 1900; and you say the correct date is the 15th of June, 1900? A Yes sir.

Examination by Mr. Mott:
Q Have you got another child enrolled? A In the Creek Nation?
Q Yes. A No sir.
Q In any other nation? A My oldest children are all enrolled in the Seminole Nation.
Q Is your wife dead? A No sir, she's living.
Q You are a Creek citizen? A Yes sir.
Q She a Seminole? A Yes sir.
Q Where is she? A She is up there about 4 miles Northwest of Wewoka.
Q How many children have you got? A About 7.
Q Why did you put Leeford Noble down here? A I just wanted to put him down; he is the next one to Stephen.
Q Why did you put only two down here and not the others down? A I didn't thought I would need to put them down; they had filed up there in the Seminole nation[sic].
Q Well, there is not any need to put Leeford down; you knew he couldn't file, didn't you? A Yes sir.
Q When did you put these down here? A I don't know exactly; I wouldn't say because I am not positive when I did write it but I written it in there myself.
Q About what time did you put it down, do you know? A No sir, I don't.
Q Has it been a year ago? A I don't think it was a year, but what date I can't tell you.
Q Was it six months? A That's what I don't know, I keep telling you.
Q Haven't you any idea when you put it down? A No sir.
Q Well, you put it down for the purpose of bringing it here for evidence, didn't you? A Yes sir.
Q And then can't tell whether you put it down 6 months or 12 months ago? A I think it aint[sic] 12 months ago; of course I don't know exactly what month I put it down and can't say.
Q Well, to your best judgment? A It can't be much more than 2 month ago since I written that in that book there.
Q You put it down for the purpose of bringing it here as evidence? A Yes sir.
Q Why didn't you bring it then? A Well; I couldn't go off then; it was a good ways and money was hard to get and we come when we could.
Q Why didn't you bring the Bible? A I didn't think that was needed; that was me hardy to fetch than the Bible.
Q It is not as good evidence as the Bible. A Well, the Bible could come if, it is needed.
Q You put this down here for the purpose of bringing it here as testimony? A Yes sir.

30

Applications for Enrollment of Seminole Newborn Freedmen
Act of 1905

Q And you don't know why you put Leeford down? A Well, I put his name cause I didn't know but what I could make application for him too; I just put him down; if I could it would be all right, if not, all right too.

Q When did you file? When did you enroll? A It must have been 1900 when I filed.

Q Did you file before or after Stephen Noble was born? A After, wasn't it? This is 1900.

Q Did you file before or after Stephen was born? A That's what I don't know; I don't know exactly what year I did file in.

By the Commission:

Q Can you remember whether or not that child was at your house when you came down to file? A I don't think he was there then.

The records of the Commission show that George Noble was listed for enrollment May 17, 1901, and that a citizenship certificate was issued to him on that day.

By Mr. Mott:

Q Now, according to that, that child was a year old when you came here? A Yes sir.

Q If this child was born, why didn't you file him when you did yourself and enrolled here? A I don't know anything about whether I could enroll him here in the Creek country until a long time after I was filed.

Q Well, you just said a bit ago that he wasn't living when you came here and filed; what have you to say about that now? A Well, it was just a mistake that's all, I just can't keep my memory right.

Q Where is that boy now? A Its[sic] home.

Q Did you have a midwife at the birth of this child? A Yes sir.

Q Have a doctor? A No sir.

Q Where is she now? A Dead.

Q Where is your wife? A She's home.

Q Was there any neighbors there when the child was born? A Yes sir.

Q -- that you can show by? A Yes sir.

Q Who are they? A One of my sisters was there.

Q Any of your neighbors? A Well, she was a neighbor.

Q Well, you have got some neighbors living right close there that knows your wife's condition about the time she was down? A Yes sir.

Q Can you get any of them to come here? A I don't know; I guess so.

Q If you didn't know you could file this child when you filed, why did you wait four or five years after it was born to come? A Well, I just had to pick my chance to come; I was a poor man and got nothing.

Q You are a poor man and your wife has an allotment and your wife has one and you have two or three children that's got allotments. A Well, they aint[sic] bringing in anything; they are all leased out; they aint[sic] bringing in any money.

Redmond Holmes being duly sworn testified as follows:

Examination by the Commission:

Q Give you name, age and post office address. A Redmond Holmes; 38; Wetumka.

Applications for Enrollment of Seminole Newborn Freedmen
Act of 1905

Q You are a citizen of the Creek Nation are you? A Yes sir.
Q Do you know George Noble? A Yes sir.
Q Know his wife, Delia? A Yes sir.
Q How far do you live from them? A About 10 miles.
Q Do you know a child of theirs named Stephen? A Yes sir.
Q Do you visit the home of George Noble occasionally? A Yes sir.
Q Any kin to him and his wife? A No sir; just pretty near raised up together.
Q Do you know how old that child is? A I went up there in 1900 along about the middle of June and this child was born; it was there the 15th or 16th; I was up there and the child was there.
Q What is it calls your attention to the exact date you were up there; what did you go up there for? A I went up there to town and stayed with him all night.
Q What did you go to town for? A To trade.
Q Do you know when George Noble came to file on his land? A No sir.
Q Do you know of his coming to file? A Yes sir, I know of his coming
Q Did you hear of it at the time? A Not at the time; I heard of it after he got back home.
Q Soon after? A No sir, not so soon.
Q Well, in a week or two weeks or a month? A I believe it was 2 or 3 weeks after he got back.
Q Was that child living when you heard he had been down here to file? A I don't know whether it was after or before; I wasn't up there at that time that I heard he had come down to file.
Q Who told you that? A A man by the name of George Add.
Q How long after he was down here to file that you was at his house? A That is just what I don't remember.

Examination by Mr. Mott:
Q What year was it he told you he had come here to file-- this man? A The other man told me.
Q His card there show that he filed in 1901; when did you hear it? A I can't tell exactly what year I heard that but I suppose its[sic] been about 1901 sometime; I don't know just what time.
Q You don't know whether the child was there then or not? A I don't remember whether it was before or after I went up there and saw the child
Q You don't know whether it was before or after he filed that you saw it? A No sir.
Q You say you fix the date as being the 15th or 16th because you went over to town to do some trading? A Yes sir.
Q What date in June were you in town trading in June, 1901? A That's what I think it was between the 15th and 16th; the exact date I don't know.
Q Well, you said you know it was the 15th or 16th because you went there to town to do some trading. A Yes sir.
Q In 1900? A Yes sir.
Q Did you do any trading in 1901? A Yes sir.
Q What date did you go over there in 1901 to do some trading? A In March.
Q What date? A Along about the last of March.
Q About the 30th? A Yes sir.
Q Did you go there in 1901? A Yes sir.

Applications for Enrollment of Seminole Newborn Freedmen
Act of 1905

Q Did you go there in 1902? A Yes sir.

Q What date? A That was in March.

q How many times did you go to town in 1902? A I don't know sir.

Q How many times did you go in 1901 to town to trade? A I don't know how many times I went.

Q How many times in 1900 did you go? A I don't know; but I went in 1900 the 3rd time I think?

Q What dates did you go on the other two times? A I don't know sir.

Q Why don't you remember them? A Well, what drawed my attention to this 1900 by him and I talking about the age of this child.

Q When were you talking about that? A When I was coming.

Q Coming up here this time? A Yes sir.

Q You and him talking about it coming up here made you think it was 1900? A Yes sir.

Q Well, it wasn't going to the town to trade that made you think so, then? A Well, it was going to the town; you see I went to the town, traded and went over to his place and stayed with him all night.

Q Well, he told you coming up here that it was 1900, didn't he? A Yes sir.

Q That's the way he refreshed your memory about it, coming up here? Told you?
A Well, I knowed[sic] it was 1900.

Q How? A I know the year I was up there.

Q Well, you go up there every year? A Yes, but I knowed[sic] all the time.

Q Well, you have gone there several times every year, don't you? A Yes but I don't go over to his place every time.

Q Well, what date was you at his place in 1902? A I wasn't there.

Q Was you there in 1901? A I don't remember being there in 1901.

Q You say you wasn't? A I don't remember; if I have, I have forgot the time.

Q Do you pretend to say that you know four years backwards without having anything to call it to your recollection- that you can tell back anywhere you spent the night?
A Sometime I can.

Q Did you put down any dates about this at that time? A No sir.

Q When did you find that he wanted you to come up here and testify about this matter?
A He told me along about a month ago.

Q You had not had any occasion to recollect it then from June 1900 until he told you about it a month ago that he wanted you to come up here? A Yes sir; we always talked about the little children and mine; they both born the same year and we would always talk about the two children near about the same age; mine born in 1900 in March.

By the Commission:

Q What's your child's name? A Jane Holmes.

Q Have you a child named Sango? A Yes sir.

Q Sango is dead, is he? A Yes sir.

Q Was this child of George Noble's born about the same time that your two children, Sango and Jane, were? A No sir, that Noble was born after mine.

Q How long after? A I guess it three months after.

Q About three months? A I believe

Applications for Enrollment of Seminole Newborn Freedmen
Act of 1905

The records of the Commission show that Sango and Jane Holmes were born March 8, 1900.

By Mr. Mott:
Q When did you file for Jane? A About a year or two ago.
Q Why didn't this man come and file this child then? A He didn't know till I told him.
Q When did you tell him? A About a year ago.
Q Where were you the 16th of June, 1901? A I don't know sir.
Q Where were you the 16th of June, 1902? A I was at home.
Q On that very day? A Yes sir; I think I was at home; I wouldn't be sure.
Q Have you and him talked about filing this boy? What talk have you and him had about filing this boy? A I just told him that I don't know but what maybe he can file for his child if he come down and see; sometime after I come and filed for mine.
Q Did he tell you that he didn't know he could file? A Yes sir.
Q Told you that about a year ago? A Yes sir.
Q What did he say about it? A Said he would try; come down here and see
Q Why did he say he didn't know he could come and file? A He didn't say.

By the Commission:
Q Your wife is a Seminole citizen like his? A Yes sir.

By Mr. Mott:
Q But he did tell you a year ago that he didn't know; he didn't know until you told him?
A I told him he ought to come down and see.

By the Commission:

The two affidavits heretofore filed are made part of the records.

Henry G. Hains being sworn on his oath states that as stenographer to the Commission to the Five Civilized Tribes he reported the above case and that this is a full, true and correct transcript of his stenographic notes in same.

Henry G. Hains

Subscribed and sworn to before me this 22 day of August, 1904.

W^m.F. Martin Jr.
Notary Public.

Applications for Enrollment of Seminole Newborn Freedmen
Act of 1905

DEPARTMENT OF THE INTERIOR
COMMISSIONER TO THE FIVE CIVILIZED TRIBES
MUSKOGEE LAND OFFICE
MUSKOGEE, I. T., November 16, 1905.

IN THE MATTER OF THE APPLICATION OF George Noble, a citizen of the Creek Nation, for the enrollment of his minor child, Stephen Noble, as a citizen by adoption of the Seminole Nation under the provisions of the Act of Congress approved March 3, 1905, Freedman Card No. 9.

GEORGE NOBLE, being sworn, testified as follows:

Q What is your name? A George Noble.
Q What is your post office address? A Wewoka.
Q How old are you? A About 43.
Q Are you a citizen of the Seminole Nation? A Creek.
Q Have your received an allotment in the Creek Nation? A Yes sir.
Q What relation are you to Delia Noble? A Delia is my wife.
Q Is she a citizen of the Creek or Seminole Nation? A Seminole.
Q Did your wife Delia Noble make application for the enrollment of Stephen Noble as a citizen of the Seminole Nation? A I don't know whether she did or not but it was understood that I was to try and get him enrolled here.
Q Is he living? A Yes sir.
Q How old is he? A 4 or 5, I don't know just how old.
Q Did you ever make application for the enrollment of this child as a citizen of the Creek Nation? A I have come here and tried to get him enrolled as a citizen of the Creek Nation.
Q When did you make application for this child as a citizen of the Creek Nation? A Last year, I don't remember just when; I don't know just what month.
Q What time last year was it that you were here to make this application? A I don't know what time it was, been a good while ago. I have got a poor recollection but I was here.
Q Was it in the summer? A I believe it was along in the Spring or Summer, I don't know which.
Q If it is possible to enroll this child as a citizen of the Creek Nation and also in the Seminole Nation, which one do you desire that he be enrolled in? A I desire to have him enrolled in the Creek Nation.

The undersigned, being sworn, states as stenographer to the Commissioner to the Five Civilized Tribes she recorded the proceedings in the above cause and that the foregoing is a true and complete transcript of her stenographic notes thereof.

Nona E Waller

Applications for Enrollment of Seminole Newborn Freedmen
Act of 1905

Subscribed and sworn to before me this 16th day of November, 1905, at Muskogee, Indian Territory.

(Illegible) Hawkins
Notary Public

Cr En 627

DEPARTMENT OF THE INTERIOR,
COMMISSIONER TO THE FIVE CIVILIZED TRIBES.

Muskogee, Indian Territory, November 16, 1905

In the matter of the application for the enrollment of Stephen Noble as a Creek Freedman.

George Noble, being duly sworn, testified as follows:

EXAMINATION BY THE COMMISSIONER:
Q What is your name? A George Noble.
Q How old are you? A About 43.
Q What is your postoffice address? A Wewoka.
Q Are you a citizen of the Creek Nation? A Yes sir.
Q Have you a child named Stephen Noble? A Yes sir.
Q Is it living? A Yes sir.
Q About how old is it? A I don't know exactly how old it is--four or five years old though. I've got his age down home.
Q What is the name of his mother? A Delia.
Q Is she a Creek? A No sir, Seminole.
Q Citizen of the Seminole Nation? A Yes sir.
Q If it should be found that your child, Stephen Noble, is entitled to be enrolled in either the Creek or Seminole Nation, in which Nation do you elect to have him enrolled that he may take his allotment of land? A For it, in the Creek, I reckon.

Q You elect for him to be enrolled in the Creek Nation, do you? A Yes sir.

The witness is instructed to have his wife go before a notary public and made affidavit to this fact.

Q You have two other children? A Yes sir.
Q What are their names? A Leeford
Q And the other? A Rachel.
Q Are they living? A Yes sir.
Q You never applied for them as Creeks, did you? A No sir; I just applied for one.
Q And you applied for the other two in the Seminole Nation? A Yes sir.

36

Applications for Enrollment of Seminole Newborn Freedmen
Act of 1905

INDIAN TERRITORY, Western District.
    I, J. Y. Miller, a stenographer to the Commissioner to the Five Civilized Tribes, do hereby certify that the above and foregoing is a true and complete translation of my notes as same appear in my stenographic report of this case.

JY Miller

Sworn to and subscribed before me
  this the 16th day of November,
  1905.   J McDermott
                        Notary Public.

Sem-Fr-NB-9
DEPARTMENT OF THE INTERIOR,
COMMISSIONER TO THE FIVE CIVILIZED TRIBES.

    In the matter of the application for the enrollment of Stephen Noble as a citizen by blood of the Seminole Nation.

D E C I S I O N.

    It appears from the record herein that on May 10, 1905, application was made to the Commission to the Five Civilized Tribes for the enrollment of Stephen Noble as a citizen of the Seminole Nation. On August 12, 1904, application was made for the enrollment of said applicant as a Creek freedman.
    It further appears from the record herein that said applicant was born on June 15, 1900, and is the son of George Noble, whose name appears as number 4920 upon the final roll of Creek freedmen approved by the Secretary of the Interior March 28, 1902, and Delia Noble, whose name appears as number 2004 upon the final roll of citizens of the Seminole Nation approved by the Secretary of the Interior April 2, 1901; and that said applicant was living on March 4, 1905.
    Under the provisions of Section 21 of the Act of Congress approved June 28, 1898 (30 Stats., 495), George Noble, father of said applicant, appeared before the Commissioner to the Five Civilized Tribes on November 16, 1905, and elected on behalf of said applicant that he be enrolled as a Creek freedman.
    The name of the applicant, Stephen Noble, appears as number 5659 upon the final roll of Creek freedmen approved by the Secretary of the Interior June 16, 1906.
    I am, therefore, of the opinion that the application for the enrollment of Stephen Noble as a citizen of the Seminole Nation should be denied under the provisions of the Act of Congress approved June 28, 1898 (30 Stats., 495), and it is so ordered.

Tams Bixby Commissioner.

Muskogee, Indian Territory.
    JAN 7- 1907

Applications for Enrollment of Seminole Newborn Freedmen
Act of 1905

Sem-Fr-NB

COPY

Muskogee, Indian Territory, January 7, 1907.

George Noble,
Wewoka, Indian Territory.

Dear Sir:

I inclose herewith a copy of the decision of the Commissioner to the Five Civilized Tribes, rendered January 7, 1907, denying the application for the enrollment of Stephen Noble as a citizen of the Seminole Nation.

The decision, with the proceedings in the case is this day transmitted to the Secretary of the Interior for review. The final decision of the Secretary will be made known to you as soon as this office is informed of the same.

Respectfully,

SIGNED   *Tams Bixby*

Registered.   Commissioner.
Sem-Fr-NB-9

Sem-Fr-NB-9

COPY

Muskogee, Indian Territory, January 7, 1907.

Wilmott[sic] & Wilhoit,
Attorneys at Law,
Wewoka, Indian Territory.

Gentlemen:

I inclose herewith a copy of the decision of the Commissioner to the Five Civilized Tribes, rendered January 7, 1907, denying the application for the enrollment of Stephen Noble as a citizen of the Seminole Nation.

The decision, with the proceedings in the case is this day transmitted to the Secretary of the Interior for review. The final decision of the Secretary will be made known to you as soon as this office is informed of the same.

Respectfully,

SIGNED   *Tams Bixby*

Commissioner.

Sem-Fr-NB-9

Applications for Enrollment of Seminole Newborn Freedmen
Act of 1905

COPY

Muskogee, Indian Territory, January 7, 1907.

The Honorable,
The Secretary of the Interior.

Sir:

There is transmitted herewith record of proceedings in the matter of the application for the enrollment of application for the enrollment of Stephen Noble as a citizen of the Seminole Nation, including the decision of the Commissioner to the Five Civilized Tribes, dated January 7, 1907, denying said application,

Respectfully,

SIGNED *Tams Bixby*
Commissioner.

Sem-Fr-NB-9

DEPARTMENT OF THE INTERIOR,
WASHINGTON

KHM

FHE

I.T.D. 3940-1907
D.C. 10646-1907

February 19, 1907.

LRS

Direct.

Commissioner to the Five Civilized Tribes,
Muskogee, Indian Territory.

Sir:

January 7, 1907, you transmitted the record in the matter of the application for the enrollment of application for the enrollment of Stephen Noble as a citizen of the Seminole Nation, including your decision of the same date, denying said application.

Reporting February 16, 1907 (Land 2525-07), the Indian Office recommends that your decision be approved. A copy of its letter is inclosed.

Your decision is hereby affirmed. The papers in the case and a carbon copy hereof have been sent to the Indian Office.

Applications for Enrollment of Seminole Newborn Freedmen
Act of 1905

Respectfully,

1 inc. and 2 for Ind. Of.

Thos. Ryan,
First Assistant Secretary.

A. F. Mc.
2-20-07.

Refer in reply to the following:

(COPY)
DEPARTMENT OF THE INTERIOR,
LAND   OFFICE OF INDIAN AFFAIRS,
2525-1907.   WASHINGTON.

February 16, 1907.

The Honorable,
The Secretary of the Interior.

Sir:

There is enclosed a report from the Commissioner to the Five Civilized Tribes, dated January 7, 1907, transmitting the record relative to the application of Stephen Noble for enrollment as a citizen of the Seminole Nation, together with the Commissioner's decision of January 7, 1907, denying the application.

The record shows that the applicant is the son of George Noble, enrolled at No. 4920, approved roll of Creek freedmen, and Delia Noble, enrolled at No. 2004, approved roll of citizens of the Seminole Nation, and that George Noble, father of the applicant, appeared before the Commissioner to the on November 16, 1905, and elected on behalf of the applicant, that he be enrolled as a Creek freedman.

It further shows that the name of Stephen Noble, this applicant, appears on the approved roll of Creek freedmen at No. 5659.

Under the provisions of the Act of June 28, 1898 (30 Stats. L., 495), the applicant is not entitled to enrollment as a Seminole, his father having elected to have him enrolled as a Creek freedman, and he approval of the Commissioner's adverse decision is recommended.

Very respectfully,

C. F. Larrabee,
GAW-GH   Acting Commissioner.

Applications for Enrollment of Seminole Newborn Freedmen
Act of 1905

Sem-Fr-NB-9

Muskogee, Indian Territory, April 16, 1907.

George Noble,
Wewoka, Indian Territory.

Dear Sir:

You are hereby advised that on February 19, 1907, the Secretary of the Interior affirmed the decision of the Commissioner to the Five Civilized Tribes, rendered January 7, 1907, denying the application for the enrollment of Stephen Noble as a citizen of the Seminole Nation.

Respectfully,

Commissioner.

Sem-Fr-NB-9.

Muskogee, Indian Territory, April 16, 1907.

Wilmott[sic] & Wilhoit,
Attorneys at Law,
Wewoka, Indian Territory.

Gentlemen:

You are hereby advised that on February 19, 1907, the Secretary of the Interior affirmed the decision of the Commissioner to the Five Civilized Tribes, rendered January 7, 1907, denying the application for the enrollment of Stephen Noble as a citizen of the Seminole Nation.

Respectfully,

Commissioner.

Applications for Enrollment of Seminole Newborn Freedmen
Act of 1905

REFER IN REPLY TO THE FOLLOWING:

Sem. NBF-9

Creek. En. 627.

DEPARTMENT OF THE INTERIOR,
COMMISSIONER TO THE FIVE CIVILIZED TRIBES.

Muskogee, Indian Territory, January 2, 1905.

Chief Clerk of Seminole Enrollment Division,
 Muskogee, Indian Territory.

Dear Sir:

Receipt is acknowledged of your letter of December 29, 1905, in which you ask to be advised as to the status of the application for the enrollment of Stephen Noble, son of George Noble, a Creek citizen, and Dilia[sic] Noble, a Seminole Freedman, as a citizen of the Creek Nation.

In reply you are advised that a decision, enrolling said Stephen Noble as a citizen of the Creek Nation, is now before the Commissioner for his approval and signature.

Respectfully,

Tams Bixby
 Commissioner.

Sem. Freed.
NB-9.

Muskogee, Indian Territory, June 29, 1905.

Commission to the Five Civilized Tribes,
 Creek Enrollment Division.

Gentlemen:

On May 10, 1905 there were filed with this Commission applications for the enrollment of Stephen Noble, born June 15, 1900, Leford Noble, born May 31, 1902, and Rachael Noble, born January 9, 1905, and Seminole freedmen. It is stated in said applications that the father of said children is George Noble, a citizen by adoption of the Creek Nation, and that their mother is Delia Noble, a Seminole freedman.

You are requested to advise the Seminole Enrollment Division as to whether any application has been made to the Commission for the enrollment of said children as citizens of the Creek Nation and if so what disposition, if any, has been made of such application.

Applications for Enrollment of Seminole Newborn Freedmen
Act of 1905

Respectfully,

Chairman.

_____

HGH

DEPARTMENT OF THE INTERIOR.
COMMISSION TO THE FIVE CIVILIZED TRIBES.

Muskogee, Indian Territory, July 11, 1905.

Seminole Enrollment Division,
General Office.

Gentlemen:

Receipt is acknowledged of your communication of June 29, 1905 (Sem.Fr.NB.9), in which you ask if application for the enrollment as citizens of the Creek Nation has been made for Stephen, Leford and Rachel Noble, children of George Noble, a citizen of the Creek Nation, and Delia Noble, a Seminole Freedman.

In reply you are advised that on August 12, 1904, George Noble appeared before the Commission to the Five Civilized Tribes and made application for the enrollment of said Stephen Noble, as a Creek Freedman; that said George Noble has this day been notified to appear at the office of the Commissioner to the Five Civilized Tribes within twenty days from date for the purpose of electing in which Nation he desires said child to be enrolled and to receive his allotment of land. When final action is had in the matter you will be duly notified.

You are further advised that the records of this office have been examined and it does not appear that application has been made for the enrollment of Leford and Rachel Noble, or either of them as citizens of the Creek Nation.

Respectfully,

Tams Bixby   Commissioner.

_____

43

Applications for Enrollment of Seminole Newborn Freedmen
Act of 1905

Sem. N B F 9

Muskogee, Indian Territory, December 29, 1905.

Chief Clerk,
Creek Enrollment Division.

Dear Sir:

On May 10, 1905, application was made to the Commission to the Five Civilized Tribes for the enrollment as a Seminole freedman under the act of Congress approved March 3, 1905, of Stephen Noble, son of George Noble, a Creek citizen, and Dilia[sic] Noble, a Seminole freedman.

It appears from the record in this case that application was also made for the enrollment of this child as a citizen of the Creek Nation, and you are requested to advise the Seminole Enrollment Division the status of his application for enrollment as a citizen of the Creek Nation; if he has been enrolled, his roll number and the date of his approval by the Secretary of the Interior.

Respectfully,

Commissioner.

Sem-Fr-NB-9   **COPY**
Muskogee, Indian Territory, January 7, 1907.

Wilmott[sic] & Wilhoit,
   Attorneys at Law,
      Wewoka, Indian Territory.

Gentlemen:

I inclose herewith a copy of the decision of the commissioner to the, rendered January 7, 1907, denying the application for the enrollment of Stephen Noble as a citizen of the Seminole Nation.

The decision, with the proceedings in the case is this day transmitted to the Secretary of the Interior for review. The final decision of the Secretary will be made known to you as soon as this office is informed of the same.

Respectfully,

SIGNED   *Tams Bixby*
Commissioner.

Sem-Fr-NB-9

Applications for Enrollment of Seminole Newborn Freedmen
Act of 1905

DEPARTMENT OF THE INTERIOR,
WASHINGTON

KHM

FHE

I.T.D. 3940-1907
D.C. 10646-1907

February 19, 1907.

LRS

Direct.

Commissioner to the Five Civilized Tribes,
    Muskogee, Indian Territory.

Sir:

January 7, 1907, you transmitted the record in the matter of the application for the enrollment of application for the enrollment of Stephen Noble as a citizen of the Seminole Nation, including your decision of the same date, denying said application.

Reporting February 16, 1907 (Land 2525-07), the Indian Office recommends that your decision be approved. A copy of its letter is inclosed.

Your decision is hereby affirmed. The papers in the case and a carbon copy hereof have been sent to the Indian Office.

Respectfully,

Thos. Ryan,
    First Assistant Secretary.

1 inc. and 2 for Ind. Of.

A. F. Mc.
2-20-07.

45

Applications for Enrollment of Seminole Newborn Freedmen
Act of 1905

Refer in reply to the following:

(COPY)
DEPARTMENT OF THE INTERIOR,
LAND OFFICE OF INDIAN AFFAIRS,
2525-1907. WASHINGTON.

February 16, 1907.

The Honorable,
 The Secretary of the Interior.
Sir:

There is enclosed a report from the Commissioner to the Five Civilized Tribes, dated January 7, 1907, transmitting the record relative to the application of Stephen Noble for enrollment as a citizen of the Seminole Nation, together with the Commissioner's decision of January 7, 1907, denying the application.

The record shows that the applicant is the son of George Noble, enrolled at No. 4920, approved roll of Creek freedmen, and Delia Noble, enrolled at No. 2004, approved roll of citizens of the Seminole Nation, and that George Noble, father of the applicant, appeared before the Commissioner to the on November 16, 1905, and elected on behalf of the applicant, that he be enrolled as a Creek freedman.

It further shows that the name of Stephen Noble, this applicant, appears on the approved roll of Creek freedmen at No. 5659.

Under the provisions of the Act of June 28, 1898 (30 Stats. L., 495), the applicant is not entitled to enrollment as a Seminole, his father having elected to have him enrolled as a Creek freedman, and he approval of the Commissioner's adverse decision is recommended.

Very respectfully,

C. F. Larrabee,
GAW-GH Acting Commissioner.

46

Applications for Enrollment of Seminole Newborn Freedmen
Act of 1905

Sem NB FR 10
BIRTH AFFIDAVIT.

DEPARTMENT OF THE INTERIOR.
COMMISSION TO THE FIVE CIVILIZED TRIBES.

IN RE APPLICATION FOR ENROLLMENT, as a citizen of the   Seminole   Nation, of
Virgil Bruner   , born on the   15   day of   April   , 1902

Name of Father: Jim Bruner   (F-1528) a citizen of the   Seminole   Nation.
Name of Mother: Bessie Bennett   (F-2013) a citizen of the   Seminole   Nation.

Postoffice   Earlsboro I.T.

Child present

AFFIDAVIT OF MOTHER.

UNITED STATES OF AMERICA, Indian Territory,
Western   DISTRICT.

I,   Dinah Walker   , on oath state that I am   47   years of age and a citizen by
adoption   , of the   Seminole   Nation; that I am the mother of Bessie Bennett,
deceased; that she was not   the lawful wife of   Jim Bruner   , who is a citizen, by
blood   of the   Seminole   Nation; that a   female   child was born to ~~me~~ her on
15th day of   April   , 1902, that said child has been named   Virgil Bruner   , and
is now living.   her
                                           Dinah x Walker
Witnesses To Mark: mark
⌠ Frank C. Sabourin
⌡ Chas E Webster

Subscribed and sworn to before me this   5th day of   April   , 1905.

Chas E Webster
Notary Public.

AFFIDAVIT OF ATTENDING PHYSICIAN OR MID-WIFE.

UNITED STATES OF AMERICA, Indian Territory,
Western   DISTRICT.
                                                   was with
I,   Eugene Walker   , ~~a~~   ——————————, on oath state that I ~~attended on~~
Mrs. Bessie Bennett   , ~~wife of~~ ——on the   15th day of   April   , 1902; that there
was born to her on said date a   female   child; that said child is now living and is said
to have been named Virgil Bruner

47

Applications for Enrollment of Seminole Newborn Freedmen
Act of 1905

Witnesses To Mark:

see sig. below

{

Subscribed and sworn to before me this 5th day of April , 1905.

           Chas E Webster   Eugene Walker
           Notary Public.   Notary Public.

Territory of Oklahoma, County of Pottawatomie, as.

We, the undersigned, Louella Jenkins and Ben Jenkins state on oath that we know Arthur Turner, son of Tom Turner and Fanny Turner, and he was born on the first day of January 1903 and was living on the fourth day of March 1905 and is still living.

Witness our hands this 19th day of July 1905

	her
Witness to mark:	Louella x Jenkins
	mark
(Name Illegible)	his
	Ben x Jenkins
R.E. Williamson	mark

Territory of Oklahoma, County of Pottawatomie, as.

Be It Remembered, That on this day came before the undersigned, a Notary Public within and for the County and Territory aforesaid duly commissioned and acting, Louella Jenkins and Ben Jenkins to me well known as the parties who signed the foregoing affidavit and stated that they executed the same for the consideration, uses and purposes therein mentioned and set forth. Witness my hand and seal as such Notary Public this 19th day of July 1905.

                             A J Grayson
My commission expires April 3d 1906.   Notary Public.

Applications for Enrollment of Seminole Newborn Freedmen
Act of 1905

Sem NB FR 11
BIRTH AFFIDAVIT.

DEPARTMENT OF THE INTERIOR.
COMMISSION TO THE FIVE CIVILIZED TRIBES.

IN RE APPLICATION FOR ENROLLMENT, as a citizen of the   Seminole   Nation, of
Arthur Turner   , born on the   1st day of   January   , 1903

Name of Father: Tom Turner   a citizen of the   U.S.   ~~Nation~~.
Name of Mother: Fanny Turner   (2021)   a citizen of the   Seminole   Nation.

Postoffice   Earlsboro, I.T.

Child not present   Father
AFFIDAVIT OF ~~MOTHER~~.

Mother dead.

UNITED STATES OF AMERICA, Indian Territory,
Western   DISTRICT.

    I,   Tom Turner   , on oath state that I am   31   years of age and a citizen ~~by~~
——— , of the   U.S.   ~~Nation~~; that I ~~am~~ was the lawful ~~wife~~ husband of   Fanny
Turner, deceased   , who is a citizen, by   adoption   of the   Seminole   Nation;
that a   male   child was born to ~~me~~ her on   1st day of   January   , 1903; that
said child has been named   Arthur Turner   , and was living March 4, 1905.

Tom Turner

Witnesses To Mark:

{

    Subscribed and sworn to before me this   9th day of   May   , 1905.

Chas E Webster
Notary Public.

AFFIDAVIT OF ATTENDING PHYSICIAN OR MID-WIFE.

UNITED STATES OF AMERICA, Indian Territory,
Western   DISTRICT.

    I,   Nina Walker   , a   midwife   , on oath state that I attended on
Mrs.   Fannie Turner   , wife of   Tom Turner   on the   1st day of   January   ,
1903; that there was born to her on said date a   male   child; that said child was living
March 4, 1905, and is said to have been named Arthur Turner
her
Nina   x   Walker
mark

49

Applications for Enrollment of Seminole Newborn Freedmen
Act of 1905

Witnesses To Mark:
{ Chas E Webster
{ Frank C. Sabourin

Subscribed and sworn to before me 16 day of   May   , 1905.

Chas E Webster
Notary Public.

Sem. Freed.
NB-11.

Muskogee, Indian Territory, June 29, 1905.

Tom Turner,
Earlsboro, Oklahoma Territory.

Dear Sir:

On May 9, 1905, you appeared before the Commission and made application for the enrollment of your son Arthur Turner, born January 1, 1903, as a Seminole freedman and submitted at that time your affidavit and the affidavit of Nina Walker, midwife, as to the birth of said child.

The mother of said child being dead it will be necessary for you to furnish in lieu of her affidavit as to the birth of said child the affidavits of two disinterested persons who know the circumstances attending his birth, when he was born, the names of his parents and whether or not it was living March 4, 1905.

You should give this matter your immediate attention.

Respectfully,

Chairman.

50

Applications for Enrollment of Seminole Newborn Freedmen
Act of 1905

Seminole NB-11. Freed

Muskogee, Indian Territory July 17, 1905.

Tom Turner,
Earlsboro, Oklahoma Territory.

Dear Sir:

Receipt is hereby acknowledged of your letter of July -- 1905 in which you state that your son Arthur Turner was born January 1, 1903 and that two disinterested parties who know of the birth of said child are Louella Jenkins and Pinkie Sutton and that said parties also know that your said said[sic] son was living March 4, 1905.

Your letter is evidently in response to a letter of the Commission to the Five Civilized Tribes of June 29, 1905 requesting you to furnish, in the matter of the application for the enrollment of your son Arthur Turner as a Seminole freedman, the affidavits of two disinterested persons who know the circumstances attending the birth of said child, when he was born, the names of his parents and whether or not it was living March 4, 1905.

You are, therefore, again advised that it will be necessary for you to furnish the Commission with the affidavits of two disinterested persons as to the birth of your son Arthur Turner and are requested to take Louella Jenkins and Pinkie Sutton, whom you state have a personal knowledge of the birth of said child, before a notary public in order that they may make affidavits as to the birth of said child and as to whether or not he was living on March 4, 1905.

When the affidavits have been made send them to this office in the inclosed envelope.

Respectfully,

Commissioner.

Env.

Sem. Freed.
NB-11.

Muskogee, Indian Territory, July 25, 1905.

Tom Turner,
Earlsboro, Oklahoma Territory.

Dear Sir:

Receipt is hereby acknowledged of the affidavits of Louella Jenkins and Ben Jenkins relative to the birth of your son Arthur Turner on January 1, 1903 and the same

51

Applications for Enrollment of Seminole Newborn Freedmen
Act of 1905

have been filed with the records of this office in the matter of the enrollment of your said son Arthur Turner as a Seminole Freedman.

Respectfully,

Commissioner.

Sem NB FR 12
BIRTH AFFIDAVIT.
DEPARTMENT OF THE INTERIOR.
COMMISSION TO THE FIVE CIVILIZED TRIBES.

IN RE APPLICATION FOR ENROLLMENT, as a citizen of the   Seminole   Nation, of
Garfield Wilson   , born on the   24   day of   Dec   , 1903

Name of Father: Jake Wilson   a citizen of the   U S   ~~Nation~~.
Name of Mother: Minerva Wilson   2035   a citizen of the   Seminole   Nation.

Postoffice

(Child present)

AFFIDAVIT OF MOTHER.

UNITED STATES OF AMERICA, Indian Territory,⎫
          Western   **DISTRICT.**   ⎭

I,   Minerva Wilson   , on oath state that I am   about 25   years of age and a citizen by   adoption   , of the   Seminole   Nation; that I am the lawful wife of Jake Wilson   , who is a citizen, ~~by~~   of the   U.S.   Nation; that a   male child was born to me on   24   day of   Dec   , 1903; that said child has been named Garfield Wilson   , and was living March 4, 1905.

                                                            her
                                              Minerva x Wilson
Witnesses To Mark: mark
⎧ Chas E Webster
⎩ Frank C. Sabourin

52

Applications for Enrollment of Seminole Newborn Freedmen
Act of 1905

Subscribed and sworn to before me this 17 day of   May   , 1905.

Chas E Webster
Notary Public.

AFFIDAVIT OF ATTENDING PHYSICIAN OR MID-WIFE.

UNITED STATES OF AMERICA, Indian Territory, ⎱
Western   DISTRICT.   ⎰

I, Mary Ann Bruner , mother of Minerva Wilson , on oath state that I attended on
Mrs.   Minerva Wilson   , wife of   Jake Wilson   on the 24 day of   Dec   ,
1903; that there was born to her on said date a   male   child; that said child was living
March 4, 1905, and is said to have been named Garfield Wilson

                                                          her
                                          Mary Ann x Bruner
Witnesses To Mark: mark
  ⎧ Chas E Webster
  ⎩ Frank C. Sabourin

Subscribed and sworn to before me 17 day of   May   , 1905.

Chas E Webster
Notary Public.

Sem NB FR 12
BIRTH AFFIDAVIT.

DEPARTMENT OF THE INTERIOR.
COMMISSION TO THE FIVE CIVILIZED TRIBES.

IN RE APPLICATION FOR ENROLLMENT, as a citizen of the   Seminole   Nation, of
Leah Wilson   , born on the 5 day of Feb , 1903

Name of Father: Jake Wilson   a citizen of the   U S   ~~Nation.~~
Name of Mother: Minerva Wilson   2035   a citizen of the   Seminole   Nation.

Postoffice   Wolf IT

Child present

AFFIDAVIT OF MOTHER.

UNITED STATES OF AMERICA, Indian Territory, ⎱
Western   DISTRICT.   ⎰

I, Minerva Wilson   , on oath state that I am about 25   years of age and a
citizen by   adoption   , of the   Seminole   Nation; that I am the lawful wife of

53

Applications for Enrollment of Seminole Newborn Freedmen
Act of 1905

Jake Wilson , who is a citizen, ~~by~~ ~~adop~~ of the U.S. Nation; that a
Female child was born to me on 5 day of Feb , 1903; that said child has
been named Leah Wilson , and was living March 4, 1905.

her
Minerva x Wilson
mark

Witnesses To Mark:
⎧ Chas E Webster
⎩ Frank C. Sabourin

Subscribed and sworn to before me this 17 day of May , 1905.

Chas E Webster
Notary Public.

AFFIDAVIT OF ATTENDING PHYSICIAN OR MID-WIFE.

UNITED STATES OF AMERICA, Indian Territory, ⎫
    Western   **DISTRICT.** ⎬

    I, Mary Ann Bruner , mother of Minerva Wilson , on oath state that I attended on
Mrs. Minerva Wilson , wife of Jake Wilson on the 5 day of Feb ,
1903; that there was born to her on said date a Female child; that said child was
living March 4, 1905, and is said to have been named Leah Wilson

her
Mary Ann x Bruner
mark

Witnesses To Mark:
⎧ Chas E Webster
⎩ Frank C. Sabourin

Subscribed and sworn to before me 17 day of May , 1905.

Chas E Webster
Notary Public.

Applications for Enrollment of Seminole Newborn Freedmen
Act of 1905

Sem NB FR 13
BIRTH AFFIDAVIT.

DEPARTMENT OF THE INTERIOR.
COMMISSION TO THE FIVE CIVILIZED TRIBES.

IN RE APPLICATION FOR ENROLLMENT, as a citizen of the   Seminole   Nation, of
Harkes Jefferson   , born on the 25   day of December   , 1903

Name of Father: Thomas Jefferson   a citizen of the   Creek   Nation.
                                    ⌠nee Williams)
Name of Mother: Julia Jefferson   ⌊   (2048)   a citizen of the   Seminole   Nation.

Postoffice   Wewoka I.T.

Child present

AFFIDAVIT OF MOTHER.

UNITED STATES OF AMERICA, Indian Territory, ⌉
     Western   DISTRICT.   ⌡

I,   Julia Jefferson (nee Williams)   , on oath state that I am 21   years of age and
a citizen by   adoption   , of the   Seminole   Nation; that I am the lawful wife
of Thomas Jefferson   , who is a citizen, by   adoption   of the   Creek   Nation;
that a   male   child was born to me on   25   day of December   , 1903, that said
child has been named   Harkes Jefferson   , and is now living.

Julia Jefferson
Witnesses To Mark:
⌠
⌊
     Subscribed and sworn to before me this 18   day of   May   , 1905.

Chas E Webster
Notary Public.

AFFIDAVIT OF ATTENDING PHYSICIAN OR MID-WIFE.

UNITED STATES OF AMERICA, Indian Territory, ⌉
     Western   DISTRICT.   ⌡

I,   Jennie Thompson   , a   midwife   , on oath state that I attended on
Mrs. Julia Jefferson   , wife of   Thomas Jefferson   on the   25   day of
December , 1903; that there was born to her on said date a   male   child; that said
child is now living and is said to have been named Harkes Jefferson

55

Applications for Enrollment of Seminole Newborn Freedmen
Act of 1905

Witnesses To Mark:
{ Frank C. Sabourin
  Chas E Webster

her
Jennie x Thompson
mark

Subscribed and sworn to before me this 18 day of   May   , 1905.

Chas E Webster
Notary Public.

Sem NB FR 13
BIRTH AFFIDAVIT.

DEPARTMENT OF THE INTERIOR.
COMMISSION TO THE FIVE CIVILIZED TRIBES.

IN RE APPLICATION FOR ENROLLMENT, as a citizen of the   Seminole   Nation, of
Ollie Renty   , born on the 6   day of   June   , 1901
(2118)
Name of Father: Robert Renty, deceased   a citizen of the   Seminole   Nation.
2048
Name of Mother: Julia Jefferson (nee Williams) a citizen of the   Seminole   Nation.

Postoffice   Wewoka I.T.

Child present

AFFIDAVIT OF MOTHER.

UNITED STATES OF AMERICA, Indian Territory,
    Western   DISTRICT.

I,   Julia Jefferson (nee Williams)   , on oath state that I am 21 years of age and
a citizen by   adoption   , of the   Seminole   Nation; that I ~am~ was not the
lawful wife of   Robert Renty, deceased   , who ~is~ was a citizen, by   adoption   of
the   Seminole   Nation; that a   female   child was born to me on   6   day of
June   , 1901, that said child has been named   Ollie Renty   , and is now living.

Julia Jefferson
Witnesses To Mark:
{

Subscribed and sworn to before me this 18   day of   May   , 1905.

Chas E Webster
Notary Public.

56

Applications for Enrollment of Seminole Newborn Freedmen
Act of 1905

UNITED STATES OF AMERICA, Indian Territory, ⎫
   Western   DISTRICT. ⎬

I,   Jennie Thompson   , a   midwife   , on oath state that I attended on Mrs. Julia Jefferson   , ~~wife of~~ then Julia Williams   on the   6   day of   June , 1901; that there was born to her on said date a   female   child; that said child is now living and is said to have been named   Ollie Renty

her
Jennie x Thompson

Witnesses To Mark: mark
⎰ Frank C. Sabourin
⎱ Chas E Webster

Subscribed and sworn to before me this   18   day of   May   , 1905.

Chas E Webster
Notary Public.

Sem Fr NB 13

Muskogee, Indian Territory, June 29, 1905.

Commission to the
      Five Civilized Tribes,
           Creek Enrollment Division.

Gentlemen:

On May 18, 1905, there was filed with the Commission application for the enrollment of Harkes Jefferson, born December 25, 1903, as a Seminole Freedman. It is stated in said application that the father of said child is Thomas Jefferson, a citizen by adoption of the Creek Nation, and that the mother is Julia Jefferson, nee Williams, a Seminole Freedman.

You are requested to inform the Seminole Enrollment Division as to whether application has been made to the Commission for the enrollment of said Harkes Jefferson as a citizen of the Creek Nation, and if so what disposition, if any, has been made of such application.

Respectfully,

Chairman.

HGH
DEPARTMENT OF THE INTERIOR.
COMMISSION TO THE FIVE CIVILIZED TRIBES.
(Sem.Fr.NB.13)

Muskogee, Indian Territory, July 10, 1905.

Seminole Enrollment Division,
General Office.

Gentlemen:

Receipt is acknowledged of your letter of June 29, 1905 (Sem.Fr.NB.13), in which you ask if application for enrollment as a citizen of the Creek Nation has been made for Harkes Jefferson, child of Thomas Jefferson, a citizen of the Creek Nation, and Julia Jefferson, (nee Williams), a Seminole Freedman

In reply you are advised that the records of this office have been examined and it does not appear that application has been made for the enrollment of said Harkes Jefferson, as a citizen of the Creek Nation.

Respectfully,

Tams Bixby
Commissioner.

Sem NB FR 14
BIRTH AFFIDAVIT.   Mother's Roll #2054 Father's Roll #2315.
DEPARTMENT OF THE INTERIOR.
COMMISSION TO THE FIVE CIVILIZED TRIBES.

IN RE APPLICATION FOR ENROLLMENT, as a citizen of the   Seminole   Nation, of
Leford Jackson   , born on the 14   day of   September , 1902

Name of Father: Davis Jackson   (#2315)   a citizen of the   Seminole   Nation.
Name of Mother: Martha Barkus (Nee Stepney) a citizen of the   Seminole   Nation.

Postoffice   Wewoka, I.T.

58

Applications for Enrollment of Seminole Newborn Freedmen
Act of 1905

_____

AFFIDAVIT OF MOTHER.

UNITED STATES OF AMERICA, Indian Territory,
Western   DISTRICT.

I,   Martha Barkus (nee Stepney)   , on oath state that I am   22   years of age
and a citizen by   adoption   , of the   Seminole   Nation; that I am not the lawful
wife of   Davis Jackson (Freedman)   , who is a citizen, by   ~~blood~~   of the
Seminole   Nation; that a   male   child was born to me on   14   day of
September   , 1902; that said child has been named   Leford Jackson   , and was
living March 4, 1905.

                              Martha Barkus
Witnesses To Mark:

{

Subscribed and sworn to before me this   2nd   day of   May   , 1905.

                    Chas E Webster
                    Notary Public.

_____

AFFIDAVIT OF ATTENDING PHYSICIAN OR MID-WIFE.

UNITED STATES OF AMERICA, Indian Territory,
Western   DISTRICT.

iss I,   Harriett Dennis   , a   midwife   , on oath state that I attended on
M~~rs~~.   Martha Stepney   now the , wife of   Sango Barkus   on the   14   day of
September   , 1902; that there was born to her on said date a   male   child; that
said child was living March 4, 1905, and is said to have been named   Leford Jackson
                              her
                    Harriett x Dennis
Witnesses To Mark: mark
    { Frank C. Sabourin
    { Ed. Merrick

Subscribed and sworn to before me   2nd   day of   May   , 1905.

                    Chas E Webster
                    Notary Public.

_____

59

Applications for Enrollment of Seminole Newborn Freedmen
Act of 1905

Sem NB FR 14   Father's Roll No. 2061
BIRTH AFFIDAVIT.   Mother's   "   "   2054

DEPARTMENT OF THE INTERIOR.
COMMISSION TO THE FIVE CIVILIZED TRIBES.

IN RE APPLICATION FOR ENROLLMENT, as a citizen of the   Seminole   Nation, of
Laddie Barkus   , born on the 26   day of   October   , 1904

Name of Father: Sango Barkus   a citizen of the   Seminole   Nation.
Name of Mother: Martha Barkus (Nee Stepney) a citizen of the   Seminole   Nation.

Postoffice   Wewoka, I.T.

Child present

AFFIDAVIT OF MOTHER.

UNITED STATES OF AMERICA, Indian Territory, ⎤
    Western   **DISTRICT.** ⎦

    I,   Martha Barkus (nee Stepney)   , on oath state that I am   22   years of age
and a citizen by   adoption   , of the   Seminole   Nation; that I am the lawful wife
of   Sango Barkus   , who is a citizen, by   adoption   of the   Seminole
Nation; that a   female   child was born to me on   26   day of   October   , 1904;
that said child has been named   Laddie Barkus   , and was living March 4, 1905.

                                         Martha Barkus
Witnesses To Mark:

⎰
⎱

    Subscribed and sworn to before me this   2nd   day of   May   , 1905.

                               Chas E Webster
                               Notary Public.

AFFIDAVIT OF ATTENDING PHYSICIAN OR MID-WIFE.

UNITED STATES OF AMERICA, Indian Territory, ⎤
    Western   **DISTRICT.** ⎦

    I,   Harriett Dennis   , a   midwife   , on oath state that I attended on
Mrs.   Martha Barkus   , wife of   Sango Barkus   on the   26 day of October   ,
1904; that there was born to her on said date a   female   child; that said child was
living March 4, 1905, and is said to have been named   Laddie Barkus
                                        her
                         Harriett x Dennis
                           mark

Applications for Enrollment of Seminole Newborn Freedmen
Act of 1905

Witnesses To Mark:
⎧ Frank C. Sabourin
⎩ Ed. Merrick

Subscribed and sworn to before me 2nd day of May , 1905.

Chas E Webster
Notary Public.

Sem NB FR 15
BIRTH AFFIDAVIT.

DEPARTMENT OF THE INTERIOR.
COMMISSION TO THE FIVE CIVILIZED TRIBES.

IN RE APPLICATION FOR ENROLLMENT, as a citizen of the   Seminole   Nation, of
Soper Barkus   , born on the 6   day of Feby , 1903

Name of Father: Jonas Barkus   (2501)   a citizen of the   Seminole   Nation.
Name of Mother: Amey Barkus   (2062)   a citizen of the   Seminole   Nation.

Postoffice   Wewoka, I.T.

(Child present)

AFFIDAVIT OF MOTHER.
Grandfather
UNITED STATES OF AMERICA, Indian Territory, ⎫   (Mother sick, father away)
Western   DISTRICT. ⎭

I,   Dosar Barkus   , on oath state that I am 55   years of age and a citizen by
adoption   , of the   Seminole   Nation; that I am the lawful wife the grandfather
of   Amey Barkus   , who is a citizen, by   adoption   of the   Seminole
Nation; that a   male   child was born to me her on 6   day of Feby   , 1903, that
said child has been named   Soper Barkus   , and is now living.

61

Applications for Enrollment of Seminole Newborn Freedmen
Act of 1905

Witnesses To Mark:
{ Chas E Webster
{ Frank C. Sabourin

his
Dosar x Barkus
mark

Subscribed and sworn to before me this 6 day of   May   , 1905.

Chas E Webster
Notary Public.

AFFIDAVIT OF ATTENDING PHYSICIAN OR MID-WIFE.

UNITED STATES OF AMERICA, Indian Territory, ⎤
    Western   **DISTRICT.** ⎦

    I,   Rhoda Cudjo   , a   midwife   , on oath state that I attended on
Mrs. Amey Barkus   , ~~wife of~~   on the 6 day of Feby , 1903; that there was
born to her on said date a   male   child; that said child is now living and is said to
have been named Soper Barkus   her

                             Rhoda x Cudjo
Witnesses To Mark: mark
{ Chas E Webster
{ Frank C. Sabourin

Subscribed and sworn to before me this 6 day of   May   , 1905.

Chas E Webster
Notary Public.

Sem NB FR 15
BIRTH AFFIDAVIT.
DEPARTMENT OF THE INTERIOR.
COMMISSION TO THE FIVE CIVILIZED TRIBES.

    IN RE APPLICATION FOR ENROLLMENT, as a citizen of the   Seminole   Nation, of
Soper Barkus   , born on the 6 day of Feby , 1903

Name of Father: Jonas Barkus   2501   a citizen of the Seminole Nation.
Name of Mother: Amey Barkus   2062   a citizen of the Seminole Nation.

Postoffice   Wewoka, I.T.

62

Applications for Enrollment of Seminole Newborn Freedmen
Act of 1905

(Child present)

AFFIDAVIT OF MOTHER.

UNITED STATES OF AMERICA, Indian Territory, ⎱
   Western   **DISTRICT.** ⎰

    I,   Amey Barkus   , on oath state that I am about 20 years of age and a citizen by   adoption   , of the   Seminole   Nation; that I am the lawful wife of Jonas Barkus   , who is a citizen, by   adoption   of the   Seminole   Nation; that a male   child was born to me on   6   day of   Feb   , 1903, that said child has been named   Soper Barkus   , and is now living.

                                      Amey Barkus

Witnesses To Mark:
⎰

    Subscribed and sworn to before me this   29 day of   May   , 1905.

                        Chas E Webster
                        Notary Public.

DEPARTMENT OF THE INTERIOR

COMMISSIONER TO THE FIVE CIVILIZED TRIBES

-o-o-o-o-o-o-o-

    In the matter of the application for the enrollment of Margaret Bruner, deceased, as a Seminole Freedman.

-o-o-o-o-

New Born Seminole Freedman Card No. 16.

-o-o-

_____

Applications for Enrollment of Seminole Newborn Freedmen
Act of 1905

S.F.N.B. 16.

DEPARTMENT OF THE INTERIOR
COMMISSIONER TO THE FIVE CIVILIZED TRIBES

In the matter of the application for the enrollment of Margaret Bruner, deceased, as a Seminole Freedman.

ORDER

The record in this case shows that on May 1, 1905, there was filed with the Commission to the Five Civilized Tribes at Wewoka, Indian Territory, the application of Lucy Bruner for the enrollment of her minor child, Margaret Bruner, deceased, as a Seminole Freedman.

The evidence shows that said Margaret Bruner was born December 16, 1902, and that she died March 29, 1903.

The Act of Congress approved March 3, 1905 (Public No. 212), provides:

"That the Commission to the Five Civilized Tribes is authorized for ninety days after the date of the approval of this act to receive and consider applications for enrollment of infant children born prior to March fourth, nineteen hundred and five, and living on said latter date, to citizens of the Seminole tribe whose enrollment has been approved by the Secretary of the Interior; and to enroll and make allotments to such children, giving to each an equal number of acres of land, and such children shall also share equally with other citizens of the Seminole tribe in the distribution of all other tribal property and funds."

It is, therefore, ordered that there is no authority of law for the enrollment of said Margaret Bruner, deceased, as a Seminole Freedman and the application for her enrollment as such should be and the same is hereby dismissed.

Tams Bixby
Commissioner.

Muskogee, Indian Territory,
December 22, 1905

Applications for Enrollment of Seminole Newborn Freedmen
Act of 1905

Sem NB FR 16
BIRTH AFFIDAVIT.
DEPARTMENT OF THE INTERIOR.
COMMISSION TO THE FIVE CIVILIZED TRIBES.

IN RE APPLICATION FOR ENROLLMENT, as a citizen of the   Seminole   Nation, of
Margaret Bruner   , born on the 16   day of   Dec , 1902

Name of Father: Douglass Bruner   2065   a citizen of the   Seminole   Nation.
Name of Mother: Lucy Bruner   2066   a citizen of the   Seminole   Nation.

Postoffice   Wewoka, I.T.

AFFIDAVIT OF MOTHER.

UNITED STATES OF AMERICA, Indian Territory, ⎫
    Western   DISTRICT.   ⎭

I,   Lucy Bruner   , on oath state that I am   28   years of age and a citizen by
adoption   , of the   Seminole   Nation; that I am the lawful wife of   Douglass
Bruner   , who is a citizen, by adoption   of the   Seminole   Nation; that a
Female   child was born to me on   16ᵗʰ   day of   December   , 1902; that said
child has been named   Margaret Bruner   , ~~and was living March 4, 1905~~. and died
29ᵗʰ March 1903
                                        Lucy Bruner
Witnesses To Mark:
  ⎰
  ⎱
    Subscribed and sworn to before me this 1ˢᵗ   day of   May   , 1905.

                            Chas E Webster
                            Notary Public.

S N B F 16
                        Muskogee, Indian Territory, January 2, 1906.

Douglass Bruner,
    Wewoka, Indian Territory.

Dear Sir:

    Inclosed herewith you will find a copy of the order of the Commissioner to the
Five Civilized Tribes, dated December 22, 1905, dismissing the application for the
enrollment of your infant child, Margaret Bruner, as a Seminole freedman.

65

Applications for Enrollment of Seminole Newborn Freedmen
Act of 1905

Respectfully,

Registered.   Commissioner.
Incl. S N B F 16

S N B F 16

Muskogee, Indian Territory, January 2, 1906.

McKennon & Wilmott[sic],
    Attorneys for Seminole Nation,
        Wewoka, Indian Territory.

Gentlemen:

    Inclosed herewith you will find a copy of the order of the Commissioner to the Five Civilized Tribes, dated December 22, 1905, dismissing the application for the enrollment of your infant child, Margaret Bruner, as a Seminole freedman.

Respectfully,

Incl. S N B F 16   Commissioner.

Sem NB FR 16
BIRTH AFFIDAVIT.
DEPARTMENT OF THE INTERIOR.
COMMISSION TO THE FIVE CIVILIZED TRIBES.

IN RE APPLICATION FOR ENROLLMENT, as a citizen of the   Seminole   Nation, of
Margaret Bruner   , born on the 16   day of   Dec , 1902

Name of Father: Douglass Bruner   2065   a citizen of the   Seminole   Nation.
Name of Mother: Lucy Bruner   2066   a citizen of the   Seminole   Nation.

Postoffice   Wewoka, I.T.

AFFIDAVIT OF MOTHER.

UNITED STATES OF AMERICA, Indian Territory, ⎫
    Western   DISTRICT. ⎰

    I,   Lucy Bruner   , on oath state that I am   28   years of age and a citizen by adoption   , of the   Seminole   Nation; that I am the lawful wife of   Douglass Bruner   , who is a citizen, by   adoption   of the   Seminole   Nation; that a

66

Female   child was born to me on   16th   day of   December   , 1902; that said child has been named   Margaret Bruner   , ~~and was living March 4, 1905~~. and died 29th March 1903

Lucy Bruner

Witnesses To Mark:

{

Subscribed and sworn to before me this 1st   day of   May   , 1905.

(Seal)   signed   Chas E Webster
                                                    Notary Public.

_____

Sem NB FR 16
BIRTH AFFIDAVIT.
DEPARTMENT OF THE INTERIOR.
COMMISSION TO THE FIVE CIVILIZED TRIBES.

_____

IN RE APPLICATION FOR ENROLLMENT, as a citizen of the   Seminole   Nation, of Zylphia Bruner   , born on the   21   day of   Jany , 1905

Name of Father: Douglass Bruner   a citizen of the   Seminole   Nation.
Name of Mother: Lucy Bruner   a citizen of the   Seminole   Nation.

Postoffice   Wewoka, I.T.

_____

Child present
AFFIDAVIT OF MOTHER.

UNITED STATES OF AMERICA, Indian Territory, }
    Western   **DISTRICT.**

      I,   Lucy Bruner   , on oath state that I am   28   years of age and a citizen by adoption   , of the   Seminole   Nation; that I am the lawful wife of   Douglass Bruner   , who is a citizen, by adoption   of the   Seminole   Nation; that a Female   child was born to me on   21   day of   Jany   , 1905; that said child has been named   Zylphia Bruner   , and was living March 4, 1905.

Lucy Bruner

Witnesses To Mark:

{

Subscribed and sworn to before me this 1st   day of   May   , 1905.

Chas E Webster
                                                    Notary Public.

Applications for Enrollment of Seminole Newborn Freedmen
Act of 1905

Husband, midwife dead

UNITED STATES OF AMERICA, Indian Territory,
Western   DISTRICT.

am the husband of

I,   Douglass Bruner   , a   , on oath state that I ~~attended on~~
Mrs.   Lucy Bruner   , ~~wife of~~ and was present   on the 21 day of   Jany   ,
1905; that there was born to her on said date a   Female   child; that said child was
living March 4, 1905, and is said to have been named   Zylphia Bruner

                                        Douglass Bruner
Witnesses To Mark:

{

    Subscribed and sworn to before me 1ˢᵗ   day of   May   , 1905.

                                        Chas E Webster
                                        Notary Public.

Sem NB FR 17
BIRTH AFFIDAVIT.
DEPARTMENT OF THE INTERIOR,
COMMISSION TO THE FIVE CIVILIZED TRIBES.

    IN RE Application for Enrollment, as a citizen of the   Seminole   Nation,
of Mary Scott , born on the 19   day of   Jan   , 1903

Name of Father: Alex Scott   a citizen of the   Creek   Nation.
Name of Mother: Tayre Davis   (2075)   a citizen of the   Seminole Nation.

                        Post-office: Wewoka

Applications for Enrollment of Seminole Newborn Freedmen
Act of 1905

UNITED STATES OF AMERICA,
   INDIAN TERRITORY.
Western   District.

I,   Tayre Scott   , on oath state that I am   about 25   years of age and a citizen by adoption , of the Seminole Nation; that I am the lawful wife of Alex Scott , who is a citizen, by adoption of the Creek Nation; that a Female child was born to me on the 19 day of January , 1903 , that said child has been named Mary Scott , and is now living.

her
Tayre x Scott nee Davis
mark

WITNESSES TO MARK:
{ John R McBeth
{ R G Gainey

Subscribed and sworn to before me this 26th *day of* April *, 1905.*

O T McConnell
NOTARY PUBLIC.

UNITED STATES OF AMERICA,
   INDIAN TERRITORY.
Western   District.

I,   Dina Davis   , a   midwife   , on oath state that I attended on Mrs. Tayre Scott , wife of Alex Scott on the 19th day of January , 1903 ; that there was born to her on said date a Female child; that said child is now living and is said to have been named Mary Scott

her
Dina x Davis
mark

WITNESSES TO MARK:
{ John R McBeth
{ R G Gainey

Subscribed and sworn to before me this 26 *day of* April *, 1905.*

O T McConnell
NOTARY PUBLIC.

Applications for Enrollment of Seminole Newborn Freedmen
Act of 1905

Sem NB FR 17

BIRTH AFFIDAVIT.

DEPARTMENT OF THE INTERIOR,
COMMISSION TO THE FIVE CIVILIZED TRIBES.

IN RE Application for Enrollment, as a citizen of the   Seminole   Nation, of   Jennie Scott , born on the   17th   day of   September , 1904

Name of Father: Alex Scott   a citizen of the   Creek   Nation.

Name of Mother: Tayre Davis   (2075)   a citizen of the   Seminole   Nation.

Post-office: Wewoka   IT

AFFIDAVIT OF MOTHER.

UNITED STATES OF AMERICA, ⎰
    INDIAN TERRITORY.   ⎱
    Western   District. ⎰

    I,   Tayre Scott   nee Davis   , on oath state that I am   about 25   years of age and a citizen by   adoption , of the   Seminole   Nation; that I am the lawful wife of Alex Scott , who is a citizen, by   adoption   of the   Creek   Nation; that a   Female   child was born to me on the   17th   day of   September , 1904 , that said child has been named Jennie Scott , and is now living.   her

                                 Tayre   x   Scott nee Davis

WITNESSES TO MARK: mark

    ⎰ John R McBeth
    ⎱ R G Gainey

Subscribed and sworn to before me this 26th *day of*   April , 1905.

                         O T McConnell
                            NOTARY PUBLIC.

AFFIDAVIT OF ATTENDING PHYSICIAN OR MID-WIFE.

UNITED STATES OF AMERICA, ⎰
    INDIAN TERRITORY.   ⎱
    Western   District. ⎰

    I,   Tayre Mills   , a   Midwife , on oath state that I attended on Mrs.   Tayre Scott , wife of   Alex Scott   on the   17th   day of   September , 1904 ; that there was born to her on said date a   Female   child; that said child is now living and is said to have been named   Jennie Scott

70

Applications for Enrollment of Seminole Newborn Freedmen
Act of 1905

  ⎰ John R McBeth
  ⎱ R G Gainey

her
Tayre x Mills
mark

Subscribed and sworn to before me this 26 *day of* April , 1905.

O T McCornell
NOTARY PUBLIC.

Sem NB FR 17
BIRTH AFFIDAVIT.

DEPARTMENT OF THE INTERIOR.
COMMISSION TO THE FIVE CIVILIZED TRIBES.

IN RE APPLICATION FOR ENROLLMENT, as a citizen of the   Seminole   Nation, of
Lucy Scott   , born on the 16 day of September , 1899

Name of Father: Alex Scott   a citizen of the ~~Seminole~~ Creek Nation.
Name of Mother: Tayre Davis   (2075)   a citizen of the Seminole Nation.

Postoffice   Wewoka I.T.

AFFIDAVIT OF MOTHER.

UNITED STATES OF AMERICA, Indian Territory,⎱
                              DISTRICT.⎰

    I,   Tayre Scott   , on oath state that I am about 25   years of age and a
citizen by   ~~Seminole~~ adoption   , of the   Seminole   Nation; that I am the
lawful wife of Alex Scott   , who is a citizen, by adoption of the   Creek
Nation; that a   Female   child was born to me on the 16th   day of   September
, 1899; that said child has been named Lucy Scott   , and was living March 4, 1905.

her
Tayre x Scott nee Davis
mark

Witnesses To Mark:
  ⎰ John R McBeth
  ⎱ R G Gainey

Subscribed and sworn to before me this 26th day of   April   , 1905.

O T McConnell
Notary Public.

Applications for Enrollment of Seminole Newborn Freedmen
Act of 1905

UNITED STATES OF AMERICA, Indian Territory, ⎫
Western   DISTRICT. ⎭

I,   Dina Davis   , a   Midwife   , on oath state that I attended on Mrs. Tayre Scott   , wife of   Alex Scott   on the 16th day of   September   , 1899; that there was born to her on said date a   Female   child; that said child was living March 4, 1905, and is said to have been named Lucy Scott

her
Dina x Davis

Witnesses To Mark: mark
⎰ John R McBeth
⎱ R G Gainey

Subscribed and sworn to before me this   26   day of   April   , 1905.

O T McConnell
Notary Public.

Sem. Freed.
NB-17.

Muskogee, Indian Territory, June 29, 1905.

Commission to the Five Civilized Tribes,
     Creek Enrollment Division.

Gentlemen:

On April 28, 1905 there were filed with the Commission applications for the enrollment of Lucy Scott, born September 16, 1899, Mary Scott, born January 19, 1903, and Jennie Scott, born September 17, 1904, as Seminole freedmen. It is stated in said application that the father of said children is Alex Scott, a citizen by adoption of the Creek Nation, and that their mother is Tayre Scott (who is identified as Tyra Davis upon the approved roll of Seminole freedmen.

You are requested to inform the Seminole Enrollment Division as to whether application has been made to the Commission for the enrollment of said children as citizens of the Creek Nation and if so what disposition, if any, has been made of such application.

Respectfully,

Chairman.

Applications for Enrollment of Seminole Newborn Freedmen
Act of 1905

HGH

DEPARTMENT OF THE INTERIOR.
COMMISSION TO THE FIVE CIVILIZED TRIBES.

Muskogee, Indian Territory, July 11, 1905.

Seminole Enrollment Division,
General Office.

Gentlemen:

Receipt is acknowledged of your communication of June 29, 1905 (Sem.Fr.NB.17), in which you ask if application for the enrollment as citizens of the Creek Nation has been made for Lucy, Mary and Jennie Scott, children of Alex Scott, a citizen of the Creek Nation, and Tayre Scott (or Tyra Davis), a Seminole Freedman.

In reply you are advised that the records of this office have been examined and it does not appear that application has been made for the enrollment of said Lucy, Mary and Jennie Scott, or either of them, as citizens of the Creek Nation.

Respectfully,

Tams Bixby Commissioner.

Sem NB FR 18
BIRTH AFFIDAVIT.
DEPARTMENT OF THE INTERIOR.
COMMISSION TO THE FIVE CIVILIZED TRIBES.

IN RE APPLICATION FOR ENROLLMENT, as a citizen of the   Seminole   Nation, of
Luther Whitfield   , born on the 3rd   day of   March   1905

Name of Father: William Whitfield   a citizen of the   U. S.   Nation.
Name of Mother: Jennie Whitfield   a citizen of the   Seminole   Nation.

73

Applications for Enrollment of Seminole Newborn Freedmen
Act of 1905

Postoffice   Emahaka, I.T.

_____

(Child present)

AFFIDAVIT OF MOTHER.

UNITED STATES OF AMERICA, Indian Territory, ⎫
Western   DISTRICT. ⎰

I,   Jennie Whitfield   , on oath state that I am 26 years of age and a citizen by adoption   , of the   Seminole   Nation; that I am the lawful wife of   William Whitfield   , who is a citizen, by - - - - - - - - - of the   U. S.   Nation; that a male   child was born to me on   3rd   day of   March   , 1905, that said child has been named   Luther Whitfield   , and is now living.

Jennie (her x mark) Whitfield

Witnesses To Mark:
⎧ Frank C. Sabourin
⎩ Chas. E. Webster.

Subscribed and sworn to before me this 15 day of   May   , 1905.

Chas. E. Webster
(SEAL)   Notary Public.

_____

AFFIDAVIT OF ATTENDING PHYSICIAN OR MID-WIFE.

UNITED STATES OF AMERICA, Indian Territory, ⎫
Western   DISTRICT. ⎰

I,   Rhoda Cudjo   , a   midwife   , on oath state that I attended on Mrs.   Jennie Whitfield   , wife of   William Whitfield   on the   3rd   day of March , 1905; that there was born to her on said date a   male   child; that said child is now living and is said to have been named   Luther Whitfield

Rhoda (her x mark) Cudjo.

Witnesses To Mark:
⎧ Frank C. Sabourin.
⎩ Chas. E. Webster.

Subscribed and sworn to before me this 15 day of   May   , 1905.

Chas E Webster
(SEAL)   Notary Public.

_____

74

Applications for Enrollment of Seminole Newborn Freedmen
Act of 1905

DEPARTMENT OF THE INTERIOR.
COMMISSION TO THE FIVE CIVILIZED TRIBES.

Wewoka, Indian Territory, May 15, 1905.

In the matter of the application for the enrollment of Luther Whitfield as a citizen of the Seminole Nation.

Jennie Whitfield, being duly sworn, testified as follows:

Q. What is your Name? A. Jennie Whitfield.
Q. How old are you? A. About 26.
Q. What is your post office? A. Emahaka.
Q. What is your husband's name? A. Will Whitfield.
Q. You desire to make application for the enrollment of your infant son, Luther Whitfield, as a citizen of the Seminole Nation? A. A.[sic] Yes sir.

The witness if identified on the records of this office as Jennie Whitfield, Seminole Freedman Card No. 666, Approved Roll No. 2081.

Q. When was Luther born? A. 3rd day of March, 1905.
Q. Do you know what day of the week that was? A. I have forgotten.
Q. What time of the day was he born? A. It was dark.
Q. You say you don't know what day of the week this child was born? A. No sir.
Q. Then how do you know it was on the 3rd day of March? A. I know it.
Q. Did you put it down anywhere? A. I didn't put it down, but my husband keeps account.
Q. Then you were told by your husband that it was on the 3rd day of March? A. Yes sir.
Q. You don't remember yourself? A. Yes, I remember it was the 3rd of March?
Q. What time of the night was this child born? A. I don't know what time of the night.
Q. About what time was it; early in the evening? A. No sir.
Q. It was in the night? A. Yes sir.
Q. About twelve o'clock? A. I reckon so; I can't say, as I haven't got a clock in the house.
Q. Who was at the house at the time this child was born? A. My granny and my husband were at the house.
Q. What was the name of your granny? A. Rhoda Cudjo.
Q. Now, you state that this child was born on the 3rd day of March, 1905; how old is the child now? A. Two months old.

William Whitfield, being duly sworn, testified as follows:

Q. What is your name? A. Will Whitfield; W. M. Whitfield is the way I sign it.
Q. How old are you? A. 37.
Q. What is your post office? A. Emahaka.
Q. Are you a citizen of the Seminole Nation? A. No sir.
Q. Are you a creek[sic] or a state man? A. A state man.

75

Applications for Enrollment of Seminole Newborn Freedmen
Act of 1905

Q. You are the husband of Jennie Whitfield? A. Yes sir, I am.

Q. You were with her at the time of the birth of Luther Whitfield? A. I was under the same roof, but not in the room.

Q. When was Luther born? A. Well, he was born on -- I disremember just the day of the month, whether it was the third or fourth, but it was on a Saturday.

Q. What time of the day was it? A. It was in the night.

Q. Do you know about what time? A. I[sic] might have been nine or ten o'clock or probably eleven o'clock. I went and laid down early and then I had to get up and go about two miles after this old lady and come back, and after we got back, the child was born.

Q. You had to go about two miles? A. Yes sir.

Q. How long after you got back was the child born? A. I don't know, it might have been half an hour or an hour I guess.

Q. You say you laid down about nine or ten o'clock and had to get up and go two miles after this granny? A. No, I didn't say I laid down about nine o'clock.

Q. What did you say? A. I said I laid down early and had to get up and go about two miles after the granny.

Q. Do you know what time it was when you went after the granny? A. No sir, I didn't notice my watch.

Q. You have a watch? A. Yes sir.

Q. Your wife stated there wasn't a clock in the house? A. There wasn't. I had my watch, it was in my clothes and not where she was.

Q. You remember it was on a Saturday night, the third of March? [sic] I am not positive e whether it was the third or fourth, but I know it was Saturday night; I can't say what day of the week March came in on.

Q. You are sure it was on Saturday night? A. I am sure of that, but I wouldn't swear whether it was on the third or fourth of March.

Q. Did you have any visitors at your home Sunday morning, the day after the child was born? A. I don't think we did.

Rhoda Cudjo, being duly sworn, testified as follows:

Q. What is your name? A. Rhoda Cudjo.

Q. How old are you? A. I don't know.

Q. Did you attend on Mrs. Jennie Whitfield at the birth of her youngest child, Luther? A. Yes sir.

Q. Do you remember what night that was? A. It was Saturday night.

Q. Do you know what day of the month it was? A. No sir, I don't know the months, when they come in or go out.

Q. What time of night was it that William Whitfield called for you? A. I couldn't tell. I was sleeping and he work me up.

Q. Had you been in bed very long? A. I had just gone to bed.

Q. How far do you live from William Whitfield? A. I couldn't tell you, because I don't know the miles.

Q. Was it twenty miles, or ten miles or five miles? A. It wasn't that far.

Q. How far do they call it from William Whitfield's to your place? A. Two miles.

Q. It was way after dark when he called for you? A. Yes sir.

Applications for Enrollment of Seminole Newborn Freedmen
Act of 1905

Q. And you had retired - had gone to bed? A. Yes sir.
Q. You don't remember the day of the month? A. I don't cunt the months.
Q. And you don't remember what time he came after you? A. No sir.
Q. You do remember it was Saturday night? A. Yes sir, because I went to meeting Sunday.
Q. Did you stay all night at the home of Jennie Whitfield? A. Yes sir.
Q. Did you see the child after you had gone to Church Sunday morning? A. Yes sir.
Q. The same Sunday? A. Yes sir.
Q. Has anyone ever told you on what day of the month or what day of the week this child was born? A. No sir.
Q. How do you know the child was born on the 3rd day of the month? A. I never count the days, and don't know. I just went and waited on her and that is all.
Q. All you remember is that the child was born on Saturday night? A. Yes sir.
Q. And the next day was Sunday? A. Yes sir.

----oOo----

Frank C. Sabourin, being duly sworn, states that the above and foregoing is a true and correct transcript of his stenographic notes taken in said case on May 15. 1905.

Frank C. Sabourin

Subscribed and sworn to before me this 16th day of May, 1905.

(seal)

Chas E Webster
Notary Public.

My Com expires April 28-1909

Sem-Fr-NB-18.

DEPARTMENT OF THE INTERIOR,
COMMISSIONER TO THE FIVE CIVILIZED TRIBES.

In the matter of the application for the enrollment of Luther Whitfield as a citizen of the Seminole Nation.

D E C I S I O N.

It appears from the record herein that on May 15, 1905, application was made to the Commission to the Five Civilized Tribes for the enrollment of Luther Whitfield as a citizen of the Seminole Nation under the provisions of the Act of Congress approved March 3, 1905 (33 Stats., 1070).

It further appears from the record herein that said applicant was born March 4, 1905, and is the son of Jennie Whitfield, whose name appears as number 2081 upon the

Applications for Enrollment of Seminole Newborn Freedmen
Act of 1905

final roll of citizens of the Seminole Nation approved by the Secretary of the Interior April 2, 1901, and William Whitfield, a non-citizen.

The Act of Congress approved March 3, 1905 (33 Stats., 1048), 1070), provides:

"That the Commission to the Five Civilized Tribes is authorized for ninety days after the date of the approval of this act to receive and consider applications for enrollment of infant children born prior to March fourth, nineteen hundred and five, and living on said latter date, to citizens of the Seminole tribe whose enrollment has been approved by the Secretary of the Interior; and to enroll and make allotments to such children, giving to each an equal number of acres of land, and such children shall also share equally with other citizens of the Seminole tribe in the distribution of all other tribal property and funds."

I am of the opinion that inasmuch as Luther Whitfield was not born prior to March 4, 1905, I am without authority to receive or consider any application for his enrollment as a citizen of the Seminole Nation of the Seminole Nation, and that, therefore, I should decline to receive or consider the same under the provisions of law above quoted, and it is so ordered.

Tams Bixby Commissioner.

Muskogee, Indian Territory.
JAN 11 1907

Sem-Fr-NB-18.

COPY

Muskogee, Indian Territory, January 11, 1907.

Jennie Whitfield,
Emahaka, Indian Territory.

Dear Madam:

Inclosed herewith you will find a copy of the decision of the Commissioner to the Five Civilized Tribes, rendered January 11, 1907, declining to receive the application for the enrollment of Luther Whitfield as a citizen of the Seminole Nation.

The decision, with the record of proceedings in the case, is this day transmitted to the Secretary of the Interior for review. The final decision of the Secretary will be made known to you as soon as this office is informed of the same.

Respectfully,

SIGNED *Tams Bixby*

Registered.   Commissioner.
Incl. Sem-Fr-NB-18.

78

Applications for Enrollment of Seminole Newborn Freedmen
Act of 1905

Sem-Fr-NB-18/[sic]   **COPY**

Muskogee, Indian Territory, January 11, 1907.

Willmott and Wilhoit,
    Attorneys for the Seminole Nation,
        Wewoka, Indian Territory.

Gentlemen:

Inclosed herewith you will find a copy of the decision of the Commissioner to the Five Civilized Tribes, rendered January 11, 1907, declining to receive the application for the enrollment of Luther Whitfield as a citizen of the Seminole Nation.

The decision, with the record of proceedings in the case, is this day transmitted to the Secretary of the Interior for review. The final decision of the Secretary will be made known to you as soon as this office is informed of the same.

Respectfully,

SIGNED *Tams Bixby*

Incl. Sem-Fr-NB-18.   Commissioner.

COPY

Muskogee, Indian Territory, January 11, 1907.

The Honorable,
    The Secretary of the Interior:

Sir:

There is transmitted herewith record of proceedings in the matter of the application for the enrollment of Luther Whitfield as a citizen of the Seminole Nation, including the decision of the Commissioner to the Five Civilized Tribes, dated January 11, 1907, declining to receive said application.

Respectfully,

SIGNED *Tams Bixby*

2 Incl. Sem-Fr-NB-18.   Commissioner.

Through the
    Commissioner of Indian Affairs.

79

Applications for Enrollment of Seminole Newborn Freedmen
Act of 1905

D.C. 12331

                                       GR

I.T.D. 5526-1907.   ELB

DEPARTMENT OF THE INTERIOR,

        WASHINGTON.   March 1, 1907.

LRS.

DIRECT.

Commissioner to the Five Civilized Tribes,
    Muskogee, Indian Territory.

Sir:

      January 11, 1907, you transmitted the record in the matter of the application for the enrollment of Luther Whitfield as a citizen of the Seminole Nation, including your decision of the same date, adverse to the applicant.

      Reporting February 25, 1907 (Land 3865), the Indian Office recommended that your decision be approved. A copy of its letter is inclosed.

      The Department concurs in said recommendation, and your decision is hereby affirmed.

      The papers in the case and a carbon copy hereof have been sent to the Indian Office.

                      Respectfully,

                            Jesse E. Wilson.

                            Assistant Secretary.

1 inc. and 2 to Ind. Of.

AFMc_____

3-107.

Applications for Enrollment of Seminole Newborn Freedmen
Act of 1905

Land.   COPY.
3865-1907.
DEPARTMENT OF THE INTERIOR,
OFFICE OF INDIAN AFFAIRS,
WASHINGTON.   February 25, 1907.

The Honorable,
The Secretary of the Interior.

Sir:-

I have the honor to transmit herewith a communication from the Commissioner to the Five Civilized Tribes, dated January 11, 1907, enclosing record in the matter of the application for the enrollment of Luther Whitfield as a citizen of the Seminole Nation, including the decision of the Commissioner, dated January 11, 1907, declining to receive the application.

It appears from the record herein that application was duly made to the Commission to the Five Civilized Tribes on May 15, 1905, for the enrollment of Luther Whitfield as a citizen of the Seminole Nation, under the provisions of the Act of Congress approved March 3, 1905 (33 Stats., 1070).

It further appears that the applicant was born on March 4, 1905, and is the son of Jennie Whitfield, whose name appears opposite No. 2081 on a final roll of citizens of the Seminole Nation approved April 2, 1901, and William Whitfield, a noncitizen.

The Act of Congress approved March 3, 1905, (33 Stat.L.,1070) provides:

That the Commission to the Five Civilized Tribes is authorized for ninety days after the approval of this Act to receive and consider applications for the enrollment of infant children born prior to March 4, 1905, and living on said latter date, to citizens of the Seminole tribe, whose enrollment has been approved by the Secretary of the Interior, and to enroll and make allotments to such children, giving to each an equal number of acres of land, and said children shall also share equally with other citizens of the Seminole tribe in the distribution of all other tribal property and funds.

Inasmuch as the applicant, Luther Whitfield, was not born prior to March 4, 1905, the Office is of the opinion that the decision of the Commissioner, dated January 11, 1907, declining to receive or consider he application for the enrollment of Luther Whitfield as a citizen of the Seminole Nation, is correct, and it is recommended that it be affirmed.

Very respectfully,

C. F. Larrabee,
Acting Commissioner.

EWE-SD

81

Applications for Enrollment of Seminole Newborn Freedmen
Act of 1905

Sem-Fr-NB-18.

Muskogee, Indian Territory, April 16, 1907.

Jennie Whitfield,
 Emahaka, Indian Territory.

Dear Madam:

You are hereby advised that on March 1, 1907, the Secretary of the Interior affirmed the decision of this office of January 11, 1907, declining to receive the application for the enrollment of Luther Whitfield as a citizen of the Seminole Nation.

Respectfully,

Commissioner.

Sem-Fr-NB-18.

Muskogee, Indian Territory, April 16, 1907.

Willmott & Withoit[sic],
 Attorneys for the Seminole Nation,
 Wewoka, Indian Territory.

Gentlemen:

You are hereby advised that on March 1, 1907, the Secretary of the Interior affirmed the decision of this office of January 11, 1907, declining to receive the application for the enrollment of Luther Whitfield as a citizen of the Seminole Nation.

Respectfully,

Commissioner.

Applications for Enrollment of Seminole Newborn Freedmen
Act of 1905

Sem NB FR 18
BIRTH AFFIDAVIT.
DEPARTMENT OF THE INTERIOR.
COMMISSION TO THE FIVE CIVILIZED TRIBES.

IN RE APPLICATION FOR ENROLLMENT, as a citizen of the   Seminole   Nation, of
Turner Whitfield   , born on the 9   day of   December , 1903

Name of Father: William Whitfield   a citizen of the   U. S.   Nation.
Name of Mother: Jennie Whitfield   (2081) a citizen of the   Seminole   Nation.

Postoffice   Emahaka, I.T.

Child present
AFFIDAVIT OF MOTHER.

UNITED STATES OF AMERICA, Indian Territory, ⎫
    Western   DISTRICT. ⎭

I,   Jennie Whitfield   , on oath state that I am   26 years of age and a citizen by
adoption   , of the   Seminole   Nation; that I am the lawful wife of   William
Whitfield   , who is a citizen, ~~by~~   of the   U. S.   ~~Nation;~~ that a   male
child was born to me on   9   day of   December   , 1903, that said child has been
named   Turner Whitfield   , and is now living.

                                        her
                                Jennie x Whitfield
Witnesses To Mark: mark
    ⎰ Frank C. Sabourin
    ⎱ Chas E Webster

Subscribed and sworn to before me this   15 day of   May   , 1905.

                            Chas. E. Webster
                                Notary Public.

AFFIDAVIT OF ATTENDING PHYSICIAN OR MID-WIFE.

UNITED STATES OF AMERICA, Indian Territory, ⎫
    Western   DISTRICT. ⎭

I,   Rhoda Cudjo   , a   midwife   , on oath state that I attended on
Mrs. Jennie Whitfield   , wife of   William Whitfield   on the 9   day of
December , 1903; that there was born to her on said date a   male   child; that said
child is now living and is said to have been named   Turner Whitfield

Applications for Enrollment of Seminole Newborn Freedmen
Act of 1905

Witnesses To Mark:
{ Frank C. Sabourin.
{ Chas E Webster

her
Rhoda x Cudjo.
mark

Subscribed and sworn to before me this 15 day of   May   , 1905.

Chas E Webster
Notary Public.

Sem NB FR 18
BIRTH AFFIDAVIT.

DEPARTMENT OF THE INTERIOR.
COMMISSION TO THE FIVE CIVILIZED TRIBES.

IN RE APPLICATION FOR ENROLLMENT, as a citizen of the   Seminole   Nation, of
Verta Whitfield   , born on the 22   day of   May   , 1902

Name of Father: William Whitfield   a citizen of the   U. S.   Nation.
Name of Mother: Jennie Whitfield   (2081) a citizen of the   Seminole   Nation.

Postoffice   Emahaka, I.T.

Child present

AFFIDAVIT OF MOTHER.

UNITED STATES OF AMERICA, Indian Territory, }
Western   **DISTRICT.** }

    I,   Jennie Whitfield   , on oath state that I am 26 years of age and a citizen by
adoption   , of the   Seminole   Nation; that I am the lawful wife of   William
Whitfield   , who is a citizen, ~~by~~   of the   U. S.   ~~Nation~~; that a   female
child was born to me on   22   day of   May   , 1902, that said child has been named
Verta Whitfield   , and is now living.

Witnesses To Mark:
{ Frank C. Sabourin
{ Chas E Webster

her
Jennie x Whitfield
mark

Subscribed and sworn to before me this 15 day of   May   , 1905.

Chas. E. Webster
Notary Public.

84

Applications for Enrollment of Seminole Newborn Freedmen
Act of 1905

UNITED STATES OF AMERICA, Indian Territory, ⎱
Western   DISTRICT.   ⎰

I,   Rhoda Cudjo   , a   midwife   , on oath state that I attended on
Mrs. Jennie Whitfield   , wife of   William Whitfield   on the 22   day of May ,
1902; that there was born to her on said date a   female   child; that said child is now
living and is said to have been named   Verta Whitfield
                                                                        her
                                                        Rhoda x Cudjo.
Witnesses To Mark: mark
    ⎰ Frank C. Sabourin
    ⎱ Chas E Webster

Subscribed and sworn to before me this 15 day of   May   , 1905.

                                        Chas E Webster
                                            Notary Public.

_____

Sem NB FR 18
BIRTH AFFIDAVIT.
DEPARTMENT OF THE INTERIOR.
COMMISSION TO THE FIVE CIVILIZED TRIBES.

_____

IN RE APPLICATION FOR ENROLLMENT, as a citizen of the   Seminole   Nation, of
Evangeline Whitfield   , born on the 25   day of   December , 1900

Name of Father: William Whitfield   a citizen of the   U. S.   Nation.
Name of Mother: Jennie Whitfield   (2081) a citizen of the   Seminole   Nation.

                    Postoffice   Emahaka, I.T.

                    _____

Child present
AFFIDAVIT OF MOTHER.

UNITED STATES OF AMERICA, Indian Territory, ⎱
Western   DISTRICT.   ⎰

I,   Jennie Whitfield   , on oath state that I am 26 years of age and a citizen by
adoption   , of the   Seminole   Nation; that I am the lawful wife of   William
Whitfield   , who is a citizen, ~~by~~   of the   U. S.   ~~Nation~~; that a   female
child was born to me on   25   day of   December   , 1900, that said child has been
named   Evangeline Whitfield   , and is now living.

85

Applications for Enrollment of Seminole Newborn Freedmen
Act of 1905

Witnesses To Mark:
⎰ Frank C. Sabourin
⎱ Chas E Webster

her
Jennie x Whitfield
mark

Subscribed and sworn to before me this   15 day of   May   , 1905.

Chas. E. Webster
Notary Public.

AFFIDAVIT OF ATTENDING PHYSICIAN OR MID-WIFE.

UNITED STATES OF AMERICA, Indian Territory, ⎱
Western   DISTRICT.   ⎰

I,   Rhoda Cudjo   , a   midwife   , on oath state that I attended on Mrs.   Jennie Whitfield   , wife of   William Whitfield   on the   25   day of December , 1900; that there was born to her on said date a   female   child; that said child is now living and is said to have been named   Evangeline Whitfield

Witnesses To Mark:
⎰ Frank C. Sabourin
⎱ Chas E Webster

her
Rhoda x Cudjo.
mark

Subscribed and sworn to before me this   15   day of   May   , 1905.

Chas E Webster
Notary Public.

Department of the Interior.
Commissioner to the Five Civilized Tribes,
MUSKOGEE, IND. TER,

~~Jennie Whitfield,~~
~~Emahaka,~~
~~Ind. Ty.~~

86

Applications for Enrollment of Seminole Newborn Freedmen
Act of 1905

AP

REFER IN REPLY TO THE FOLLOWING:

Sem. NB-18

DEPARTMENT OF THE INTERIOR,
COMMISSIONER TO THE FIVE CIVILIZED TRIBES.

Muskogee, Indian Territory, July 23, 1906.

Jennie Whitfield,
Emahaka, Indian Territory.

Dear Madam:

Receipt is hereby acknowledged of your letter of July 12, 1906, asking relative to the enrollment of your son Luther Whitfield.

In reply you are advised that it appears from your testimony taken at Wewoka, Indian Territory, May 15, 1905, that you were not positive as to the date of the birth of your child, Luther Whitfield, but stated that he was born March 3, 1905. The only testimony introduced in support of this case was the testimony of yourself, William Whitfield, the father, and Rhoda Cudjo, and Rhoda Cudjo is not positive as to the date of the birth of our child.

You are advised that before further action can be taken in the matter of the application for the enrollment of your child, Luther Whitfield, it will be necessary that you introduce additional testimony of disinterested witnesses as to the exact date of his birth.

Respectfully,

Tams Bixby
Commissioner.

Department of the Interior.
Commissioner to the Five Civilized Tribes,
MUSKOGEE, IND. TER,

Jennie Whitfield,
~~Emahaka~~, Indian Territory.
Holdenville

87

Applications for Enrollment of Seminole Newborn Freedmen
Act of 1905

AP

REFER IN REPLY TO THE FOLLOWING:

Sem-Fr-NB-18.

DEPARTMENT OF THE INTERIOR,
COMMISSIONER TO THE FIVE CIVILIZED TRIBES.

Muskogee, Indian Territory, January 11, 1907.

Jennie Whitfield,
Emahaka, Indian Territory.

Dear Madam:

Inclosed herewith you will find a copy of the decision of the Commissioner to the Five Civilized Tribes, rendered January 11, 9107, declining to receive the application for the enrollment of Luther Whitfield as a citizen of the Seminole Nation.

The decision, with the record of proceedings in the case, is this day transmitted to the Secretary of the Interior for review. The final decision of the Secretary will be made known to you as soon as this office is informed of the same.

Respectfully,

Tams Bixby
Commissioner.

Registered.
Incl. Sem-Fr-NB-18.

Department of the Interior.
Commissioner to the Five Civilized Tribes,
MUSKOGEE, IND. TER,

Jennie Whitfield,
Emahaka, Indian Territory.

Applications for Enrollment of Seminole Newborn Freedmen
Act of 1905

AP

REFER IN REPLY TO THE FOLLOWING:

Sem-Fr-NB-18.

DEPARTMENT OF THE INTERIOR,
COMMISSIONER TO THE FIVE CIVILIZED TRIBES.

Muskogee, Indian Territory, April 16, 1907.

Jennie Whitfield,
Emahaka, Indian Territory.

Dear Madam:
You are hereby advised that on March 1, 1907, the Secretary of the Interior affirmed the decision of this office of January 11, 1907, declining to receive the application for the enrollment of Luther Whitfield as a citizen of the Seminole Nation.

Respectfully,

Tams Bixby

Commissioner.

DEPARTMENT OF THE INTERIOR,
COMMISSION TO THE FIVE CIVILIZED TRIBES.,
Wewoka, Indian Territory, May 8, 1905.

In the matter of the application for the enrollment of Sam Dindy as a citizen by adoption of the Seminole Nation.

Rebecca Dindy, being duly sworn, testified as follows:

Q. What is your name? A. Rebecca Dindy.
Q. How old are you? A. 23.
Q. Your former name was Thomas? A. Yes sir.
Q. You state in this application that on the 4th day of March, 1905, a male child was born to you, and was named Sam Dindy; is that correct? A. Yes sir.
Q. Do you remember what day of the week he was born? A. On Monday.
Q. What time on Monday? A. Monday morning.

89

Applications for Enrollment of Seminole Newborn Freedmen
Act of 1905

Q. About what time Monday morning? A. About six o'clock.
Q. And you are sure it was on Monday morning? A. Yes sir.
Q. March 4, 1905? A. Yes sir.

Frank C. Sabourin, being duly sworn, states that he is a stenographer to the Commission to the Five Civilized Tribes, and that the above and foregoing is a true transcript of his stenographic notes taken in said case on said date.

Frank C. Sabourin

Subscribed and sworn to before me this 9th day of May, 1905.

Chas E Webster
Notary Public.

(seal)

My Com expires April 28-1909

Sem NB FR
BIRTH AFFIDAVIT.
DEPARTMENT OF THE INTERIOR.
COMMISSION TO THE FIVE CIVILIZED TRIBES.
(COPY)

IN RE APPLICATION FOR ENROLLMENT, as a citizen of the   Seminole   Nation, of
Sam Dindy   , born on the   4   day of   March   , 1905

Name of Father: Wilson Dindy   a citizen of the   Creek   Nation.
                                                2095
Name of Mother: Rebecca Dindy, Nee Thomas   a citizen of the   Seminole   Nation.

Postoffice   Sasakwa

(Child present)

AFFIDAVIT OF MOTHER.

UNITED STATES OF AMERICA, Indian Territory,
     Western   **DISTRICT.**

I,   Rebecca Dindy nee Thomas   , on oath state that I am   23   years of age and a citizen by   adoption   , of the   Seminole   Nation; that I am the lawful wife of   Wilson Dindy   , who is a citizen, by   adoption   of the   Creek Nation; that a   Male   child was born to me on   4   day of   March   , 1905; that said child has been named   Sam Dindy   , and was living March 4, 1905.

90

Applications for Enrollment of Seminole Newborn Freedmen
Act of 1905

her
Rebecca Dindy x
mark

Witnesses To Mark:
{ Chas. E. Webster
{ Frank C. Sabourin

Subscribed and sworn to before me this 8 day of   May   , 1905.

(SEAL)

Chas. E. Webster
Notary Public.

AFFIDAVIT OF ATTENDING PHYSICIAN OR MID-WIFE.

UNITED STATES OF AMERICA, Indian Territory, }
    Western   DISTRICT.

I,   Nellie Thomas   , a   midwife   , on oath state that I attended on Mrs.   Rebecca Dindy   , wife of   Wilson Dindy   on the 4 day of   March   , 1905; that there was born to her on said date a   Male   child; that said child was living March 4, 1905, and is said to have been named   Sam Dindy

her
Nellie x Thomas
mark

Witnesses To Mark:
{ Chas. E. Webster
{ Frank C. Sabourin

Subscribed and sworn to before me this 8 day of   May   , 1905.

(SEAL)

Chas. E. Webster
Notary Public.

DEPARTMENT OF THE INTERIOR,
COMMISSIONER TO THE FIVE CIVILIZED TRIBES.

In the matter of the application for the enrollment of Sam Dindy as a Seminole citizen.

DECISION.

It appears from the record in this case that on May 8, 1905, there was filed with the Commission to the Five Civilized Tribes an application for the enrollment of Sam Dindy as a Seminole citizen.

It further appears from the record herein and the records of the Commission to the Five Civilized Tribes that the applicant was born the first part of March, 1905 (not earlier than March 4, 1905), and is a son of Rebecca Dindy, a recognized and enrolled citizen of

Applications for Enrollment of Seminole Newborn Freedmen
Act of 1905

the Seminole Nation whose name (as Rebecca Thomas) appears as number 2095 upon the final roll of Seminole citizens approved by the Secretary of the Interior April 2, 1901, and Wilson Dindy, a Creek citizen.

The Act of Congress approved March 3, 1905 (33 Stat., 1070), provides:

"That the Commission to the Five Civilized Tribes is authorized for ninety days after the date of the approval of this act to receive and consider applications for enrollment of infant children <u>born prior to March fourth, nineteen hundred and five</u>, and living on said latter date, to citizens of the Seminole tribe whose enrollment has been approved by the Secretary of the Interior; and to enroll and make allotments to such children, giving to each an equal number of acres of land, and such children shall also share equally with other citizens of the Seminole tribe in the distribution of all other tribal property and funds."

I am of the opinion that, inasmuch as Sam Dindy was not born prior to March 4, 1905, I am without authority to receive or consider the application for his enrollment as a Seminole citizen, and that, therefore, I should decline to receive or consider the same, and it is so ordered.

Tams Bixby Commissioner.

Muskogee, Indian Territory.
JUL 25 1906

AP

REFER IN REPLY TO THE FOLLOWING:

S.F.N.B. 19

DEPARTMENT OF THE INTERIOR,
COMMISSIONER TO THE FIVE CIVILIZED TRIBES.

Muskogee, Indian Territory, July 28, 1906.

Rebecca Dindy,
Emahaka, Indian Territory.

Dear Madam:

Inclosed herewith you will find a copy of the decision of the Commissioner to the Five Civilized Tribes, rendered July 28, 1906, declining to receive or consider the application for the enrollment of Sam Dindy as a Seminole citizen.

The decision, with the record of proceedings in the case, is this day transmitted to the Secretary of the Interior for review. The final decision of the Secretary will be made known to you as soon as this office is informed of the same.

Respectfully,
Tams Bixby
Commissioner.

Incl. S.F.N.B.-19
Registered.

Applications for Enrollment of Seminole Newborn Freedmen
Act of 1905

S.F.N.B. 19

Muskogee, Indian Territory, July 28, 1906.

Wilmott[sic] & Wilhoit
~~McKennon & Wilmott~~
    Attorneys for Seminole Nation,
        Wewoka, Indian Territory.

Gentlemen:

Inclosed herewith you will find a copy of the decision of the Commissioner to the Five Civilized Tribes, rendered July 28, 1906, declining to receive or consider the application for the enrollment of Sam Dindy as a Seminole citizen.

The decision, with the record of proceedings in the case, is this day transmitted to the Secretary of the Interior for review. The final decision of the Secretary will be made known to you as soon as this office is informed of the same.

Respectfully,

SIGNED   *Tams Bixby*
Commissioner.

Incl. S.F.N.B.19.

Muskogee, Indian Territory, July 28, 1906.

The Honorable,
    The Secretary of the Interior.

Sir:

There is herewith transmitted the record of proceedings in the matter of the application for the enrollment of Sam Dindy as a Seminole citizen, including the decision of the Commissioner to the Five Civilized Tribes, dated July 28k[sic], 1906, declining to receive or consider said application.

Respectfully,

SIGNED   *Tams Bixby*
Commissioner.

2 Incl. S.F.N.B.-19

Through the
    Commissioner of Indian Affairs.

93

Applications for Enrollment of Seminole Newborn Freedmen
Act of 1905

KHN

DEPARTMENT OF THE INTERIOR,
WASHINGTON   FHE

D.C. 5187-1907.   January 22, 1907.
I.T.D. 872-1907.

LRS

Commissioner to the Five Civilized Tribes,
Muskogee, Indian Territory.

Sir:

July 28, 1906, you transmitted the record in the matter of the application for the enrollment of application for the enrolment[sic] of Sam Dindy as a Seminole citizen, including your decision of the same date, declining to receive or consider said application.

Reporting January 12, 1907 (Land 65697-06), the Indian Office recommends that said decision be approved. A copy of its letter is inclosed.

The Department concurs in said recommendation, and your decision is hereby affirmed.

The papers in the matter have been returned to the Indian Office for its files.

Respectfully,

Thos Ryan

Through the Commissioner   First Assistant Secretary.
   of Indian Affairs.
1 inc. and 2 for Ind. Of.

———————

Refer in reply to the following:

COPY

DEPARTMENT OF THE INTERIOR,
LAND   OFFICE OF INDIAN AFFAIRS,
65697-1906.   WASHINGTON.

January 12, 1907.

The Honorable,
   The Secretary of the Interior.

94

Applications for Enrollment of Seminole Newborn Freedmen
Act of 1905

Sir:

There is enclosed a report from the Commissioner to the Five Civilized Tribes, dated July 28, 1906, transmitting the record relative to the application of Sam Dindy for enrollment as a citizen of the Seminole Nation.

On May 8, 1905, application was made to the Commission to the Five Civilized Tribes for the enrollment of Sam Dindy as a citizen.

On July 28, 1906, the Commissioner decided that the applicant was not entitled to such enrollment.

The record shows that the applicant was born on March 4, 1905, and is the son of Wilson Dindy, a citizen of the Creek Nation, and Rebecca Dindy, identified as Rebecca Thomas, at number 2095 on the final roll of citizens of the Seminole Nation approved by the Department on April 2, 1901.

In view of the Act of March 3, 1905 (33 Stat. L., 1060), the decision of the Commissioner adverse to the applicant is recommended for approval.

Very respectfully,

C. F. Larrabee,
HRD   Acting Commissioner.
    C

SF-NB-19

Muskogee, Indian Territory, February 8, 1907.

Rebecca Dindy,
    Holdenville, Indian Territory.

Dear Madam:

You are hereby notified that on January 22, 1907, the Secretary of the Interior affirmed the decision of the Commissioner to the Five Civilized Tribes, rendered July 28, 1906, declining to receive the application for the enrollment of Sam Dindy as a Seminole citizen.

Respectfully,

Commissioner.

Applications for Enrollment of Seminole Newborn Freedmen
Act of 1905

SF-NB-19

Muskogee, Indian Territory, February 8, 1907.

Wilmott[sic] & Wilhoit,
Attorneys at Law,
Wewoka, Indian Territory.

Gentlemen:

You are hereby notified that on January 22, 1907, the Secretary of the Interior affirmed the decision of the Commissioner to the Five Civilized Tribes, rendered July 28, 1906, declining to receive the application for the enrollment of Sam Dindy as a Seminole citizen.

Respectfully,

Commissioner.

_____

Sem. Freed.
NB-19.

Muskogee, Indian Territory, June 29, 1905.

Commission to the Five Civilized Tribes,
Creek Enrollment Division.

Gentlemen:

On May 8, 1905 there were filed with this Commission applications for the enrollment of Levi Dindy, born April 1, 1900, Mary Dindy, born May 9, 1903, and Sam Dindy, born about March 4, 1905, as Seminole freedmen. It is stated in said applications that the father of said children is Wilson Dindy, a citizen by adoption of the Creek Nation, and that their mother is Rebecca Dindy, who is identified as Rebecca Thomas upon the approved roll of Seminole freedmen.

You are requested to inform the Seminole Enrollment Division as to whether application has been made to the Commission for the enrollment of said children as citizens of the Creek Nation and if so what disposition, if any, has been made of such application.

Respectfully,

Chairman.

_____

Applications for Enrollment of Seminole Newborn Freedmen
Act of 1905

HGH

DEPARTMENT OF THE INTERIOR.

COMMISSION TO THE FIVE CIVILIZED TRIBES.

Muskogee, Indian Territory, July 10, 1905.

Seminole Enrollment Division,
    General Office.

Gentlemen:

Receipt is acknowledged of your communication of June 29, 1905 (Sem.Fr.NB.19), in which you ask if application for the enrollment as citizens of the Creek Nation has been made for Levi, Mary and Sam Dindy, children of Wilson Dindy, a citizen of the Creek Nation, and Rebecca Dindy, a Seminole Freedman.

In reply you are advised that the records of this office have been examined and it does not appear that application has been made for the enrollment of said Levi, Mary and Sam Dindy, or either of them, as citizens of the Creek Nation.

Respectfully,

Tams Bixby   Commissioner.

_____

Sem NB FR 19
BIRTH AFFIDAVIT.

DEPARTMENT OF THE INTERIOR.

COMMISSION TO THE FIVE CIVILIZED TRIBES.

_____

IN RE APPLICATION FOR ENROLLMENT, as a citizen of the   Seminole   Nation, of
Levi Dindy   , born on the 1   day of   April , 1900

Name of Father: Wilson Dindy   a citizen of the   Creek   Nation.
Name of Mother: Rebecca Dindy   2095   a citizen of the   Seminole   Nation.
            nee Thomas
                Postoffice   Sasakwa, I.T.

_____

(Child present)
AFFIDAVIT OF MOTHER.

UNITED STATES OF AMERICA, Indian Territory, ⎱
    Western   **DISTRICT.** ⎰

I,   Rebecca Dindy nee Thomas   , on oath state that I am   23   years of age
and a citizen by   adoption   , of the   Seminole   Nation; that I am the lawful wife

97

Applications for Enrollment of Seminole Newborn Freedmen
Act of 1905

of   Wilson Dindy   , who is a citizen, by adoption   of the   Creek
Nation; that a   male   child was born to me on   1   day of April   , 1900; that
said child has been named   Levi Dindy   , and was living March 4, 1905.

her
Rebecca x Dindy

Witnesses To Mark: mark   nee Thomas
  { Chas E Webster
  { Frank C. Sabourin

Subscribed and sworn to before me this 8   day of   May   , 1905.

Chas E Webster
Notary Public.

AFFIDAVIT OF ATTENDING PHYSICIAN OR MID-WIFE.

UNITED STATES OF AMERICA, Indian Territory, }
    Western   DISTRICT.

    I, Nellie Thomas   , a   midwife   , on oath state that I attended on
Mrs. Rebecca Dindy   , wife of   Wilson Dindy   on the 1 day of   April   ,
1900; that there was born to her on said date a   male   child; that said child was living
March 4, 1905, and is said to have been named Levi Dindy

her
Nellie x Thomas

Witnesses To Mark: mark
  { Chas E Webster
  { Frank C. Sabourin

Subscribed and sworn to before me 8 day of   May   , 1905.

Chas E Webster
Notary Public.

98

Applications for Enrollment of Seminole Newborn Freedmen
Act of 1905

Sem NB FR 19
BIRTH AFFIDAVIT.

DEPARTMENT OF THE INTERIOR.
COMMISSION TO THE FIVE CIVILIZED TRIBES.

_____

IN RE APPLICATION FOR ENROLLMENT, as a citizen of the   Seminole   Nation, of
Mary Dindy   , born on the 9   day of   May , 1903

Name of Father: Wilson Dindy   a citizen of the   Creek   Nation.
Name of Mother: Rebecca Dindy   2095   a citizen of the   Seminole   Nation.
               nee Thomas
                         Postoffice   Sasakwa, IT

_____

(Child present)
AFFIDAVIT OF MOTHER.

UNITED STATES OF AMERICA, Indian Territory, ⎤
     Western   DISTRICT.   ⎦

        I,   Rebecca Dindy nee Thomas   , on oath state that I am   23   years of age
and a citizen by   adoption   , of the   Seminole   Nation; that I am the lawful wife
of   Wilson Dindy   , who is a citizen, by   adoption   of the   Creek
Nation; that a   Female   child was born to me on   9 day of May   , 1903; that
said child has been named   Mary Dindy   , and was living March 4, 1905.
                                   her
                         Rebecca x Dindy
Witnesses To Mark: mark   nee Thomas
  ⎧ Chas E Webster
  ⎩ Frank C. Sabourin

        Subscribed and sworn to before me this 8 day of   May   , 1905.

                         Chas E Webster
                           Notary Public.

_____

AFFIDAVIT OF ATTENDING PHYSICIAN OR MID-WIFE.

UNITED STATES OF AMERICA, Indian Territory, ⎤
     Western   DISTRICT.   ⎦

        I, Nellie Thomas   , a   midwife   , on oath state that I attended on
Mrs. Rebecca Dindy   , wife of   Wilson Dindy   on the 9 day of May   ,
1903; that there was born to her on said date a   Female   child; that said child was
living March 4, 1905, and is said to have been named Mary Dindy

99

Applications for Enrollment of Seminole Newborn Freedmen
Act of 1905

Witnesses To Mark:
  { Chas E Webster
  { Frank C. Sabourin

her
Nellie x Thomas
mark

Subscribed and sworn to before me   8   day of   May   , 1905.

Chas E Webster
Notary Public.

Sem NB FR 20
BIRTH AFFIDAVIT.
DEPARTMENT OF THE INTERIOR.
COMMISSION TO THE FIVE CIVILIZED TRIBES.

———

IN RE APPLICATION FOR ENROLLMENT, as a citizen of the   Seminole   Nation, of
Sherman Barkus   , born on the   23   day of   April   , 1900

Name of Father: Willie Barkus   2568   a citizen of the   Seminole   Nation.
Name of Mother: Jennie Thomas   2096   a citizen of the   Seminole   Nation.

Postoffice   Sasakwa, I.T.

———

Child present

AFFIDAVIT OF ~~MOTHER~~.
Sister

UNITED STATES OF AMERICA, Indian Territory, }
    Western   **DISTRICT.**

(Mother dead)

     I,   Rebecca Dindy   nee Thomas   , on oath state that I am   23   years of age
and a citizen by   adoption   , of the   Seminole   Nation; that I am the lawful wife
of   Wilson Dean[sic]   , who is a citizen, by   adoption   of the   Creek
Nation; that a   male   child was born to ~~me~~ Jennie Thomas my sister on   23   day of
April 1900; that said child has been named Sherman Barkus   , and was living March 4,
1905.

her
Rebecca x Dindy
mark   nee Thomas

100

Applications for Enrollment of Seminole Newborn Freedmen
Act of 1905

Witnesses To Mark:
{ Chas E Webster
{ Frank C. Sabourin

Subscribed and sworn to before me this 8 day of   May   , 1905.

Chas E Webster
Notary Public.

AFFIDAVIT OF ATTENDING PHYSICIAN OR MID-WIFE.

UNITED STATES OF AMERICA, Indian Territory, ⎱
   Western   DISTRICT.   ⎰

I, Nellie Thomas   , a   midwife   , on oath state that I attended on
~~Mrs.~~ Jennie Thomas   , ~~wife of~~ my daughter   on the 23 day of April   ,
1900; that there was born to her on said date a   male   child; that said child was living
March 4, 1905, and is said to have been named Sherman ~~Thomas~~ Barkus
                                                    her
                                          Nellie x Thomas
Witnesses To Mark: mark
{ Chas E Webster
{ Frank C. Sabourin

Subscribed and sworn to before me 8 day of   May   , 1905.

Chas E Webster
Notary Public.

(The above Birth Affidavit given again.)

101

Applications for Enrollment of Seminole Newborn Freedmen
Act of 1905

Sem NB FR 21
BIRTH AFFIDAVIT.
DEPARTMENT OF THE INTERIOR.
COMMISSION TO THE FIVE CIVILIZED TRIBES.

IN RE APPLICATION FOR ENROLLMENT, as a citizen of the   Seminole   Nation, of
Levi Cudjo   , born on the   11   day of   Sept   , 1904

Name of Father: Ned Cudjo   (2087)   a citizen of the   Seminole   Nation.
Name of Mother: Nancy Barkus   (2101)   a citizen of the   Seminole   Nation.

Postoffice   Sasakwa, IT

(Child present)
AFFIDAVIT OF MOTHER.

UNITED STATES OF AMERICA, Indian Territory,
    Western   DISTRICT.

    I,   Nancy Barkus   , on oath state that I am   26   years of age and a citizen by
adoption   , of the   Seminole   Nation; that I am not the lawful wife of   Ned
Cudjo   , who is a citizen, by   adoption   of the   Seminole   Nation; that a
male   child was born to me on   11   day of   September   , 1904, that said child has
been named   Levi Cudjo   , and is now living.

Witnesses To Mark: Nancy Barkus

{

    Subscribed and sworn to before me this   6   day of   May   , 1905.

Chas E Webster
Notary Public.

AFFIDAVIT OF ATTENDING PHYSICIAN OR MID-WIFE.

UNITED STATES OF AMERICA, Indian Territory,
    Western   DISTRICT.

    I,   Rhoda Cudjo   , a   midwife   , on oath state that I attended on
~~Mrs.~~ Nancy Barkus   , ~~wife of~~   on the   11   day of   Sept , 1904; that there was
born to her on said date a   male   child; that said child is now living and is said to
have been named Levi Cudjo

her
Rhoda x Cudjo
mark

102

Applications for Enrollment of Seminole Newborn Freedmen
Act of 1905

Witnesses To Mark:
  ⎰ Chas E Webster
  ⎱ Frank C. Sabourin

    Subscribed and sworn to before me this 6 day of   May   , 1905.

                      Chas E Webster
                          Notary Public.

Sem NB FR 21
BIRTH AFFIDAVIT.
DEPARTMENT OF THE INTERIOR.
COMMISSION TO THE FIVE CIVILIZED TRIBES.

IN RE APPLICATION FOR ENROLLMENT, as a citizen of the   Seminole   Nation, of
Peter Cudjo   , born on the 27 day of July , 1902

Name of Father: Ned Cudjo   (2368)   a citizen of the Seminole Nation.
Name of Mother: Nancy Barkus   (2101)   a citizen of the Seminole Nation.

                Postoffice   Sasakwa, IT

(Child present)
AFFIDAVIT OF MOTHER.

UNITED STATES OF AMERICA, Indian Territory, ⎱
    Western   **DISTRICT.** ⎰

    I,   Nancy Barkus , on oath state that I am 26 years of age and a citizen by adoption   , of the   Seminole   Nation; that I am not the lawful wife of   Ned Cudjo   , who is a citizen, by   adoption   of the   Seminole   Nation; that a male   child was born to me on 27 day of   July   , 1902, that said child has been named Peter Cudjo   , and is now living.

                      Nancy Barkus
Witnesses To Mark:
  ⎰

    Subscribed and sworn to before me this 6 day of May   , 1905.

                      Chas E Webster
                        Notary Public.

Applications for Enrollment of Seminole Newborn Freedmen
Act of 1905

AFFIDAVIT OF ATTENDING PHYSICIAN OR MID-WIFE.

UNITED STATES OF AMERICA, Indian Territory, ⎱
    Western   DISTRICT. ⎰

I,   Rhoda Cudjo   , a   midwife   , on oath state that I attended on
~~Mrs.~~ Nancy Barkus   , ~~wife of~~   on the   27   day of   July , 1902; that there was
born to her on said date a   male   child; that said child is now living and is said to
have been named Peter Cudjo   her
                                      Rhoda x Cudjo
                                            mark

Witnesses To Mark:
    ⎰ Chas E Webster
    ⎱ Frank C. Sabourin

Subscribed and sworn to before me this 6 day of   May   , 1905.

                                   Chas E Webster
                                        Notary Public.

Sem NB FR 22
BIRTH AFFIDAVIT.
DEPARTMENT OF THE INTERIOR.
COMMISSION TO THE FIVE CIVILIZED TRIBES.

IN RE APPLICATION FOR ENROLLMENT, as a citizen of the   Seminole   Nation, of
Patton Cudjo   , born on the 14   day of June , 1904
                              by adoption
Name of Father: Gardner Cudjo   F2367   a citizen of the   Seminole   Nation.
Name of Mother: Polly Cudjo   F2101   a citizen of the   Seminole   Nation.
                    nee Barkus
                         Postoffice   Sasakwa IT

104

Applications for Enrollment of Seminole Newborn Freedmen
Act of 1905

(Child present)

UNITED STATES OF AMERICA, Indian Territory,
Western   DISTRICT.

I,   Polly Cudjo   , on oath state that I am   24   years of age and a citizen by adoption   , of the   Seminole   Nation; that I am the lawful wife of   Gardner Cudjo   , who is a citizen, by adoption   of the   Seminole   Nation; that a male   child was born to me on   14   day of   June   , 1904; that said child has been named   Patton Cudjo   , and was living March 4, 1905.

Polly Cudjo

Witnesses To Mark:

{

Subscribed and sworn to before me this 2   day of   May   , 1905.

Chas E Webster
Notary Public.

AFFIDAVIT OF ATTENDING PHYSICIAN OR MID-WIFE.

UNITED STATES OF AMERICA, Indian Territory,
Western   DISTRICT.

I,   Harriett Dennis   , a   midwife   , on oath state that I attended on Mrs.   Polly Cudjo   , wife of   Gardner Harjo   on the 14   day of   June   , 1904; that there was born to her on said date a   male   child; that said child was living March 4, 1905, and is said to have been named   Patton Cudjo

her
Harriett x Dennis
mark

Witnesses To Mark:
⌠ Frank C. Sabourin
⌡ Chas E Webster

Subscribed and sworn to before me 2 day of   May   , 1905.

Chas E Webster
Notary Public.

105

Applications for Enrollment of Seminole Newborn Freedmen
Act of 1905

Sem NB FR 23
BIRTH AFFIDAVIT.
DEPARTMENT OF THE INTERIOR.
COMMISSION TO THE FIVE CIVILIZED TRIBES.

IN RE APPLICATION FOR ENROLLMENT, as a citizen of the   Seminole   Nation, of
Elry Barkus   , born on the 6th day of   July , 1904

Name of Father: Willie Barkus   2568   a citizen of the   Seminole   Nation.
Name of Mother: Mary Barkus   2104   a citizen of the   Seminole   Nation.

Postoffice   Sasakwa IT

Child present

AFFIDAVIT OF MOTHER.

UNITED STATES OF AMERICA, Indian Territory,
    Western   DISTRICT.

I,   Mary Barkus   , on oath state that I am   22   years of age and a citizen by
adoption   , of the   Seminole   Nation; that I am not the lawful wife of   Willie
Barkus   , who is a citizen, by   adoption   of the   Seminole   Nation; that a
male   child was born to me on   6   day of   July   , 1904; that said child has been
named   Elry Barkus   , and was living March 4, 1905.

Mary Barkus

Witnesses To Mark:

Subscribed and sworn to before me this 2 day of   May   , 1905.

Chas E Webster
Notary Public.

AFFIDAVIT OF ATTENDING PHYSICIAN OR MID-WIFE.

UNITED STATES OF AMERICA, Indian Territory,
    Western   DISTRICT.

iss   I,   Nancy Barkus   , a   midwife   , on oath state that I attended on
M~~rs~~.   Mary Barkus   , ~~wife of~~   on the 6th day of   July   , 1904; that
there was born to her on said date a   male   child; that said child was living March 4,
1905, and is said to have been named   Elry Barkus

Nancy Barkus

106

Applications for Enrollment of Seminole Newborn Freedmen
Act of 1905

Witnesses To Mark:

{

Subscribed and sworn to before me 2 day of   May   , 1905.

Chas E Webster
Notary Public.

Sem NB FR 24
BIRTH AFFIDAVIT.
DEPARTMENT OF THE INTERIOR.
COMMISSION TO THE FIVE CIVILIZED TRIBES.

IN RE APPLICATION FOR ENROLLMENT, as a citizen of the   Seminole   Nation, of
Sillah Sango   , born on the 18   day of April   , 1901

Name of Father: Jackson Sango   a citizen of the   Creek   Nation.
Name of Mother: Delilah Sango   2111   a citizen of the   Seminole   Nation.

Postoffice   Holdenville, IT

Child at home
AFFIDAVIT OF MOTHER.

UNITED STATES OF AMERICA, Indian Territory,
Western   **DISTRICT.**

    I, Delilah Sango   , on oath state that I am 27 years of age and a citizen by
adoption   , of the   Seminole   Nation; that I am the lawful wife of Jackson
Sango   , who is a citizen, by   adoption   of the   Creek   Nation; that a
female   child was born to me on   18 day of   April   , 1901, that said child has
been named   Sillah Sango   , and is now living.

her
Delilah x Sango
mark

107

Applications for Enrollment of Seminole Newborn Freedmen
Act of 1905

Witnesses To Mark:
    { Chas E Webster
    { A. B. Davis

    Subscribed and sworn to before me this 31 day of May , 1905.

                       Chas E Webster
                       Notary Public.

AFFIDAVIT OF ATTENDING PHYSICIAN OR MID-WIFE.

                       Had no midwife

UNITED STATES OF AMERICA, Indian Territory, }
   Western   **DISTRICT.**

                                   saw

    I, August Cyrus , ~~a~~ , on oath state that I ~~attended on~~
Mrs. Delilah Sango , wife of Jackson Sango on the 18 day of April , 1901;
that there was born to her on said date a female child; that said child is now living
and is said to have been named Sillah Sango

                           his
                    August x Cyrus
Witnesses To Mark: mark
    { Chas E Webster
    { A. B. Davis

    Subscribed and sworn to before me this 31 day of May , 1905.

                       Chas E Webster
                       Notary Public.

                                  AP

COMMISSIONERS:
TAMS BIXBY,   **DEPARTMENT OF THE INTERIOR,**   REFER IN REPLY TO THE FOLLOWING:
THOMAS B. NEEDLES,
C.R. BRECKINBRIDGE. **COMMISSIONER TO THE FIVE CIVILIZED TRIBES.**   Sem. Freed.

WM. O. BEALL   NB-24.
Secretary

        ADDRESS ONLY THE
  COMMISSION TO THE FIVE CIVILIZED TRIBES.   Muskogee, Indian Territory, June 29, 1905.

Delilah Sango,
    Holdenville, Indian Territory.

Dear Madam:

    On May 31, 1905 you appeared before the Commission and made application for
the enrollment of your daughter Sillah Sango, born April 18, 1901, as a Seminole
freedman and at that time submitted your affidavit and the affidavit of August Cyrus as to

the birth of said child stating that there was no midwife in attendance when said child was born.

You are advised that it will be necessary for you to furnish the Commission with the affidavit of an additional disinterested party relative to the birth of said child. Said affidavit must state the name of said child, the date of her birth, the names of her parents and whether or not she was living on March 4, 1905 and must also set forth the source of the knowledge of the affiant.

Respectfully,

Tams Bixby   Chairman.

_____

Sem. Freed.
NB-24.

Muskogee, Indian Territory, June 29, 1905.

Commission to the Five Civilized Tribes,
Creek Enrollment Division.

Gentlemen:

On May 31, 1905 there was filed with the Commission application for the enrollment of Sillah Sango, born April 18, 1901, as a Seminole freedman. It is stated in said application that the father of said child is Jackson Sango, a citizen by adoption of the Creek Nation and that her mother is Delilah Sango, a Seminole freedman.

You are requested to advise the Seminole Enrollment Division as to whether any application has been made to the Commission for the enrollment of said Sillah Sango as a citizen of the Creek Nation and if so what disposition, if any, has been made of such application.

Respectfully,

Chairman.

_____

Applications for Enrollment of Seminole Newborn Freedmen
Act of 1905

HGH
DEPARTMENT OF THE INTERIOR.
COMMISSION TO THE FIVE CIVILIZED TRIBES.

Muskogee, Indian Territory, July 11, 1905.

Seminole Enrollment Division,
    General Office.

Gentlemen:

Receipt is acknowledged of your communication of June 29, 1905 (Sem.NB.24), in which you ask if application for the enrollment as a citizen of the Creek Nation has been made for Sillah Sango, child of Jackson Sango, a citizen of the Creek Nation, and Delilah Sango, a Seminole Freedman.

In reply you are advised that the records of this office have been examined and it does not appear that application has been made for the enrollment of said Sillah Sango, as a citizen of the Creek Nation.

Respectfully,

Tams Bixby   Commissioner.

REFER IN REPLY TO THE FOLLOWING:
————————————

DEPARTMENT OF THE INTERIOR,
COMMISSIONER TO THE FIVE CIVILIZED TRIBES.

Muskogee, Indian Territory, December 24, 1906.

Chief Clerk,
    Seminole Enrollment Division.

Dear Sir:

Receipt is hereby acknowledged of your letter under date of December 15, 1906, requesting information as to whether application has been made for the enrollment of Sillah Sango child of Jackson Sango, a citizen of the Creek Nation, and Delilah Sango, a citizen of the Seminole Nation, as a citizen of the Creek Nation under the Act of Congress approved April 26, 1906.

In reply you are advised that it does not appear from the records of this office that application has been made for the enrollment of said Sillah Sango as a citizen of the Creek Nation.

Respectfully,

Tams Bixby   Commissioner.

110

Applications for Enrollment of Seminole Newborn Freedmen
Act of 1905

Department of the Interior.
Commissioner to the Five Civilized Tribes,
MUSKOGEE, IND. TER,

Delilah Sango,
Holdenville, Indian Territory.

AP

REFER IN REPLY TO THE FOLLOWING:

Sem Fr NB-24

DEPARTMENT OF THE INTERIOR,
COMMISSIONER TO THE FIVE CIVILIZED TRIBES.

Muskogee, Indian Territory, March 4, 1907.

Delilah Sango,
   Holdenville, Indian Territory.

Dear Madam:

   You are hereby advised that on February 12, 1907, the Secretary of the Interior approved the enrollment of your child Sillah Sango as a Seminole Freedman, under the Act of Congress approved March 3, 1905, and her name appears upon the roll of such freedmen enrolled under said Act, opposite No. 124.

   Respectfully,

   Tams Bixby   Commissioner.

Department of the Interior.
Commissioner to the Five Civilized Tribes,
MUSKOGEE, IND. TER,

Jackson Sango,
Holdenville, Indian Territory.

111

Applications for Enrollment of Seminole Newborn Freedmen
Act of 1905

AP

REFER IN REPLY TO THE FOLLOWING:

Sem-Fr-NB-NB-24.

DEPARTMENT OF THE INTERIOR,
COMMISSIONER TO THE FIVE CIVILIZED TRIBES.

Muskogee, Indian Territory, April 15, 1907.

Jackson Sango,
Holdenville, Indian Territory.

Dear Madam:

You are hereby advised that on February 12, 1907, the Secretary of the Interior approved the enrollment of your minor child, Sillah Sango, as a new born Seminole freedman, and her name appears upon the final roll of such citizens of the Seminole Nation opposite No. 124.

Respectfully,

Tams Bixby Commissioner.

Sem NB FR 25
BIRTH AFFIDAVIT.
DEPARTMENT OF THE INTERIOR.
COMMISSION TO THE FIVE CIVILIZED TRIBES.

IN RE APPLICATION FOR ENROLLMENT, as a citizen of the   Seminole   Nation, of
Cynda Barkus   , born on the 27th day of July , 1903

Name of Father: Hackless Barkus   (2565)   a citizen of the Seminole   Nation.
(nee Steward 2136)
Name of Mother: Lousanna Cudjoe   a citizen of the Seminole   Nation.

Postoffice   Tidmore, IT

112

Applications for Enrollment of Seminole Newborn Freedmen
Act of 1905

Child present

AFFIDAVIT OF MOTHER.

UNITED STATES OF AMERICA, Indian Territory, ⎱
  Western   DISTRICT. ⎰

I,   Lousanna Cudjoe (nee Stewart) , on oath state that I am 21 years of age and a citizen by   adoption   , of the   Seminole   Nation; that I am not the lawful wife of   Hackless Barkus   , who is a citizen, by   adoption   of the   Seminole Nation; that a   female   child was born to me on   27th day of   July   , 1903, that said child has been named   Cynda Barkus   , and is now living.

Lousanna Cudjoe

Witnesses To Mark:

⎧
⎩

Subscribed and sworn to before me this 12 day of   May   , 1905.

Chas E Webster
Notary Public.

AFFIDAVIT OF ATTENDING PHYSICIAN OR MID-WIFE.

UNITED STATES OF AMERICA, Indian Territory, ⎱
  Western   DISTRICT. ⎰

I,   Venus Davis   , a   midwife   , on oath state that I attended on Mrs. Lousanna Cudjoe   , ~~wife of~~ (then Lousanna Stewart)   on the 27   day of July , 1903; that there was born to her on said date a   female   child; that said child is now living and is said to have been named Cynda Barkus

her
Venus x Davis
mark

Witnesses To Mark:
⎧ Frank C. Sabourin
⎩ Chas E Webster

Subscribed and sworn to before me this 12 day of   May   , 1905.

Chas E Webster
Notary Public.

113

Applications for Enrollment of Seminole Newborn Freedmen
Act of 1905

Sem NB FR 26
BIRTH AFFIDAVIT.

DEPARTMENT OF THE INTERIOR.
COMMISSION TO THE FIVE CIVILIZED TRIBES.

IN RE APPLICATION FOR ENROLLMENT, as a citizen of the   Seminole   Nation, of
Remonia Bruner   , born on the   15   day of   July   , 1904

Name of Father: Solomon Bruner   (2562)   a citizen of the   Seminole   Nation.
Name of Mother: Rachel Jackson   (2137)   a citizen of the   Seminole   Nation.

Postoffice   Emahaka IT

Child present

AFFIDAVIT OF MOTHER.

UNITED STATES OF AMERICA, Indian Territory, ⎱
   Western   DISTRICT. ⎰

I,   Rachel Jackson   , on oath state that I am   20   years of age and a citizen
by   adoption   , of the   Seminole   Nation; that I am not the lawful wife of
Solomon Bruner   , who is a citizen, by   adoption   of the   Seminole
Nation; that a   female   child was born to me on   15th   day of   July   , 1904;
that said child has been named   Remonia Bruner   , and was living March 4, 1905.

Rachel Jackson

Witnesses To Mark:

⎰

   Subscribed and sworn to before me this   8th   day of   May   , 1905.

Chas E Webster
Notary Public.

AFFIDAVIT OF ATTENDING PHYSICIAN OR MID-WIFE.

UNITED STATES OF AMERICA, Indian Territory, ⎱
   Western   DISTRICT. ⎰

I,   Harriett Dennis   , a   midwife   , on oath state that I attended on
~~Mrs.~~   Rachel Jackson   , ~~wife of~~   on the   15th   day of   July   , 1904; that
there was born to her on said date a   female   child; that said child was living March
4, 1905, and is said to have been named   Remonia Bruner

her
Harriett x Dennis
mark

114

Applications for Enrollment of Seminole Newborn Freedmen
Act of 1905

Witnesses To Mark:
{ Frank C. Sabourin
{ Chas E Webster

Subscribed and sworn to before me 8th day of   May   , 1905.

Chas E Webster
Notary Public.

Sem NB FR 26
BIRTH AFFIDAVIT.
DEPARTMENT OF THE INTERIOR.
COMMISSION TO THE FIVE CIVILIZED TRIBES.

IN RE APPLICATION FOR ENROLLMENT, as a citizen of the   Seminole   Nation, of
Pearline Bruner   , born on the 9th day of July , 1902

Name of Father: Solomon Bruner   (2562)   a citizen of the   Seminole   Nation.
Name of Mother: Rachel Jackson   (2137)   a citizen of the   Seminole   Nation.

Postoffice   Emahaka IT

Child present
AFFIDAVIT OF MOTHER.

UNITED STATES OF AMERICA, Indian Territory, }
Western   DISTRICT. }

I,   Rachel Jackson   , on oath state that I am   20   years of age and a citizen
by   adoption   , of the   Seminole   Nation; that I am not the lawful wife of
Solomon Bruner   , who is a citizen, by   adoption   of the   Seminole
Nation; that a   female   child was born to me on 9th day of   July   , 1902;
that said child has been named   Pearline Bruner   , and was living March 4, 1905.

Rachel Jackson
Witnesses To Mark:
{
{
Subscribed and sworn to before me this 8th day of   May   , 1905.

Chas E Webster
Notary Public.

115

Applications for Enrollment of Seminole Newborn Freedmen
Act of 1905

AFFIDAVIT OF ATTENDING PHYSICIAN OR MID-WIFE.

UNITED STATES OF AMERICA, Indian Territory, ⎱
Western   DISTRICT. ⎰

I,   Harriett Dennis   , a   midwife   , on oath state that I attended on ~~Mrs.~~ Rachel Jackson   , ~~wife of~~   on the 9th day of   July   , 1902; that there was born to her on said date a   child; that said child was living March 4, 1905, and is said to have been named   Pearline Bruner

her
Harriett   x   Dennis
mark

Witnesses To Mark:
   ⎰ Frank C. Sabourin
   ⎱ Chas E Webster

Subscribed and sworn to before me   8th day of   May   , 1905.

Chas E Webster
Notary Public.

Sem NB FR 27
BIRTH AFFIDAVIT.
DEPARTMENT OF THE INTERIOR.
COMMISSION TO THE FIVE CIVILIZED TRIBES.

IN RE APPLICATION FOR ENROLLMENT, as a citizen of the   Seminole   Nation, of Lethia Jackson   , born on the   17th day of   Feb , 1903

Name of Father: Davis Jackson	2315	a citizen of the	Seminole	Nation.
Name of Mother: Fannie Jackson	2142	a citizen of the	Seminole	Nation.
nee Johnson				

Postoffice   Tidmore IT

Applications for Enrollment of Seminole Newborn Freedmen
Act of 1905

(Child present)

AFFIDAVIT OF MOTHER.

UNITED STATES OF AMERICA, Indian Territory, ⎱
    Western   DISTRICT. ⎰

    I, Fannie Jackson , on oath state that I am about 31 years of age and a citizen by   adoption   , of the   Seminole   Nation; that I am the lawful wife of Davis Jackson , who is a citizen, by   adoption   of the   Seminole   Nation; that a female   child was born to me on 17   day of Feb   , 1903, that said child has been named Lethia Jackson   , and is now living.

Fannie Jackson

Witnesses To Mark:

{

    Subscribed and sworn to before me this 31 day of   May   , 1905.

Chas E Webster
Notary Public.

AFFIDAVIT OF ATTENDING PHYSICIAN OR MID-WIFE.

UNITED STATES OF AMERICA, Indian Territory, ⎱
    Western   DISTRICT. ⎰

    I,   Ida Grayson   , a midwife   , on oath state that I attended on Mrs. Fannie Jackson , wife of Davis Jackson   on the 17 day of Feb , 1903; that there was born to her on said date a   female   child; that said child is now living and is said to have been named Lethia Jackson

her
Ida x Grayson

Witnesses To Mark: mark
⎰ Chas E Webster
⎱ A. B. Davis

    Subscribed and sworn to before me this   31 day of   May   , 1905.

Chas E Webster
Notary Public.

Applications for Enrollment of Seminole Newborn Freedmen
Act of 1905

Sem NB FR 28 270

BIRTH AFFIDAVIT.

DEPARTMENT OF THE INTERIOR.
COMMISSION TO THE FIVE CIVILIZED TRIBES.

IN RE APPLICATION FOR ENROLLMENT, as a citizen of the   Seminole   Nation, of
Ruthie Butler   , born on the   13   day of   August   , 1901

Name of Father: Tom Butler   (2145)   a citizen of the   Seminole   Nation.
Name of Mother: Lizzie Butler   (2146)   a citizen of the   Seminole   Nation.

Postoffice   Tidmore, IT

AFFIDAVIT OF ATTENDING PHYSICIAN OR MID-WIFE.

UNITED STATES OF AMERICA, Indian Territory, ⎫
     Western   **DISTRICT.** ⎭

     I,   Dollie Jacobs   , a   midwife   , on oath state that I attended
on Mrs.   Lizzie Butler   , wife of   Tom Butler   on the   13th   day of   August ,
1901; that there was born to her on said date a   Female   child; that said child is now
living and is said to have been named   Ruthie Butler

her
Dollie   x   Jacobs

Witnesses To Mark: mark
     ⎰ Ida Rentie
     ⎱ Julia Rentie

     Subscribed and sworn to before me this   19th   day of   May   , 1905.

W.E. Grisso
Notary Public.

Wewoka, Indian Territory, May 19, 1905.

Lizzie Butler,
     Care Tom Butler,
         Tidmore, Indian Territory.

Madam:

     On May 12, 1905, you appeared before this office and made application for the
enrollment of your minor daughter, Ruthie Butler, as a citizen of the Seminole Nation,
but no affidavit was made by the attending physician or midwife.

Applications for Enrollment of Seminole Newborn Freedmen
Act of 1905

It will be necessary, therefore, to furnish this office with such affidavit, said person either to appear before the Seminole Enrollment Office at Wewoka, Indian Territory, prior to June 1, 1905, or to have the inclosed blank affidavit filled out and properly executed before a Notary Public, returning same to this office in the inclosed envelope, which requires no postage.

Respectfully,

Enc.   Clerk in Charge.

Sem NB FR 28
BIRTH AFFIDAVIT.

DEPARTMENT OF THE INTERIOR.
COMMISSION TO THE FIVE CIVILIZED TRIBES.

IN RE APPLICATION FOR ENROLLMENT, as a citizen of the   Seminole   Nation, of Ruthie Butler   , born on the   13   day of   August , 1901

Name of Father: Tom Butler	(2145)	a citizen of the Seminole	Nation.
Name of Mother: Lizzie Butler	(2146)	a citizen of the Seminole	Nation.

Postoffice   Tidmore, IT

Child present

AFFIDAVIT OF MOTHER.

UNITED STATES OF AMERICA, Indian Territory, ⎫
    Western   **DISTRICT.** ⎬

I,   Lizzie Butler   , on oath state that I am 26   years of age and a citizen by adoption   , of the   Seminole   Nation; that I am the lawful wife of   Tom Butler , who is a citizen, by   adoption   of the   Seminole   Nation; that a   female child was born to me on   13   day of   August , 1901, that said child has been named ~~Lizzie~~ Ruthie Butler   , and is now living.

Lizzie Butler

Witnesses To Mark:

⎧
⎩

Subscribed and sworn to before me this 12 day of   May   , 1905.

Chas E Webster
Notary Public.

119

Applications for Enrollment of Seminole Newborn Freedmen
Act of 1905

Sem NB FR 29
BIRTH AFFIDAVIT.

DEPARTMENT OF THE INTERIOR.
COMMISSION TO THE FIVE CIVILIZED TRIBES.

IN RE APPLICATION FOR ENROLLMENT, as a citizen of the   Seminole   Nation, of
Rebecca Dindy   , born on the   16   day of   December   , 1902

Name of Father: Ben Dindy   (2439)   a citizen of the   Seminole   Nation.
                                  2153
Name of Mother: Leitha Dindy (Nee Mundy)   a citizen of the   Seminole   Nation.

                       Postoffice   Sasakwa, IT

Child present

AFFIDAVIT OF MOTHER.

UNITED STATES OF AMERICA, Indian Territory, ⎫
    Western   **DISTRICT.** ⎬

     I,   Leitha Dindy   , on oath state that I am   28   years of age and a citizen by
adoption   , of the   Seminole   Nation; that I am the lawful wife of   Ben Dindy   ,
who is a citizen, by   adoption   of the   Seminole   Nation; that a   female
child was born to me on   16   day of   December   , 1902; that said child has been
named   Rebecca Dindy   , and was living March 4, 1905.
                                       her
                            Leitha   Dindy
Witnesses To Mark: mark
   ⎧ Frank C. Sabourin
   ⎩ Chas E Webster

     Subscribed and sworn to before me this 3   day of   May   , 1905.

                         Chas E Webster
                         Notary Public.

AFFIDAVIT OF ATTENDING PHYSICIAN OR MID-WIFE.

UNITED STATES OF AMERICA, Indian Territory, ⎫
    Western   **DISTRICT.** ⎬

     I,   Affie Lottie   , a   , on oath state that I attended on
Mrs. Leitha Dindy   , ~~wife of~~   my daughter   on the   16   day of   December   ,
1902; that there was born to her on said date a   female   child; that said child was
living March 4, 1905, and is said to have been named   Rebecca Dindy

Applications for Enrollment of Seminole Newborn Freedmen
Act of 1905

Witnesses To Mark:
⎰ Frank C. Sabourin
⎱ Chas E Webster

her
Affie x Lottie
mark

Subscribed and sworn to before me 3 day of   May   , 1905.

Chas E Webster
Notary Public.

Sem NB FR 29
BIRTH AFFIDAVIT.

DEPARTMENT OF THE INTERIOR.
COMMISSION TO THE FIVE CIVILIZED TRIBES.

IN RE APPLICATION FOR ENROLLMENT, as a citizen of the   Seminole   Nation, of Nelson Dindy   , born on the   day of April   , 1904

Name of Father: Ben Dindy   (2439)   a citizen of the   Seminole   Nation.
(2153)
Name of Mother: Leitha Dindy (Nee Mundy)   a citizen of the   Seminole   Nation.

Postoffice   Sasakwa, IT

Child present

AFFIDAVIT OF MOTHER.

UNITED STATES OF AMERICA, Indian Territory, ⎱
   Western   DISTRICT.   ⎰

I,   Leitha Dindy   , on oath state that I am   28   years of age and a citizen by adoption   , of the   Seminole   Nation; that I am the lawful wife of   Ben Dindy   , who is a citizen, by   adoption   of the   Seminole   Nation; that a   male child was born to me on   day of   April   , 1904; that said child has been named Nelson Dindy   , and was living March 4, 1905.

her
Leitha Dindy
mark

Witnesses To Mark:
⎰ Frank C. Sabourin
⎱ Chas E Webster

Subscribed and sworn to before me this 3rd   day of   May   , 1905.

Chas E Webster
Notary Public.

121

Applications for Enrollment of Seminole Newborn Freedmen
Act of 1905

UNITED STATES OF AMERICA, Indian Territory,
Western   DISTRICT.

I,   Affie Lottie   , a   , on oath state that I attended on
Mrs. Leitha Dindy   , ~~wife of~~ my daughter   on the   day of   April   , 1904;
that there was born to her on said date a   male   child; that said child was living March
4, 1905, and is said to have been named Nelson Dindy

                                                    her
                                          Affie x Lottie
Witnesses To Mark: mark
  ⌠ Frank C. Sabourin
  ⌡ Chas E Webster

    Subscribed and sworn to before me 3ʳᵈ   day of   May   , 1905.

                                          Chas E Webster
                                          Notary Public.

Sem NB FR 30
BIRTH AFFIDAVIT.
DEPARTMENT OF THE INTERIOR.
COMMISSION TO THE FIVE CIVILIZED TRIBES.

IN RE APPLICATION FOR ENROLLMENT, as a citizen of the   Seminole   Nation, of
Mary Etta Denmark   , born on the 24   day of   December   , 1903

Name of Father: Charles Denmark   a citizen of the   U. S.   ~~Nation~~.
Name of Mother: Mary Ella Denmark   a citizen of the   Seminole   Nation.
                  (Nee Winton 2163)
                            Postoffice   Kidmore[sic] IT

122

Applications for Enrollment of Seminole Newborn Freedmen
Act of 1905

Child present

AFFIDAVIT OF MOTHER.

UNITED STATES OF AMERICA, Indian Territory, ⎤
 Western   DISTRICT. ⎦

I,   Mary Ella Denmark (Winton)   , on oath state that I am   16   years of age
and a citizen by   adoption   , of the   Seminole   Nation; that I am the lawful wife
of   Charles Denmark   , who is a citizen, by   of the   U.S.   ~~Nation~~; that
a   female   child was born to me on   24   day of   December   , 1903; that said
child has been named   Mary Etta Denmark   , and was living March 4, 1905.

her
Mary Ella x Denmark
mark

Witnesses To Mark:
 ⎰ Frank C. Sabourin
 ⎱ Chas E Webster

Subscribed and sworn to before me this   3   day of   May   , 1905.

Chas E Webster
Notary Public.

AFFIDAVIT OF ATTENDING PHYSICIAN OR MID-WIFE.

UNITED STATES OF AMERICA, Indian Territory, ⎤
 Western   DISTRICT. ⎦

I,   Betsy Winton   , a   midwife   , on oath state that I attended on
Mrs.   Mary Ella Denmark   , wife of   Charles Denmark   on the   24   day of
December   , 1903; that there was born to her on said date a   female   child; that
said child was living March 4, 1905, and is said to have been named   Mary Etta
Denmark

Betsy Winton

Witnesses To Mark:
 ⎰

Subscribed and sworn to before me   3rd   day of   May   , 1905.

Chas E Webster
Notary Public.

123

Applications for Enrollment of Seminole Newborn Freedmen
Act of 1905

Sem NB FR 31
BIRTH AFFIDAVIT.

DEPARTMENT OF THE INTERIOR.
COMMISSION TO THE FIVE CIVILIZED TRIBES.

IN RE APPLICATION FOR ENROLLMENT, as a citizen of the   Seminole   Nation, of
Walter Abraham   , born on the   7   day of   Jan , 1904

Name of Father: Pompey Abraham   2214   a citizen of the   Seminole   Nation.
Name of Mother: Betsy Abraham   2196   a citizen of the   Seminole   Nation.
            nee Toney
                Postoffice   Sasakwa, I.T.

AFFIDAVIT OF ATTENDING PHYSICIAN OR MID-WIFE.

UNITED STATES OF AMERICA, Indian Territory, ⎱
      Western   DISTRICT. ⎰

      I,   Bessie Carolina   , a   midwife   , on oath state that I attended on
Mrs.   Betsy Abraham   , wife of   Pompey Abraham   on the   7th   day of
January , 1904; that there was born to her on said date a   male   child; that said child
is now living and is said to have been named   Walter Abraham
                               her
                  Bessie x Carolina
Witnesses To Mark: mark
   ⎰ Eddie Payne
   ⎱ Edward Cox

      Subscribed and sworn to before me this 31st   day of   May   , 1905.

My commission   Edward Cox
expires May 3d 1907   Notary Public.

Sem NB FR 31
BIRTH AFFIDAVIT.

DEPARTMENT OF THE INTERIOR.
COMMISSION TO THE FIVE CIVILIZED TRIBES.

IN RE APPLICATION FOR ENROLLMENT, as a citizen of the   Seminole   Nation, of
Walter Abraham   , born on the   7   day of   Jan , 1904

Name of Father: Pompey Abraham   2214   a citizen of the   Seminole   Nation.
Name of Mother: Betsy Abraham   2196   a citizen of the   Seminole   Nation.
            nee Toney

124

Applications for Enrollment of Seminole Newborn Freedmen
Act of 1905

Postoffice   Sasakwa, I.T.

_____

(Child present)

AFFIDAVIT OF MOTHER.

UNITED STATES OF AMERICA, Indian Territory, ⎱
     Western   **DISTRICT.** ⎰

   I,   Betsey Abraham   , on oath state that I am   27   years of age and a citizen by adoption   , of the   Seminole   Nation; that I am the lawful wife of   Pompey Abraham   , who is a citizen, by   adoption   of the   Seminole   Nation; that a male   child was born to me on   7   day of   Jan   , 1904, that said child has been named   Walter Abraham   , and is now living.

her
Betsey x Abraham
mark   nee Toney

Witnesses To Mark:
⎰ Chas E Webster
⎱ A. B. Davis

   Subscribed and sworn to before me this   29   day of   May   , 1905.

Chas E Webster
Notary Public.

───────────────────────────────────────

HGH

DEPARTMENT OF THE INTERIOR.
COMMISSION TO THE FIVE CIVILIZED TRIBES.
Sem.Fr.NB.32.

Muskogee, Indian Territory, July 10, 1905.

Seminole Enrollment Division,
     General Office.

Gentlemen:

   Receipt is acknowledged of your communication of June 29, 1905 (Sem.Fr.NB.32), in which you ask if application for enrollment as a citizen of the Creek

Nation has been made for William Cox, child of Ed Cox, a citizen of the Creek Nation, and Zylphia Cox, a Seminole Freedman.

In reply you are advised that the records of this office have been examined and it does not appear that application has been made for the enrollment of said William Cox, as a citizen of the Creek Nation.

Respectfully,

Tams Bixby Commissioner.

Sem NB FR 32
BIRTH AFFIDAVIT.

DEPARTMENT OF THE INTERIOR.
COMMISSION TO THE FIVE CIVILIZED TRIBES.

IN RE APPLICATION FOR ENROLLMENT, as a citizen of the Seminole Nation, of William Cox , born on the 10 day of July , 1904

Name of Father: Ed Cox a citizen of the Creek Nation.
Name of Mother: Zylphia Cox (2201) a citizen of the Seminole Nation.
nee Payne
Postoffice Sasakwa

Child present

AFFIDAVIT OF MOTHER.

UNITED STATES OF AMERICA, Indian Territory,
Western DISTRICT.

I, Zylphia Cox nee Payne , on oath state that I am 26 years of age and a citizen by adoption , of the Seminole Nation; that I am the lawful wife of Ed Cox , who is a citizen, by adoption of the Seminole Nation; that a male child was born to me on 10 day of July , 1904; that said child has been named William Cox , and was living March 4, 1905.

Zylphia Cox
nee Payne

Witnesses To Mark:

Subscribed and sworn to before me this 5 day of May , 1905.

Chas E Webster
Notary Public.

Applications for Enrollment of Seminole Newborn Freedmen
Act of 1905

UNITED STATES OF AMERICA, Indian Territory,
Western   DISTRICT.

I, Mandy Payne   , a midwife   , on oath state that I attended on
Mrs. Zylphia Cox   , wife of   Ed Cox   on the 10 day of   July   , 1904; that
there was born to her on said date a   male   child; that said child was living March 4,
1905, and is said to have been named   William Cox

                                    Mandy Payne
Witnesses To Mark:

{

    Subscribed and sworn to before me 5   day of   May   , 1905.

                                    Chas E Webster
                                    Notary Public.

Sem NB FR 33
BIRTH AFFIDAVIT.

DEPARTMENT OF THE INTERIOR,
COMMISSION TO THE FIVE CIVILIZED TRIBES.

IN RE Application for Enrollment, as a citizen of the   Seminole   Nation,
of   Stella Manuel , born on the   21st day of   May   , 1899

Name of Father: Sam Manuel   a citizen of the   Creek   Nation.
                                                                 United States
Name of Mother: Nancy Manuel   a citizen of the   ~~Creek~~   ~~Nation~~.

                        Post-office: Muscogee[sic] Ind Ter

127

Applications for Enrollment of Seminole Newborn Freedmen
Act of 1905

AFFIDAVIT OF MOTHER.

UNITED STATES OF AMERICA, ⎫
    INDIAN TERRITORY. ⎬
Northern   District. ⎭

    I, Nancy Manuel   , on oath state that I am 36 years of age and a citizen by Birth , of the State of Missouri ~~Nation~~; that I am the lawful wife of Samuel Manuel , who is a citizen, by Birth of the Creek Nation; that a Girl child was born to me on 21st day of May , 1899 , that said child has been named Stella Manuel , and is now living.

Nancy Manuel

Subscribed and sworn to before me this 3 *day of* June , 1899.

W. H. Davidson
NOTARY PUBLIC.

───────────   My commission expires
May 10th 1903.

AFFIDAVIT OF ATTENDING PHYSICIAN OR MID-WIFE.

UNITED STATES OF AMERICA, ⎫
    INDIAN TERRITORY. ⎬
Northern   District. ⎭

    I, Amy Jackson   , a Midwife   , on oath state that I attended on Mrs. Sam Manuel , wife of Sam Manuel on the 21st day of May , 1899 ; that there was born to her on said date a girl child; that said child is now living and is said to have been named Stella Manuel

her
Amy + Jackson
mark

Subscribed and sworn to before me this 27" *day of* May , 1899.

M. G. Butler
NOTARY PUBLIC.
My commission expires
January 27, 1903.

───────────

Applications for Enrollment of Seminole Newborn Freedmen
Act of 1905

Sem NB FR 33
BIRTH AFFIDAVIT.

DEPARTMENT OF THE INTERIOR.
COMMISSION TO THE FIVE CIVILIZED TRIBES.

IN RE APPLICATION FOR ENROLLMENT, as a citizen of the   Seminole   Nation, of
Serethia Turner   , born on the   15   day of   December   , 1904

Name of Father: Andrew Turner   a citizen of the   U.S.   ~~Nation~~.
                                    Bruner)(2204)
Name of Mother: Eliza Turner (formerly Eliza   a citizen of the   Seminole   Nation.

Postoffice   Earlsboro IT

Child present

AFFIDAVIT OF MOTHER.

UNITED STATES OF AMERICA, Indian Territory, ⎫
     Western   DISTRICT. ⎭

     I,   Eliza Turner (formerly Eliza Bruner)   , on oath state that I am   24   years
of age and a citizen by   adoption   , of the   Seminole   Nation; that I am the
lawful wife of   Andrew Turner   , who is a citizen, by   ~~adoption~~   of the   U. S.
Nation; that a   female   child was born to me on   15   day of   December   , 1904;
that said child has been named   Serethia Turner   , and was living March 4, 1905.

Eliza Turner

Witnesses To Mark:
   {

     Subscribed and sworn to before me this 9th   day of   May   , 1905.

Chas E Webster
Notary Public.

AFFIDAVIT OF ATTENDING PHYSICIAN OR MID-WIFE.

UNITED STATES OF AMERICA, Indian Territory, ⎫
     Western   DISTRICT. ⎭

     I,   Nina Walker   , a   midwife   , on oath state that I attended on
Mrs.   Eliza Turner formerly Eliza Bruner   , wife of   Andrew Turner   on the
15   day of   Dec   , 1904; that there was born to her on said date a   female   child;
that said child was living March 4, 1905, and is said to have been named   Serethia Turner

129

Applications for Enrollment of Seminole Newborn Freedmen
Act of 1905

Witnesses To Mark:
    ⌠ Chas E Webster
    ⌡ Frank C. Sabourin

her
Nina x Walker
mark

Subscribed and sworn to before me 16   day of   May   , 1905.

                     Chas E Webster
                     Notary Public.

Sem NB FR 33
BIRTH AFFIDAVIT.

DEPARTMENT OF THE INTERIOR.
COMMISSION TO THE FIVE CIVILIZED TRIBES.

IN RE APPLICATION FOR ENROLLMENT, as a citizen of the   Seminole   Nation, of Willie Bruner   , born on the   19   day of   March   , 1901

Name of Father: Douglass Bruner   (2203)   a citizen of the   Seminole   Nation.
                            Bruner (2204)
Name of Mother: Eliza Turner formerly Eliza   a citizen of the   Seminole   Nation.

                 Postoffice   Earlsboro, I.T.

Child present

AFFIDAVIT OF MOTHER.

UNITED STATES OF AMERICA, Indian Territory, ⌉
     Western   **DISTRICT.** ⌡

     I,   Eliza Turner (formerly Eliza Bruner)   , on oath state that I am   24   years of age and a citizen by   adoption   , of the   Seminole   Nation; that I am not the lawful wife of   Douglass Bruner   , who is a citizen, by   adoption   of the Seminole   Nation; that a   male   child was born to me on   19th   day of   March , 1901; that said child has been named   Willie Bruner   , and was living March 4, 1905.

                     Eliza Turner

Witnesses To Mark:
     ⌠ (Parents divorced)
     ⌡

Subscribed and sworn to before me this 9th   day of   May   , 1905.

                     Chas E Webster
                     Notary Public.

130

Applications for Enrollment of Seminole Newborn Freedmen
Act of 1905

UNITED STATES OF AMERICA, Indian Territory, ⎱
    Western   DISTRICT. ⎰

I,   Nina Walker   , a   midwife   , on oath state that I attended on Mrs. Eliza Turner former Bruner   former wife of Douglass Bruner   on the   19 day of   March   , 1901; that there was born to her on said date a   male   child; that said child was living March 4, 1905, and is said to have been named Willie Bruner

her
Nina x Walker
mark

Witnesses To Mark:
 ⎰ Chas E Webster
 ⎱ Frank C. Sabourin

Subscribed and sworn to before me 16 day of   May   , 1905.

Chas E Webster
Notary Public.

Sem NB FR 34
BIRTH AFFIDAVIT.
DEPARTMENT OF THE INTERIOR.
COMMISSION TO THE FIVE CIVILIZED TRIBES.

IN RE APPLICATION FOR ENROLLMENT, as a citizen of the   Seminole   Nation, of Charley Glass   , born on the 31 day of March , 1904

Name of Father: Bob Glass   a citizen of the United States Nation.
Name of Mother: Mollie Glass   2226   a citizen of the Seminole Nation.
                 nee Alexander
                 Postoffice   Earlsboro O.T.

Applications for Enrollment of Seminole Newborn Freedmen
Act of 1905

Charley present

UNITED STATES OF AMERICA, Indian Territory, ⎱
Western   DISTRICT. ⎰

    I,   Mollie Glass   , on oath state that I am   27   years of age and a citizen by Blood   , of the   Seminole   Nation; that I am the lawful wife of   Bob Glass   , who is a citizen, by   marriage   of the   Seminole   Nation; that a   mail[sic] child was born to me on   31   day of   March   , 1904; that said child has been named Charley Glass   , and was living March 4, 1905.

Mollie Glass
nee Alexander

Witnesses To Mark:
  ⎰ Annie O. Payne
  ⎱ Rosie Alexander

    Subscribed and sworn to before me this 10 day of   May   , 1905.

My commission expires Oct. 10-1906   R.N. Bruner
                                                   Notary Public.

UNITED STATES OF AMERICA, Indian Territory, ⎱
Western   DISTRICT. ⎰

    I,   Rachel Bruner   , a   mid wife   , on oath state that I attended on Mrs.   Mollie Glass   , wife of   Bob Glass   on the 31 day of   March   , 1904; that there was born to her on said date a   mail[sic]   child; that said child was living March 4, 1905, and is said to have been named   Charley Glass

her
Rachel x Bruner
mark

Witnesses To Mark:
  ⎰ Annie O. Payne
  ⎱ Rosie Alexander

    Subscribed and sworn to before me this 10 day of   May   , 1905.

My commission expires Oct. 10-1906   R.N. Bruner
                                                   Notary Public.

Applications for Enrollment of Seminole Newborn Freedmen
Act of 1905

Sem NB FR 34
BIRTH AFFIDAVIT.

DEPARTMENT OF THE INTERIOR.
COMMISSION TO THE FIVE CIVILIZED TRIBES.

IN RE APPLICATION FOR ENROLLMENT, as a citizen of the   Seminole   Nation, of
Lucy Glass   , born on the 28   day of   September   , 1902

Name of Father: Bob Glass   a citizen of the United States Nation.
Name of Mother: Mollie Glass   2226   a citizen of the   Seminole   Nation.
                        nee Alexander
                        Postoffice   Earlsboro O.T.

Lucy at home

AFFIDAVIT OF MOTHER.

UNITED STATES OF AMERICA, Indian Territory,
    Western   **DISTRICT.**

I,   Mollie Glass   , on oath state that I am   27   years of age and a citizen by
Blood   , of the   Seminole   Nation; that I am the lawful wife of   Bob Glass   ,
who is a citizen, by   marriage   of the   Seminole   Nation; that a   female
child was born to me on   28   day of   September   , 1902; that said child has been
named   Lucy Glass   , and was living March 4, 1905.

                                        Mollie Glass
Witnesses To Mark: nee Alexander
    Annie O. Payne
    Rosie Alexander

        Subscribed and sworn to before me this 10   day of   May   , 1905.

My commission expires Oct. 10-1906   R.N. Bruner
                                    Notary Public.

AFFIDAVIT OF ATTENDING PHYSICIAN OR MID-WIFE.

UNITED STATES OF AMERICA, Indian Territory,
    Western   **DISTRICT.**

I,   Rachel Bruner   , a   mid wife   , on oath state that I attended on
Mrs.   Mollie Glass   , wife of Bob Glass   on the 28 day of   September   ,
1902; that there was born to her on said date a   female   child; that said child was
living March 4, 1905, and is said to have been named Lucy Glass

133

Applications for Enrollment of Seminole Newborn Freedmen
Act of 1905

Witnesses To Mark:
  ⎧ Annie O. Payne
  ⎩ Rosie Alexander

her
Rachel x Bruner
mark

Subscribed and sworn to before me this 10 day of May , 1905.

My commission expires Oct. 10-1906   R.N. Bruner
                                    Notary Public.

Sem NB FR 35
BIRTH AFFIDAVIT.
DEPARTMENT OF THE INTERIOR.
COMMISSION TO THE FIVE CIVILIZED TRIBES.

_____

IN RE APPLICATION FOR ENROLLMENT, as a citizen of the   Seminole   Nation, of
Gladys Shuny Crain   , born on the 13 day of Aug , 1901

Name of Father: William A Crain   (1993)   a citizen of the Seminole Nation.
Name of Mother: Polly Crain   (2228)   a citizen of the Seminole Nation.

Postoffice   Neal, Okla. Terry

_____

(Child brought to office)
AFFIDAVIT OF MOTHER.

UNITED STATES OF AMERICA, Indian Territory, ⎤
    Western   **DISTRICT.** ⎦

    I, Polly Crain , on oath state that I am 24 years of age and a citizen by
birth , of the Seminole Nation; that I am the lawful wife of William A Crain ,
who is a citizen, by birth of the Seminole Nation; that a Female child
was born to me on 13 day of August , 1901; that said child has been named
Gladys Shuny Crain , and was living March 4, 1905.

                        Polly Crain

Applications for Enrollment of Seminole Newborn Freedmen
Act of 1905

Witnesses To Mark:
   { Fay Carolina
    Hagar Bruner

    Subscribed and sworn to before me this 2 day of   May   , 1905.

                          R N Bruner
                          Notary Public.

AFFIDAVIT OF ATTENDING PHYSICIAN OR MID-WIFE.

UNITED STATES OF AMERICA, Indian Territory, ⎤
    Western   **DISTRICT.** ⎦

    I,   Rosa Ella Fay   , a midwife   , on oath state that I attended on
Mrs. Polly Crain   , wife of William A Crain   on the 13th day of Aug   ,
1901; that there was born to her on said date a   Female   child; that said child was
living March 4, 1905, and is said to have been named Gladys S Crain
                                           her
                            Rose Ella x Fay
Witnesses To Mark: mark
   { Fay Carolina
    Hagar Bruner

    Subscribed and sworn to before me 2 day of   May   , 1905.

                          R N Bruner
                          Notary Public.

Sem NB FR 35
BIRTH AFFIDAVIT.
DEPARTMENT OF THE INTERIOR.
COMMISSION TO THE FIVE CIVILIZED TRIBES.

    IN RE APPLICATION FOR ENROLLMENT, as a citizen of the   Seminole   Nation, of
Albert Alex Crain   , born on the 18   day of Feb , 1904

Name of Father: William A Crain   1993   a citizen of the Seminole   Nation.
Name of Mother: Polly Crain   2228   a citizen of the Seminole   Nation.

                    Postoffice   Neal, Okla. Terry

135

Applications for Enrollment of Seminole Newborn Freedmen
Act of 1905

UNITED STATES OF AMERICA, Indian Territory, ⎱
                     DISTRICT. ⎰

     I,   Polly Crain   , on oath state that I am 24   years of age and a citizen by birth , of the   Seminole   Nation; that I am the lawful wife of   William A Crain , who is a citizen, by birth   of the   Seminole   Nation; that a   male   child was born to me on   18th day of   Feb   , 1904; that said child has been named Albert Alex Crain   , and was living March 4, 1905.

                                               Polly Crain

Witnesses To Mark:
⎰ Fay Carolina
⎱ Hagar Bruner

     Subscribed and sworn to before me this 2 day of   May   , 1905.

                              R N Bruner
                              Notary Public.

UNITED STATES OF AMERICA, Indian Territory, ⎱
   Western   DISTRICT. ⎰

     I,   Rosa Ella Fay   , a midwife   , on oath state that I attended on Mrs. Polly Crain   , wife of   William A Crain   on the 18th day of   Feb , 1904; that there was born to her on said date a   male   child; that said child was living March 4, 1905, and is said to have been named Albert Alex Crain

                                             her
                                 Rose Ella x Fay
Witnesses To Mark: mark
⎰ Fay Carolina
⎱ Hagar Bruner

     Subscribed and sworn to before me 2 day of   May   , 1905.

                              R N Bruner
                              Notary Public.

Applications for Enrollment of Seminole Newborn Freedmen
Act of 1905

Sem NB FR 36

BIRTH AFFIDAVIT.

DEPARTMENT OF THE INTERIOR.
COMMISSION TO THE FIVE CIVILIZED TRIBES.

IN RE APPLICATION FOR ENROLLMENT, as a citizen of the   Seminole   Nation, of
George Wesley Stewart   , born on the   5   day of   April   , 1901

Name of Father: Henry Stewart	2231	a citizen of the Seminole	Nation.
Name of Mother: Mary Stewart	2232	a citizen of the Seminole	Nation.

Postoffice   Wewoka, IT

Child present

AFFIDAVIT OF MOTHER.

(Mother dead)

UNITED STATES OF AMERICA, Indian Territory, ⎱   Grandmother's affidavit
Western   **DISTRICT.** ⎰

I,   Grace Wisner   , on oath state that I am   43   years of age and a citizen by
adoption   , of the   Seminole   Nation; that I am the lawful wife of   Henry Wisner ,
who is a citizen, by   adoption   of the   Seminole   Nation; that a   male
child was born to ~~me~~ my daughter Mary Stewart on   5   day of   April   , 1901; that
said child has been named   George Wesley Stewart   , and was living March 4, 1905.

Grace Wisner

Witnesses To Mark:
{

Subscribed and sworn to before me this 3   day of   May   , 1905.

Chas E Webster
Notary Public.

AFFIDAVIT OF ATTENDING PHYSICIAN OR MID-WIFE.

UNITED STATES OF AMERICA, Indian Territory, ⎱
Western   **DISTRICT.** ⎰

I,   Peggie Kelley   , a   midwife   , on oath state that I attended on
Mrs.   Mary Stewart   , wife of   Henry Stewart   on the   5   day of   April   ,
1901; that there was born to her on said date a   male   child; that said child was living
March 4, 1905, and is said to have been named   George Wesley Stewart
her
Peggie x Kelley
mark

137

Applications for Enrollment of Seminole Newborn Freedmen
Act of 1905

Witnesses To Mark:
  { Chas E Webster
   Frank C. Sabourin

   Subscribed and sworn to before me 3 day of   May   , 1905.

                                  Chas E Webster
                                    Notary Public.
Note: Mary Dead Henry in pen. 10 years

Sem NB FR 37
BIRTH AFFIDAVIT.
DEPARTMENT OF THE INTERIOR.
COMMISSION TO THE FIVE CIVILIZED TRIBES.

_____

IN RE APPLICATION FOR ENROLLMENT, as a citizen of the   Seminole   Nation, of
Ollie Fay   , born on the 14   day of Nov , 1901

Name of Father: Plenty Fay   2238   a citizen of the Seminole   Nation.
Name of Mother: Rosa Fay   2233   a citizen of the   Seminole   Nation.

                         Postoffice   Little, I.T.

Child is at home sick
_____
AFFIDAVIT OF MOTHER.

UNITED STATES OF AMERICA, Indian Territory, ⎫
    Western   DISTRICT. ⎰

     I,   Rosa Fay   , on oath state that I am 42 years of age and a citizen by
adoption   , of the   Seminole   Nation; that I am the lawful wife of Plenty Fay ,
who is a citizen, by   adoption   of the   Seminole   Nation; that a   Female
child was born to me on   14   day of   Nov   , 1901, that said child has been named
Ollie Fay   , and is now living.   her
                                   Rosa x Fay
Witnesses To Mark: mark
  { Chas E Webster
   A. B. Davis

138

Applications for Enrollment of Seminole Newborn Freedmen
Act of 1905

Subscribed and sworn to before me this 24   day of   May   , 1905.

Chas E Webster
Notary Public.

UNITED STATES OF AMERICA, Indian Territory, ⎱
Western   DISTRICT.   ⎰

I,   Rachael Bruner   , a   midwife   , on oath state that I attended on
Mrs.   Rosa Fay   , wife of   Plenty Fay   on the   14   day of   Nov , 1901; that
there was born to her on said date a   Female   child; that said child is now living and
is said to have been named Ollie Fay   her

Rachael x Bruner
Witnesses To Mark: mark
⎰ Chas E Webster
⎱ A. B. Davis

Subscribed and sworn to before me this 24   day of   May   , 1905.

Chas E Webster
Notary Public.

Sem. Freed. NB-38.

Muskogee, Indian Territory, July 6, 1905.

Silvey Beard,
c/o Ben Beard,
Neal, Oklahoma Territory.

Dear Madam:

In the matter of the application for the enrollment of your son John D. Beard as a
Seminole freedman it will be necessary for you to file with this office properly verified
affidavits as to the birth of said child. You are therefore requested to appear before a
notary public and have the inclosed affidavit executed.

Applications for Enrollment of Seminole Newborn Freedmen
Act of 1905

Be careful to see that the notary public, before whom the affidavits are sworn to attaches his name and seal to each affidavit. In case any signature is by mark it must be attested by two disinterested witnesses.

Please sign your name to the affidavit as it appears in the body thereof.

Respectfully,

Commissioner.

CTD-1

Sem NB FR 38
BIRTH AFFIDAVIT.

DEPARTMENT OF THE INTERIOR.
COMMISSION TO THE FIVE CIVILIZED TRIBES.

IN RE APPLICATION FOR ENROLLMENT, as a citizen of the   Seminole   Nation, of
John D Beard   , born on the 2   day of   Dec   , 1902

Name of Father: Ben Beard   a citizen of the   U.S.   ~~Nation~~.
Name of Mother: Silvey Beard nee   2254   a citizen of the   Seminole   Nation.
                       Lincoln
                       Postoffice   Neal, O.T.

(Child present)
AFFIDAVIT OF MOTHER.

UNITED STATES OF AMERICA, Indian Territory, ⎫
        Western   DISTRICT. ⎰

I,   Silvie[sic] Beard   , on oath state that I am 31 years of age and a citizen by
Blood   , of the   Seminole   Nation; that I am the lawful wife of   Ben Beard   ,
who is a citizen, by   marriage   of the   Seminole   Nation; that a   mail[sic]
child was born to me on   2   day of   December   , 1902, that said child has been
named   John D Beard   , and is now living.

Silvya[sic] Byard[sic]

Witnesses To Mark:
  ⎰ Hagar Bruner
  ⎱ Ben Beard

Subscribed and sworn to before me this 22 day of   May   , 1905.

my commission expires Oct 10 1906   R. N. Bruner
                                               Notary Public.

140

Applications for Enrollment of Seminole Newborn Freedmen
Act of 1905

AFFIDAVIT OF ATTENDING PHYSICIAN OR MID-WIFE.

UNITED STATES OF AMERICA, Indian Territory,
    Western   DISTRICT.

I, Eliza Lincoln   , a mid woman   , on oath state that I attended on Mrs. Silvie Beard , wife of Ben Beard   on the 2 day of December , 1902; that there was born to her on said date a ~~mail~~ male   child; that said child is now living and is said to have been named John D Beard

her
Eliza x Lincoln
mark

Witnesses To Mark:
   { Hagar Bruner
   { Ben Beard

Subscribed and sworn to before me this 22 day of May   , 1905.

R. N. Bruner
Notary Public.

By mail 5/24/05

Sem NB FR 38
BIRTH AFFIDAVIT.

DEPARTMENT OF THE INTERIOR.
COMMISSION TO THE FIVE CIVILIZED TRIBES.

IN RE APPLICATION FOR ENROLLMENT, as a citizen of the   Seminole   Nation, of John D Byard   , born on the 2 day of Dec , 1902

Name of Father: Ben x Byard   a citizen of the United States Nation.
            his mark
Name of Mother: Silvey Byard   a citizen of the Seminole Nation.
           (nee Lincoln)
               Postoffice   Neal O.T.

AFFIDAVIT OF MOTHER.

UNITED STATES OF AMERICA, Indian Territory,
    Western   DISTRICT.

I, Silvey Byard   , on oath state that I am 31 years of age and a citizen by adoption , of the Seminole Nation; that I am the lawful wife of Ben his x mark Byard   , who is a citizen, ~~by~~ of the United States Nation; that a

141

Applications for Enrollment of Seminole Newborn Freedmen
Act of 1905

male   child was born to me on 2nd   day of   December   , 1902; that said child
has been named   John D Byard   , and was living March 4, 1905.

Silvy Byard

Witnesses To Mark:
   { WM Jarvis
     John Labords

Subscribed and sworn to before me this 18th   day of   July   , 1905.

Nettie Jarvis
Notary Public.

AFFIDAVIT OF ATTENDING PHYSICIAN OR MID-WIFE.

UNITED STATES OF AMERICA, Indian Territory, ⎱
     Western   DISTRICT. ⎰

     I,   Eliza Lincoln   , a mid-wife   , on oath state that I attended on
Mrs.   Silvey Byard   , wife of   Ben Byard   on the 2nd day of   December   ,
1902; that there was born to her on said date a   male   child; that said child was living
March 4, 1905, and is said to have been named John D Byard

her mark
Eliza Lincoln x

Witnesses To Mark:
   { John Labors
     WM Jarvis

Subscribed and sworn to before me 18   day of   July   , 1905.

Nettie Jarvis
Notary Public.

142

Applications for Enrollment of Seminole Newborn Freedmen
Act of 1905

Sem NB FR 39
BIRTH AFFIDAVIT.

DEPARTMENT OF THE INTERIOR.
COMMISSION TO THE FIVE CIVILIZED TRIBES.

IN RE APPLICATION FOR ENROLLMENT, as a citizen of the   Seminole   Nation, of
Lorlie Bruner   , born on the   28   day of   March   , 1898

Name of Father: Grant Bruner   2260   a citizen of the   Seminole   Nation.
Name of Mother: Polly Bruner   2261   a citizen of the   Seminole   Nation.

Postoffice   Earlsboro O.T.

(Child not present)

AFFIDAVIT OF MOTHER.

UNITED STATES OF AMERICA, Indian Territory, ⎱
      Western   DISTRICT.   ⎰

I,   Polly Bruner   , on oath state that I am   29   years of age and a citizen by
adoption   , of the   Seminole   Nation; that I am the lawful wife of   Grant
Bruner   , who is a citizen, by   adoption   of the   Seminole   Nation; that a
female   child was born to me on   28   day of   March   , 1898, that said child has
been named   Lorlie Bruner   , and is now living.

Polly Bruner
Witnesses To Mark:
⎰

Subscribed and sworn to before me this   29   day of   May   , 1905.

Chas E Webster
Notary Public.

AFFIDAVIT OF ATTENDING PHYSICIAN OR MID-WIFE.

UNITED STATES OF AMERICA, Indian Territory, ⎱
      Western   DISTRICT.   ⎰

I,   Dinah Walker   , a   midwife   , on oath state that I attended on
Mrs. Polly Bruner   , wife of   Grant Bruner   on the   28   day of   March , 1898;
that there was born to her on said date a   female   child; that said child is now living
and is said to have been named Lorlie Bruner

her
Dinah x Walker
mark

143

Applications for Enrollment of Seminole Newborn Freedmen
Act of 1905

Witnesses To Mark:
{ Chas E Webster
{ A. B. Davis

   Subscribed and sworn to before me this 29 day of   May   , 1905.

                                        Chas E Webster
                                             Notary Public.

Sem NB FR 39
BIRTH AFFIDAVIT.

DEPARTMENT OF THE INTERIOR.
COMMISSION TO THE FIVE CIVILIZED TRIBES.

IN RE APPLICATION FOR ENROLLMENT, as a citizen of the   Seminole   Nation, of
Ella Bruner   , born on the 19 day of   July , 1901

Name of Father: Grant Bruner   (2260)   a citizen of the   Seminole   Nation.
Name of Mother: Polly Bruner   (2261)   a citizen of the   Seminole   Nation.

                     Postoffice   Earlsboro, O.T.

Child not present

AFFIDAVIT OF MOTHER.

UNITED STATES OF AMERICA, Indian Territory, }
     Western   **DISTRICT.** }

     I,   Polly Bruner   , on oath state that I am   28   years of age and a citizen by
adoption   , of the   Seminole   Nation; that I am the lawful wife of   Grant
Bruner, who is a citizen, by   adoption   of the   Seminole   Nation; that a
female   child was born to me on   19"   day of   July   , 1901; that said child has
been named   Ella Bruner   , and was living March 4, 1905.

                                        Polly Bruner
Witnesses To Mark:
{
{
   Subscribed and sworn to before me this 3 day of   May   , 1905.

                                        Chas E Webster
                                             Notary Public.

144

Applications for Enrollment of Seminole Newborn Freedmen
Act of 1905

AFFIDAVIT OF ATTENDING PHYSICIAN OR MID-WIFE.

UNITED STATES OF AMERICA, Indian Territory,　⎤
　　Western　　　DISTRICT.　⎦

I,　Rachel Bruner　　, a　midwife　　, on oath state that I attended on
Mrs.　Polly Bruner　　, wife of　Grant Bruner　　on the　19　day of　July　　,
1901; that there was born to her on said date a　female　child; that said child was
living March 4, 1905, and is said to have been named　Ella Bruner
　　　　　　　　　　　　　　　　　　her
　　　　　　　　　　　　　　　Rachel x Bruner
Witnesses To Mark:　　　　　　　　mark
　⎰ Frank C. Sabourin
　⎱ Chas E Webster

Subscribed and sworn to before me　3　day of　May　　, 1905.

　　　　　　　　　　Chas E Webster
　　　　　　　　　　Notary Public.

Sem NB FR 39
BIRTH AFFIDAVIT.
DEPARTMENT OF THE INTERIOR.
COMMISSION TO THE FIVE CIVILIZED TRIBES.

IN RE APPLICATION FOR ENROLLMENT, as a citizen of the　　Seminole　　Nation, of
Rachel Bruner　　, born on the　28　day of　July　, 1904

Name of Father: Grant Bruner　　(2260)　a citizen of the　Seminole　Nation.
Name of Mother: Polly Bruner　　(2261)　a citizen of the　Seminole　Nation.

　　　　　　　Postoffice　　Earlsboro, O.T.

Child present
AFFIDAVIT OF MOTHER.

UNITED STATES OF AMERICA, Indian Territory,　⎤
　　Western　　　DISTRICT.　⎦

I,　Polly Bruner　　, on oath state that I am　28　years of age and a citizen by
adoption　　, of the　Seminole　Nation; that I am the lawful wife of　　Grant
Bruner, who is a citizen, by　adoption　of the　　Seminole　　Nation; that a
female　child was born to me on　28　day of　July　　, 1904; that said child has
been named　Rachel Bruner　　, and was living March 4, 1905.

　　　　　　　Polly Bruner

145

Applications for Enrollment of Seminole Newborn Freedmen
Act of 1905

Witnesses To Mark:

{

Subscribed and sworn to before me this 3 day of   May   , 1905.

Chas E Webster
Notary Public.

AFFIDAVIT OF ATTENDING PHYSICIAN OR MID-WIFE.

UNITED STATES OF AMERICA, Indian Territory, ⎱
    Western   DISTRICT. ⎰

I,   Rachel Bruner   , a midwife   , on oath state that I attended on
Mrs. Polly Bruner   , wife of   Grant Bruner   on the 28 day of   July   ,
1904; that there was born to her on said date a   female   child; that said child was
living March 4, 1905, and is said to have been named   Rachel Bruner
                                    her
                         Rachel x Bruner
Witnesses To Mark: mark
  { Frank C. Sabourin
    Chas E Webster

Subscribed and sworn to before me 3 day of   May   , 1905.

Chas E Webster
Notary Public.

Sem NB FR 39
BIRTH AFFIDAVIT.
DEPARTMENT OF THE INTERIOR.
COMMISSION TO THE FIVE CIVILIZED TRIBES.

IN RE APPLICATION FOR ENROLLMENT, as a citizen of the   Seminole   Nation, of
Lorlie Bruner   , born on the 28   day of   March , 1898

Name of Father: Grant Bruner   (F 2260) a citizen of the   Seminole   Nation.
Name of Mother: Polly Bruner   (F 2261) a citizen of the   Seminole   Nation.

Postoffice   Earlsboro, O.T.

146

Applications for Enrollment of Seminole Newborn Freedmen
Act of 1905

Child not present

UNITED STATES OF AMERICA, Indian Territory, ⎱
Western   DISTRICT. ⎰

    I,   Polly Bruner   , on oath state that I am   28   years of age and a citizen by adoption   , of the   Seminole   Nation; that I am the lawful wife of   Grant Bruner, who is a citizen, by   adoption   of the   Seminole   Nation; that a female   child was born to me on   28th   day of   March   , 1898; that said child has been named   Lorlie Bruner   , and was living March 4, 1905.

                                        Polly Bruner

Witnesses To Mark:

⎧
⎨
⎩

    Subscribed and sworn to before me this   3   day of   May   , 1905.

                                Chas E Webster
                                  Notary Public.

                                    Sem Fr N B 40

             Muskogee, Indian Territory, June 29, 1905.

Commission to the
    Five Civilized Tribes,
        Creek Enrollment Division.

Gentlemen:

    On May 26, 1905, there was filed with the Commission application for the enrollment of Oscar Willis, born January 13, 1903, as a Seminole Freedman. It is stated in said application that the father of said child is John Willis a citizen by adoption of the Creek Nation and that the mother of said child is Tilly Willis identified as Tilly Sancho upon the approved roll of Seminole Freedman.

    You are requested to inform the Seminole Enrollment Division as to whether application has been made to the Commission for the enrollment of said Oscar Willis as a

147

Applications for Enrollment of Seminole Newborn Freedmen
Act of 1905

citizen of the Creek Nation, and if so what disposition, if any, has been made of such application.

Respectfully,

Chairman.

———————

HGH

DEPARTMENT OF THE INTERIOR.
COMMISSION TO THE FIVE CIVILIZED TRIBES.

Muskogee, Indian Territory, July 10, 1905.

Seminole Enrollment Division,
General Office.

Gentlemen:

Receipt is acknowledged of your communication of June 29, 1905 (Sem.NB.40), in which you ask if application for the enrollment as a citizen of the Creek Nation has been made for Oscar Willis, child of John Willis, a citizen of the Creek Nation, and Tillie Willis, a Seminole Freedman.

In reply you are advised that the records of this office have been examined and it does not appear that application has been made for the enrollment of said Oscar Willis as a citizen of the Creek Nation.

Respectfully,

Tams Bixby   Commissioner.

———————

Sem NB FR 40
BIRTH AFFIDAVIT.

DEPARTMENT OF THE INTERIOR.
COMMISSION TO THE FIVE CIVILIZED TRIBES.

———————

IN RE APPLICATION FOR ENROLLMENT, as a citizen of the   Seminole   Nation, of Oscar Willis   , born on the   13   day of   Jan   , 1903

Name of Father: John Willis   a citizen of the   Creek   Nation.
Name of Mother: Tilly Willis   2277   a citizen of the   Seminole Nation.

nee Sancho

Postoffice   Bearden IT

———————

148

Applications for Enrollment of Seminole Newborn Freedmen
Act of 1905

Child home

UNITED STATES OF AMERICA, Indian Territory, ⎱
Western   DISTRICT. ⎰

I, Tilly Willis , on oath state that I am about 34 years of age and a citizen by adoption , of the Seminole Nation; that I am the lawful wife of John Willis, who is a citizen, by adoption of the Creek Nation; that a male child was born to me on 13 day of Jan , 1903, that said child has been named Oscar Willis , and is now living.

her
Tilly x Willis
mark

Witnesses To Mark:
⎰ Chas E Webster
⎱ A. B. Davis

Subscribed and sworn to before me this 26 day of May , 1905.

Chas E Webster
Notary Public.

UNITED STATES OF AMERICA, Indian Territory, ⎱
Western   DISTRICT. ⎰

I, Lucy Sancho , a midwife , on oath state that I attended on Mrs. Tilly Willis , wife of John Willis on the 13 day of Jan , 1903; that there was born to her on said date a male child; that said child is now living and is said to have been named Oscar Willis

her
Lucy x Sancho
mark

Witnesses To Mark:
⎰ Chas E Webster
⎱ A. B. Davis

Subscribed and sworn to before me this 26 day of May , 1905.

Chas E Webster
Notary Public.

149

Applications for Enrollment of Seminole Newborn Freedmen
Act of 1905

Sem NB FR 41
BIRTH AFFIDAVIT.

DEPARTMENT OF THE INTERIOR.
COMMISSION TO THE FIVE CIVILIZED TRIBES.

———————

IN RE APPLICATION FOR ENROLLMENT, as a citizen of the   Seminole   Nation, of
Sillah Jackson   , born on the   31   day of   March , 1901

Name of Father: Davis Jackson   2315   a citizen of the   Seminole   Nation.
Name of Mother: Rhina Jackson   2286   a citizen of the   Seminole   Nation.

Postoffice   Tidmore, I.T.

———————

Child at home

AFFIDAVIT OF MOTHER.

UNITED STATES OF AMERICA, Indian Territory,
Western   DISTRICT.

     I,   Rhina Jackson , on oath state that I am   about 29   years of age and a citizen
by   adoption   , of the   Seminole   Nation; that I am the lawful wife of
Davis Jackson   , who is a citizen, by   adoption   of the   Seminole   Nation;
that a   female   child was born to me on   31   day of   March   , 1901, that said
child has been named   Sillah Jackson   , and is now living.

Rhina Jackson

Witnesses To Mark:

     Subscribed and sworn to before me this   31   day of   May   , 1905.

Chas E Webster
Notary Public.

———————

AFFIDAVIT OF ATTENDING PHYSICIAN OR MID-WIFE.

UNITED STATES OF AMERICA, Indian Territory,
Western   DISTRICT.

     I,   Ida Grayson   , a   midwife   , on oath state that I attended on
Mrs.   Rhina Jackson , wife of   Davis Jackson   on the   31   day of March ,
1901; that there was born to her on said date a   female   child; that said child is now
living and is said to have been named   Sillah Jackson

her
Ida x Grayson
mark

150

Applications for Enrollment of Seminole Newborn Freedmen
Act of 1905

Witnesses To Mark:
    ⎰ Chas E Webster
    ⎱ A. B. Davis

    Subscribed and sworn to before me this 31 day of   May   , 1905.

                         Chas E Webster
                           Notary Public.

Sem NB FR 41
BIRTH AFFIDAVIT.
DEPARTMENT OF THE INTERIOR.
COMMISSION TO THE FIVE CIVILIZED TRIBES.

IN RE APPLICATION FOR ENROLLMENT, as a citizen of the   Seminole   Nation, of
Raymond Jackson   , born on the 2 day of April , 1903

Name of Father: Davis Jackson   2315   a citizen of the Seminole Nation.
Name of Mother: Rhina Jackson   2286   a citizen of the Seminole Nation.

                  Postoffice   Tidmore, I.T.

Child at home
AFFIDAVIT OF MOTHER.

UNITED STATES OF AMERICA, Indian Territory, ⎱
    Western   **DISTRICT.** ⎰

    I, Rhina Jackson , on oath state that I am about 29 years of age and a citizen
by   adoption   , of the   Seminole   Nation; that I am the lawful wife of
Davis Jackson   , who is a citizen, by   adoption   of the   Seminole   Nation;
that a   male   child was born to me on 2 day of April   , 1903, that said child
has been named   Raymond Jackson   , and is now living.

                      Rhina Jackson
Witnesses To Mark:

    ⎰
    ⎱

    Subscribed and sworn to before me this 31 day of   May   , 1905.

                         Chas E Webster
                           Notary Public.

Applications for Enrollment of Seminole Newborn Freedmen
Act of 1905

AFFIDAVIT OF ATTENDING PHYSICIAN OR MID-WIFE.

UNITED STATES OF AMERICA, Indian Territory, ⎱
    Western   DISTRICT. ⎰

I,   Ida Grayson   , a   midwife   , on oath state that I attended on
Mrs.   Rhina Jackson   , wife of   Davis Jackson   on the 2   day of April , 1903;
that there was born to her on said date a   male   child; that said child is now living
and is said to have been named Raymond Jackson

her
Ida x Grayson
mark

Witnesses To Mark:
   ⎰ Chas E Webster
   ⎱ A. B. Davis

Subscribed and sworn to before me this 31 day of   May   , 1905.

Chas E Webster
Notary Public.

Sem NB FR 42
BIRTH AFFIDAVIT.
DEPARTMENT OF THE INTERIOR.
COMMISSION TO THE FIVE CIVILIZED TRIBES.

IN RE APPLICATION FOR ENROLLMENT, as a citizen of the   Seminole   Nation, of
Vibert Barkus   , born on the 4   day of June   , 1901

Name of Father: Willie Barkus   2568   a citizen of the   Seminole   Nation.
Name of Mother: Adeline Barkus   2299   a citizen of the   Seminole   Nation.

nee Foster
Postoffice   Sasakwa, I.T.

Applications for Enrollment of Seminole Newborn Freedmen
Act of 1905

(Child present)

UNITED STATES OF AMERICA, Indian Territory, ⎱
   Western   DISTRICT. ⎰

     I, Adeline Barkus   , on oath state that I am 24 years of age and a citizen by adoption   , of the   Seminole   Nation; that I am the lawful wife of Willie Barkus   , who is a citizen, by   adoption   of the   Seminole   Nation; that a male   child was born to me on 4 day of June   , 1901, that said child has been named   Vibert Barkus   , and is now living.

Adeline Barkus nee Foster

Witnesses To Mark:

{

     Subscribed and sworn to before me this 23 day of   May   , 1905.

Chas E Webster
Notary Public.

UNITED STATES OF AMERICA, Indian Territory, ⎱
   Western   DISTRICT. ⎰

saw

     I, Mandy Payne   , a   , on oath state that I ~~attended on~~ Mrs. Adeline Barkus   , wife of Willie Barkus   ~~on~~ two or three days after the 4 day of June , 1901; that there was born to her on said date a   male   child; that said child is now living and is said to have been named Vibert Barkus

Mandy Payne

Witnesses To Mark:

{

     Subscribed and sworn to before me this 23 day of   May   , 1905.

Chas E Webster
Notary Public.

Applications for Enrollment of Seminole Newborn Freedmen
Act of 1905

Sem NB FR 42
BIRTH AFFIDAVIT.

DEPARTMENT OF THE INTERIOR.
COMMISSION TO THE FIVE CIVILIZED TRIBES.

IN RE APPLICATION FOR ENROLLMENT, as a citizen of the   Seminole   Nation, of
Vibert Barkus   , born on the   4   day of   June   , 1901

Name of Father: Willie Barkus   2568   a citizen of the   Seminole   Nation.
Name of Mother: Adeline Barkus   2299   a citizen of the   Seminole   Nation.
          nee Foster
               Postoffice   Sasakwa, I.T.

AFFIDAVIT OF ATTENDING PHYSICIAN OR MID-WIFE.

UNITED STATES OF AMERICA, Indian Territory, ⎫
     Western   DISTRICT.   ⎭

     I,   Rose Cudjo   , a   mid wife   , on oath state that I attended on
Mrs.   Adeline Barkus   , wife of   Willie Barkus   on the   4   day of June , 1901;
that there was born to her on said date a   male   child; that said child is now living
and is said to have been named Vibert Barkus
                                her
                     Rose   x   Cudjo
Witnesses To Mark: mark
    ⎰ Eddie Payne
    ⎱ Edward Cox

     Subscribed and sworn to before me this 24   day of   May   , 1905.

My commission expires   Edward Cox
   May 20, 1907   Notary Public.

Applications for Enrollment of Seminole Newborn Freedmen
Act of 1905

Sem NB FR 43
BIRTH AFFIDAVIT.

DEPARTMENT OF THE INTERIOR.
COMMISSION TO THE FIVE CIVILIZED TRIBES.

IN RE APPLICATION FOR ENROLLMENT, as a citizen of the   Seminole   Nation, of
Lela Stephenson   , born on the   9th   day of   Sept   , 1900

Name of Father: Leaford Stephenson   a citizen of the   Chickasaw   Nation.
Name of Mother: Patsie Stephenson   2202   a citizen of the   Seminole   Nation.

Postoffice   Milo, I.T.

AFFIDAVIT OF MOTHER.

UNITED STATES OF AMERICA, Indian Territory, ⎫
    Southern   **DISTRICT.** ⎭

    I,   Patsie Stephenson   , on oath state that I am   about 30   years of age and a
citizen by   birth   , of the   Seminole   Nation; that I am the lawful wife of
Leaford Stephenson   , who is a citizen, by   birth   of the   Chickasaw Nation;
that a   female   child was born to me on   9th   day of   Sept   , 1900; that said
child has been named   Lela Stephenson   , and was living March 4, 1905.

                   (signed) Patsie Stephenson
Witnesses To Mark:
   ⎰ Laura Murray
   ⎱ ? Murray

    Subscribed and sworn to before me this   10th   day of   May   , 1905.

(Seal)   (signed) M. F. Moss
                         Notary Public.

AFFIDAVIT OF ATTENDING PHYSICIAN OR MID-WIFE.

UNITED STATES OF AMERICA, Indian Territory, ⎫
    Southern   **DISTRICT.** ⎭

    I,   Nancy Wilson   , a   midwife   , on oath state that I attended on
Mrs.   Patsie Stephenson   , wife of   Leaford Stephenson   on the   9th   day of
Sept   , 1900; that there was born to her on said date a   female   child; that said
child was living March 4, 1905, and is said to have been named   Lela Stephenson

Applications for Enrollment of Seminole Newborn Freedmen
Act of 1905

<pre>
                                               her
                                        Nancy x Wilson
Witnesses To Mark: mark
  ⌠ John W. Hall   his
  ⌡ Lehman Wilson   x
                   mark
</pre>

Subscribed and sworn to before me this 10th   day of   May   , 1905.

(Seal)   signed   M. F. Moss
                                                   Notary Public.

A. B.

19--561
Sem Fr NB

Muskogee, Indian Territory, June 29, 1905.

Commission to the
    Five Civilized Tribes,
        Seminole Enrollment Division.

Gentlemen:

      Replying to verbal inquiry relative to Lela Stephenson, born September 9, 1900, daughter of Leaford Stephenson a Chickasaw Freedman and Patsy Stephenson a Seminole Freedman you are advised that the name of Lela Stevenson[sic], daughter of Leford Stevenson, a Chickasaw Freedman, and Patsy Stevenson, a Seminole Freedman has been placed on a partial roll of Chickasaw Freedmen which has been forwarded to the Honorable Secretary of the Interior for approval.

      Respectfully,

           (signed)   Tams Bixby
                  Chairman.

19-561

Muskogee, Indian Territory, November 28, 1905.

Chief Clerk,
    Seminole Enrollment Division.

Dear Sir:

Applications for Enrollment of Seminole Newborn Freedmen
Act of 1905

Receipt is hereby acknowledged of your letter of November 24, 1905, asking if the name of Lela Stephenson, daughter of Leford Stephenson a Chickasaw Freedman, and Patsy a Seminole freedman has been approved by the Secretary of the Interior.

In reply to your letter you are advised that Lela Stephenson, daughter of Leford Stephenson, a Chickasaw freedman, and Patsy Stephenson a Seminole freedman has been enrolled as a Chickasaw freedman and her enrollment as such was approved by the Secretary of the Interior July 20, 1905.

Respectfully,

Geo. D. Rodgers
Acting Commissioner.

S.N.B.F.43.

DEPARTMENT OF THE INTERIOR
COMMISSIONER TO THE FIVE CIVILIZED TRIBES
SEMINOLE DIVISION

In the matter of the application for the enrollment of Lela Stephenson as a Seminole Freedman.

D E C I S I O N.

The record in this case shows that on May 20, 1905, there was filed with the Commission to the Five Civilized Tribes at Muskogee, Indian Territory, the application for the enrollment of Lela Stephenson as a Seminole Freedman.

The evidence shows that the said Lela Stephenson was born September 9, 1900; that she is the daughter of Patsie Stephenson, a Seminole Freedman, and Leaford Stephenson, a Chickasaw Freedman.

Paragraph 8 of the Act of Congress of June 28, 1898 (30 Stat. L. 495) provides:

"The several tribes may, by agreement, determine the right of persons who for any reason may claim citizenship in two or more tribes, and to allotment of lands and distribution of moneys belonging to each tribe; but if no such agreement be made, then such claimant shall be entitled to such rights in one tribe only, and may elect in which tribe he will take such right; but if he fail or refuse to make such selection in due time, he shall be enrolled in the tribe with whom he has resided, and there be given such allotment and distributions, and not elsewhere."

It is, therefore, ordered and adjudged that there is no authority of law for the enrollment of said Lela Stephenson as a Seminole Freedman, and that the application for her enrollment as such is accordingly denied.

Tams Bixby Commissioner.

Muskogee, Indian Territory.
December 22, 1905

Applications for Enrollment of Seminole Newborn Freedmen
Act of 1905

Seminole NB
Freedman 43   **COPY**
                    Muskogee, Indian Territory, January 2, 1906.

Leaford Stephenson,
     Milo, Indian Territory.

Dear Sir:

     Inclosed herewith you will find a copy of the decision of the Commissioner to the Five Civilized Tribes, rendered December 22, 1905, denying the application for the enrollment of your infant child, Lela Stephenson, as a Seminole freedman.

     The decision, with the record of proceedings in the case, is this day transmitted to the Secretary of the Interior for review. The final decision of the Secretary will be made known to you as soon as this office is informed of the same.

                          Respectfully,

                          SIGNED   *Tams Bixby*
Registered.   Commissioner.
Incl. S N B F 43

S. NB F 43.   **COPY**
                    Muskogee, Indian Territory, January 2, 1906.

McKennon & Wilmott[sic],
     Attorneys for Seminole Nation,
          Wewoka, Indian Territory.
Gentlemen:

     Inclosed herewith you will find a copy of the decision of the Commissioner to the Five Civilized Tribes, rendered December 22, 1905, denying the application for the enrollment of your infant child, Lela Stephenson, as a Seminole freedman.

     The decision, with the record of proceedings in the case, is this day transmitted to the Secretary of the Interior for review. The final decision of the Secretary will be made known to you as soon as this office is informed of the same.

                          Respectfully,

                          SIGNED   *Tams Bixby*
Incl. S NB F 43   Commissioner.

Applications for Enrollment of Seminole Newborn Freedmen
Act of 1905

COPY

Muskogee, Indian Territory, January 2, 1906.

The Honorable,
The Secretary of the Interior.

Sir:

There is herewith transmitted the record of proceedings in the matter of the application for the enrollment of Lela Stephenson as a Seminole Freedman, including the decision of the Commissioner to the Five Civilized Tribes, dated December 22, 1905, denying said application.

Respectfully,

SIGNED *Tams Bixby*

2 Incl. S N B F 43   Commissioner.

Through the
Commissioner of Indian Affairs.

SECRETARY'S OFFICE

DEPARTMENT OF THE INTERIOR.

WASHINGTON, D.C.

D.C.   5277-1906.   February 3, 1906.
I T D   1416-1906.

LRS

Commissioner to the Five Civilized Tribes,
Muskogee, Indian Territory.

Sir:

January 2, 1906, you transmitted the record in the matter of the application for the enrollment of Lela Stephenson as a Seminole freedman.

Reporting January 24, 1906, the Indian Office recommended that your decision, adverse to the applicant, be approved. A copy of its letter is inclosed.

Applications for Enrollment of Seminole Newborn Freedmen
Act of 1905

The Department concurs in said recommendation, and your decision dated December 22, 1905, is hereby affirmed.

Respectfully,

THOS. RYAN,
First Assistant Secretary.

1 inclosure.

Land:
1783-1906.

DEPARTMENT OF THE INTERIOR,
OFFICE OF INDIAN AFFAIRS,
WASHINGTON.

January 24, 1906.

The Honorable,
The Secretary of the Interior.

Sir:

I have the honor to enclose a report from the Commissioner to the Five Civilized Tribes dated January 2, 1906, transmitting the record of the application for enrollment as a Seminole Freedman of Lela Stephenson.

December 22, 1905, the Commissioner decided adversely to the application.

The record shows that Lela Stephenson was born September 9, 1900 and is the daughter of Patsie Stephenson, a Seminole Freedman, and Leaford Stephenson, a Chickasaw Freedman; that application was made for the enrollment of Lela Stephenson as a Chickasaw freedman, and that her name appears at Number 4624 on the Chickasaw Freedman roll approved by the Department July 20, 1905.

In view of the record and of the act of June 28, 1898 (30 Stats. 495) the approval of the Commissioner's decision adverse to the application is recommended.

Very respectfully,

MMM

C

C. F. Larrabee,
Acting Commissioner.

Applications for Enrollment of Seminole Newborn Freedmen
Act of 1905

Seminole NB
Freedman 43

Muskogee, Indian Territory, February 10, 1906.

Leaford Stephenson,
Milo, Indian Territory.

Dear Sir:

You are hereby notified that the Secretary of the Interior under date of February 3, 1906, affirmed the decision of this office dated December 22, 1905, denying the application for the enrollment of your infant child, Lela Stephenson, as a Seminole Freedman.

Respectfully,

Acting Commissioner.

_____

Seminole NB
Freedman 43

Muskogee, Indian Territory, February 10, 1906.

McKennon & Wilmott[sic],
Attorneys for Seminole Nation,
Wewoka, Indian Territory.

Gentlemen:

You are hereby notified that the Secretary of the Interior under date of February 3, 1906, affirmed the decision of this office dated December 22, 1905, denying the application for the enrollment of your infant child, Lela Stephenson, as a Seminole Freedman.

Respectfully,

Acting Commissioner.

_____

Applications for Enrollment of Seminole Newborn Freedmen
Act of 1905

S.N.B.F.43.

DEPARTMENT OF THE INTERIOR   **COPY**
COMMISSIONER TO THE FIVE CIVILIZED TRIBES
SEMINOLE DIVISION

In the matter of the application for the enrollment of Lela Stephenson as a Seminole Freedman.

D E C I S I O N.

The record in this case shows that on May 20, 1905, there was filed with the Commission to the Five Civilized Tribes at Muskogee, Indian Territory, the application for the enrollment of Lela Stephenson as a Seminole Freedman.

The evidence shows that the said Lela Stephenson was born September 9, 1900; that she is the daughter of Patsie Stephenson, a Seminole Freedman, and Leaford Stephenson, a Chickasaw Freedman.

Paragraph 8 of the Act of Congress of June 28, 1898 (30 Stat. L. 495) provides:

"The several tribes may, by agreement, determine the right of persons who for any reason may claim citizenship in two or more tribes, and to allotment of lands and distribution of moneys belonging to each tribe; but if no such agreement be made, then such claimant shall be entitled to such rights in one tribe only, and may elect in which tribe he will take such right; but if he fail or refuse to make such selection in due time, he shall be enrolled in the tribe with whom he has resided, and there be given such allotment and distributions, and not elsewhere."

It is, therefore, ordered and adjudged that there is no authority of law for the enrollment of said Lela Stephenson as a Seminole Freedman, and that the application for her enrollment as such is accordingly denied.

SIGNED   *Tams Bixby*
Commissioner.

Muskogee, Indian Territory.
DEC 22 1905

(The above letter of February 3, 1906, from Thos. Ryan, given again.)

(The above letter of January 24, 1906, from C.F. Larrabee, given again.)

162

Applications for Enrollment of Seminole Newborn Freedmen
Act of 1905

Sem NB FR 44
BIRTH AFFIDAVIT.

DEPARTMENT OF THE INTERIOR.
COMMISSION TO THE FIVE CIVILIZED TRIBES.

_____

IN RE APPLICATION FOR ENROLLMENT, as a citizen of the   Seminole   Nation, of
Langston Payne , born on the 3 day of Jan , 1902

Name of Father: Caesar Payne   2150   a citizen of the Seminole Nation.
Name of Mother: Nancy Bruner   2303   a citizen of the Seminole Nation.

Postoffice   Sasakwa I.T.

_____

(Child present)

AFFIDAVIT OF MOTHER.

UNITED STATES OF AMERICA, Indian Territory,⎱
Western   **DISTRICT.**⎰

    I, Nancy Bruner , on oath state that I am 30 years of age and a citizen by adoption , of the   Seminole   Nation; that I am not the lawful wife of Caesar Payne , who is a citizen, by   adoption   of the   Seminole   Nation; that a male   child was born to me on 3 day of   Jan   , 1902, that said child has been named Langston Payne , and is now living.

                           her
                 Nancy x Bruner
Witnesses To Mark: mark
  ⎰ Chas E Webster
  ⎱ Frank C. Sabourin

    Subscribed and sworn to before me this 16 day of   May   , 1905.

                       Chas E Webster
                       Notary Public.

_____

AFFIDAVIT OF ATTENDING PHYSICIAN OR MID-WIFE.
midwife dead

UNITED STATES OF AMERICA, Indian Territory,⎱
Western   **DISTRICT.**⎰

                                        saw
    I, Dindy Foster   , ~~a~~   , on oath state that I ~~attended on~~
~~Mrs.~~ Nancy Bruner , ~~wife of~~ my sister ~~on the   day of , 1~~; the day after
Jan 3-1902 that there was born to her on said date a   male   child; that said child is now living and is said to have been named Langston Payne

163

Applications for Enrollment of Seminole Newborn Freedmen
Act of 1905

Witnesses To Mark:
⌠ Chas E Webster
⌡ Frank C. Sabourin

his
Dindy x Foster
mark

Subscribed and sworn to before me this 16 day of   May   , 1905.

Chas E Webster
Notary Public.

———————

Sem NB FR 44
BIRTH AFFIDAVIT.

DEPARTMENT OF THE INTERIOR.
COMMISSION TO THE FIVE CIVILIZED TRIBES.

———————

IN RE APPLICATION FOR ENROLLMENT, as a citizen of the   Seminole   Nation, of
Ethel Payne   , born on the 3   day of April   , 1904

Name of Father: Caesar Payne	2150	a citizen of the	Seminole	Nation.
Name of Mother: Nancy Bruner	2303	a citizen of the	Seminole	Nation.

Postoffice   Sasakwa I.T.

———————

(Child present)

AFFIDAVIT OF MOTHER.

UNITED STATES OF AMERICA, Indian Territory, ⌉
    Western   DISTRICT.   ⌡

I,   Nancy Bruner   , on oath state that I am 30 years of age and a citizen by
adoption   , of the   Seminole   Nation; that I am not the lawful wife of Caesar
Payne   , who is a citizen, by   adoption   of the   Seminole   Nation; that a
Female   child was born to me on 3   day of   April   , 1904, that said child has
been named   Ethel Payne   , and is now living.

her
Nancy x Bruner
mark

Witnesses To Mark:
⌠ Chas E Webster
⌡ Frank C. Sabourin

Subscribed and sworn to before me this 16   day of   May   , 1905.

Chas E Webster
Notary Public.

———————

164

Applications for Enrollment of Seminole Newborn Freedmen
Act of 1905

midwife dead

UNITED STATES OF AMERICA, Indian Territory, ⎫
    Western   DISTRICT. ⎭

saw

    I,   Dindy Foster   , a   , on oath state that I ~~attended on~~
~~Mrs.~~   Nancy Bruner   , ~~wife of~~   my sister   ~~on the   day of , 1~~; a couple of
days after April 3-1904 that there was born to her on said date a   Female   child; that
said child is now living and is said to have been named Ethel Payne

                                          his
                                 Dindy x Foster
Witnesses To Mark: mark
    ⎧ Chas E Webster
    ⎩ Frank C. Sabourin

    Subscribed and sworn to before me this 16 day of   May   , 1905.

                                  Chas E Webster
                                  Notary Public.

Sem NB FR 45
DEPARTMENT OF THE INTERIOR.
COMMISSION TO THE FIVE CIVILIZED TRIBES.

IN RE APPLICATION FOR ENROLLMENT, as a citizen of the   Seminole   Nation, of
Noah Pompey   , born on the 10 day of March , 1901

Name of Father: Passy Pompey   2307   a citizen of the Seminole Nation.
Name of Mother: Matilda Pompey   2308   a citizen of the Seminole Nation.

                          Postoffice   Sasakwa

165

Applications for Enrollment of Seminole Newborn Freedmen
Act of 1905

(Child present)   father
AFFIDAVIT OF <s>MOTHER</s>.
mother dead

UNITED STATES OF AMERICA, Indian Territory, ⎫
   Western   DISTRICT. ⎰

I,   Passy Pompey   , on oath state that I am   35   years of age and a citizen by   adoption   , of the   Seminole   Nation; that I am the lawful <s>wife</s> husband of Matilda Pompey   , who is a citizen, by   adoption   of the   Seminole Nation; that a   male   child was born to <s>me</s> her on   10   day of   March   , 1901; that said child has been named   Noah Pompey   , and was living March 4, 1905.

his
Passy x Pompey

Witnesses To Mark: mark
  ⎰ Chas E Webster
  ⎱ Frank C. Sabourin

Subscribed and sworn to before me this 8   day of   May   , 1905.

Chas E Webster
Notary Public.

AFFIDAVIT OF ATTENDING PHYSICIAN OR MID-WIFE.

UNITED STATES OF AMERICA, Indian Territory, ⎫
   Western   DISTRICT. ⎰

I,   Nellie Thomas   , a   midwife   , on oath state that I attended on Mrs.   Matilda Pompey   , wife of   Passy Pompey   on the   10   day of   March   , 1901; that there was born to her on said date a   male   child; that said child was living March 4, 1905, and is said to have been named   Noah Pompey

her
Nellie x Thomas

Witnesses To Mark: mark
  ⎰ Chas E Webster
  ⎱ Frank C. Sabourin

Subscribed and sworn to before me   8   day of   May   , 1905.

Chas E Webster
Notary Public.

Applications for Enrollment of Seminole Newborn Freedmen
Act of 1905

DEPARTMENT OF THE INTERIOR

COMMISSIONER TO THE FIVE CIVILIZED TRIBES

In the matter of the application for the enrollment of Hagar Eckals, Laura Jones, Emanuel Eckals, Andrew Eckals, Nancy Eckals, George Eckals, Elnora Eckals and Addilina Eckals as Seminole Freedmen.

Seminole New Born Freedmen Card No. 46.
_____

United States of America, Indian Territory,)
)   PETITION.
    Western Judicial District.   )

In re, the application of Hagar Eckals, to be enrolled as a citizen of the Seminole Tribe of Indian, in the Indian Territory, by adoption, as provided for by an agreement between the United States and Seminole Tribe of Indians, and by act of United States Congress, approved June 2, 1900; 31st Stat. 250 and Act March 3rd 1905.

The United States Commission to the Five Civilized Tribes,
      Muskogee, Indian Territory.

Your petitioner, Hagar Eckals, et al, respectfully makes application under Acts of Congress, June 2, 1900, 31 stat 250; for enrollment as a citizen of the Seminole Tribe of Indians in the Indian Territory, and to have and enjoy all the rights and benefits as such citizen[sic] of the said Seminole Tribe of Indians as is accorded to any citizen or citizens of said tribe, according to the acts herein mentioned: Wherefore, comes now your petitioner, the said Hagar Eckals, and by her attorneys, says, she makes this application for the following reasons.

1st. That she is uneducated, and has no knowledge of literal value, from which fact she is wholly incapable of understanding the laws, or construing any part thereof, or knowing how to undertake an action that would bring to her the relief and benefits guaranteed by the law.

2nd. Because she is the daughter of Hannah Haley, was a Seminole Freedman, and Sharper Haley, was a Creek Freedman, Seminole freedman,[sic] and entitled to inherit in the Seminole Nation, under the laws and treaties of said Nation, which said laws and treaties are fully set forth and made public in 31st Stat. 250, and that she is rightfully entitled to all the benefits as given under such treaties and laws.

167

Applications for Enrollment of Seminole Newborn Freedmen
Act of 1905

3rd. Because, she is ready to produce good and sufficient proof in support of her allegations, above set forth.

Wherefore, comes not your petitioner and prays that she be given the right as provided in act of June 2nd, 1900, March 3, 1905, and that her name with all of her living children, Laura Jones, Emanuel Eckals, Andrew Eckals, Nancy Eckals, George Eckals, Elnora Eckals, Addilina Eckals, be placed upon the roll with the Seminole Freedmen as citizens of the Seminole Nation, Indian Territory, and that she may share in the division of all the lands and funds or moneys or any other thing of value to the same extent and to the same purpose that any citizen of the Seminole Nation is now or may hereafter be given.

her
Hagar x Eckals
mark

Witnesses to mark
John R McBeth   . . . .
Chas E Webster   . . . .

. . . .

Subscribed and sworn to before me a Notary Public for and within the Western District, Indian Territory, on this 1st day of June 1905.

Chas E Webster
Notary Public.

DEPARTMENT OF THE INTERIOR,
COMMISSIONER TO THE FIVE CIVILIZED TRIBES.
SEMINOLE DIVISION.

In the matter of the application for the enrollment of Hagar Eckals, Laura Jones, Emanuel Eckals, Andrew Eckals, Nancy Eckals, George Eckals, Elnora Eckals and Addilina Eckals as Seminole Freedmen.

DECISION.

The evidence in this case shows that on June 1, 1905, there was filed with the Commission to the Five Civilized Tribes at Muskogee, Indian Territory, the application for the enrollment of Hagar Eckals, Laura Jones, Emanuel Eckals, Andrew Eckals, Nancy Eckals, George Eckals, Elnora Eckals and Addilina Eckals as Seminole Freedmen; that Laura Jones, Emanuel Eckals, Andrew Eckals, Nancy Eckals, George Eckals, Elnora Eckals and Addilina Eckals are children of the said Hagar Eckals and that Hagar Eckals is the daughter of Hannah Haley, alleged to be a Seminole Freedman, and Sharper Haley alleged to be a Creek Freedman.

It does not appear from an examination of the records in the possession of the Commissioner to the Five Civilized Tribes, that any of the applicants or Hannah and Sharper Haley, the parents of the principal applicant, Hagar Eckals, have ever been enrolled as citizens of either the Seminole or Creek Nations, nor have they or any of

Applications for Enrollment of Seminole Newborn Freedmen
Act of 1905

them, or the said Hannah and Sharper Haley ever been admitted to citizenship in either of said nations, by the Tribal authorities thereof, the Commission to the Five Civilized Tribes or the United States Court in Indian Territory.

It is, therefore, ordered and adjudged that there be no authority of law for the enrollment of said Hagar Eckals, Laura Jones, Emanuel Eckals, Andrew Eckals, Nancy Eckals, George Eckals, Elnora Eckals and Addilina Eckals as Freedmen citizens of either the Seminole or Creek Nation, and the application for their enrollment as such, is accordingly denied.

Tams Bixby
Commissioner.

Muskogee, Indian Territory.
JAN 16 1907

---

sem-Fr-46

COPY
Muskogee, Indian Territory, January 16, 1907.

Hagar Eckals,
Wewoka, Indian Territory.

Dear Sir:

Inclosed herewith you will find a copy of the decision of the Commissioner to the Five Civilized Tribes, rendered January 16, 1907, denying the applications for the enrollment of Hagar Eckals, Laura Jones, Emanuel Eckals, Andrew Eckals, Nancy Eckals, George Eckals, Elnora Eckals, and Addilina Eckals as Freedmen citizens of either the Seminole or Creek Nation.

The decision, with the record of proceedings in the case, is this day transmitted to the Secretary of the Interior for review. The final decision of the Secretary will be made known to you as soon as this office is informed of the same.

Respectfully,

SIGNED *Tams Bixby*
Commissioner.

Registered.
Incl. Sem-Fr-46

Applications for Enrollment of Seminole Newborn Freedmen
Act of 1905

Sem-Fr-46

COPY

Muskogee, Indian Territory, January 16, 1907.

Willmott and Wilhoit,
Attorneys for the Seminole Nation,
Wewoka, Indian Territory.

Gentlemen:

Inclosed herewith you will find a copy of the decision of the Commissioner to the Five Civilized Tribes, rendered January 16, 1907, denying the applications for the enrollment of Hagar Eckals, Laura Jones, Emanuel Eckals, Andrew Eckals, Nancy Eckals, George Eckals, Elnora Eckals, and Addilina Eckals as Freedmen citizens of either the Seminole or Creek Nation.

The decision, with the record of proceedings in the case, is this day transmitted to the Secretary of the Interior for review. The final decision of the Secretary will be made known to you as soon as this office is informed of the same.

Respectfully,

SIGNED *Tams Bixby*

Incl. SempFr-46.[sic]

Commissioner.

COPY

Muskogee, Indian Territory, January 16, 1907.

The Honorable,
The Secretary of the Interior.

Sir:

There is transmitted herewith record of proceedings in the matter of the application for the enrollment of Hagar Eckals, Laura Jones, Emanuel Eckals, Andrew Eckals, Nancy Eckals, George Eckals, Elnora Eckals, and Addilina Eckals as Freedmen citizens of either the Seminole or Creek Nations[sic], including the decision of the Commissioner to the Five Civilized Tribes, dated January 16, 1907, denying said applications.

Respectfully,

SIGNED *Tams Bixby*

2 incl. Sem-Fr-46

Commissioner.

Through the
Commissioner of Indian Affairs.

170

Applications for Enrollment of Seminole Newborn Freedmen
Act of 1905

CRW

DEPARTMENT OF THE INTERIOR,   S.P.
WASHINGTON.

I.T.D. 4174-1907.   February 25, 1907.
D.C. 11761

LRS

DIRECT

Commissioner to the Five Civilized Tribes
    Muskogee, Indian Territory.

Sir:

       February 18, 1907, the Indian Office transmitted the record in the matter of the application for the enrollment of Hagar Eckals, Laura Jones, Emanuel Eckals, Andrew Eckals, Nancy Eckals, George Eckals, Elnora Eckals and Addilina Eckals as freedmen citizens of either the Seminole or Creek nations[sic], concurring in your decision of January 16, 1907, denying the application. A copy of its letter is inclosed.

       The Department also concurs in your decision and it is hereby affirmed.

       The papers have been sent to the Indian Office for its files, together with a copy hereof.

                        Respectfully,

                              Jesse E. Wilson

                              Assistant Secretary

1 inc. and
2 to Ind. Of.

Applications for Enrollment of Seminole Newborn Freedmen
Act of 1905

Refer in reply to the following.   --Copy--

DEPARTMENT OF THE INTERIOR,
Land.   OFFICE OF INDIAN AFFAIRS,
6297-1907.   WASHINGTON. February 18, 1907.
D. C. 11761.

The Honorable,
    The Secretary of the Interior.

Sir:

I have the honor to transmit herewith a communication from the Commissioner to the Five Civilized Tribes, dated January 16, 1907, enclosing record of the proceedings in the matter of the application for the enrollment of applications for the enrollment of Hagar Eckals, Laura Jones, Emanuel Eckals, Andrew Eckals, Nancy Eckals, George Eckals, Elnora Eckals, and Addilina Eckals as Freedmen citizens of either the Seminole or Creek Nations, including the decision of the Commissioner to the Five Civilized Tribes, dated January 16, 1907, denying the application.

It is shown from the record herein that application was filed with the Commission to the Five Civilized Tribes on June 1, 1905, for the enrollment of Hagar Eckals, Laura Jones, Emanuel Eckals, Andrew Eckals, Nancy Eckals, George Eckals, Elnora Eckals, and Addilina Eckals as Seminole Freedmen; that Laura Jones, Emanuel Eckals, Andrew Eckals, Nancy Eckals, George Eckals, Elnora Eckals, and Addilina Eckals are the children of Hagar Eckals; and that Hagar Eckals is the daughter of Hannah Haley, alleged to be a Seminole Freedman, and Sharper Haley, alleged to be a Creek Freedman.

The records in the office of the Commissioner do not show that any of the applicants, or Hannah and Sharper Haley, the parents of the principal applicant, Hagar Eckals, have ever been enrolled as citizens of either the Seminole or the Creek Nation nor have they, or any of them, nor Hannah and Sharper Haley, ever been admitted to citizenship in either of these nations by the tribal authorities thereof, the Commission to the Five Civilized Tribes, or the United States Courts in the Indian Territory.

The Office is of the opinion that under the facts shown by the record there is no authority of law for the enrollment of the applicants and that the decision of the Commissioner to the Five Civilized Tribes denying their enrollment as Freedmen citizens of either the Seminole or Creek Nation is correct; and it is therefore recommended that it be affirmed.

Very respectfully,

C. F. Larrabee,

Acting Commissioner.

EWE-D

172

Applications for Enrollment of Seminole Newborn Freedmen
Act of 1905

SEM FR.-46

Muskogee, Indian Territory, April 18, 1907.

Hagar Eckals,
Wewoka, Indian Territory.

Dear Sir:

You are hereby advised that on February 25, 1907, the Secretary of the Interior affirmed the decision of this office of January 16, 1907, denying the applications for the enrollment of Hager[sic] Eckals, Laura Jones, Emanuel Eckals, Andrew Eckals, Nancy Eckals, George Eckals, Elnora Eckals, and Addilina Eckals as freedmen citizens of either the Seminole or Creek Nations.

Respectfully,

Commissioner.

Sem-Fr-46

Muskogee, Indian Territory, April 18, 1907.

Willmott & Willhoit,
Attorneys at Law,
Wewoka, Indian Territory.

Gentlemen:

You are hereby advised that on February 25, 1907, the Secretary of the Interior affirmed the decision of this office of January 16, 1907, denying the applications for the enrollment of Hager[sic] Ackals[sic], Laura Jones, Emanuel Eckals, Andrew Eckals, Nancy Eckals, George Eckals, Elnora Eckals and Addilina Eckals as freedmen citizens of either the Seminole or Creek Nations.

Respectfully,

Commissioner.

173

Applications for Enrollment of Seminole Newborn Freedmen
Act of 1905

S.N.B.F.46.

DEPARTMENT OF THE INTERIOR,
COMMISSIONER TO THE FIVE CIVILIZED TRIBES.
SEMINOLE DIVISION.

In the matter of the application for the enrollment of Hagar Eckals, Laura Jones, Emanuel Eckals, Andrew Eckals, Nancy Eckals, George Eckals, Elnora Eckals and Addilina Eckals as Seminole Freedmen.

D E C I S I O N.

The evidence in this case shows that on June 1, 1905, there was filed with the Commission to the Five Civilized Tribes at Muskogee, Indian Territory, the application for the enrollment of Hagar Eckals, Laura Jones, Emanuel Eckals, Andrew Eckals, Nancy Eckals, George Eckals, Elnora Eckals and Addilina Eckals as Seminole Freedmen; that Laura Jones, Emanuel Eckals, Andrew Eckals, Nancy Eckals, George Eckals, Elnora Eckals and Addilina Eckals are children of the said Hagar Eckals; that neither Hagar Eckals or any of her children herein named have ever been recognized as citizens of the Seminole Nation.

The Act of Congress of March 3, 1905 (33 Stat., 1048) provides:

"That the Commission to the Five Civilized Tribes is authorized for ninety days after the date of the approval of this act to receive and consider applications for enrollment of infant children born prior to March fourth, nineteen hundred and five, and living on said latter date, to citizens of the Seminole tribe whose enrollment has been approved by the Secretary of the Interior; and to enroll and make allotments to such children, giving to each an equal number of acres of land, and such children shall also share equally with other citizens of the Seminole tribe in the distribution of all other tribal property and funds."

It is, therefore, ordered and adjudged that there is no authority of law for the enrollment of said Hagar Eckals, Laura Jones, Emanuel Eckals, Andrew Eckals, Nancy Eckals, George Eckals, Elnora Eckals and Addilina Eckals as Freedmen citizens of the Seminole Nation, and the application for their enrollment as such is accordingly denied.

_____
Commissioner.

Muskogee, Indian Territory,
_____

_____

Applications for Enrollment of Seminole Newborn Freedmen
Act of 1905

Semp-Fr-46.[sic]

Muskogee, Indian Territory, January 16, 1907.

Willmott and Wilhoit,
    Attorneys for the Seminole Nation,
        Wewoka, Indian Territory.

Gentlemen:

    Inclosed herewith you will find a copy of the decision of the Commissioner to the Five Civilized Tribes, rendered January 16, 1907, denying the applications for the enrollment of Hagar Eckals, Laura Jones, Emanuel Eckals, Andrew Eckals, Nancy Eckals, George Eckals, Elnora Eckals, and Addilina Eckals as Freedmen citizens of either the Seminole or Creek Nation.

    The decision, with the record of proceedings in the case, is this day transmitted to the Secretary of the Interior for review. The final decision of the Secretary will be made known to you as soon as this office is informed of the same.

Respectfully,

SIGNED Tams Bixby

Incl. Semp-Fr-46.[sic]   Commissioner.

CRW

DEPARTMENT OF THE INTERIOR,   S.P.
WASHINGTON.

I.T.D. 4174-1907.   February 25, 1907.
D.C. 11761

LRS

<u>DIRECT</u>

Commissioner to the Five Civilized Tribes
    Muskogee, Indian Territory.

Sir:

    February 18, 1907, the Indian Office transmitted the record in the matter of the application for the enrollment of Hagar Eckals, Laura Jones, Emanuel Eckals, Andrew Eckals, Nancy Eckals, George Eckals, Elnora Eckals and Addilina Eckals as freedmen citizens of either the Seminole or Creek nations[sic], concurring in your decision of January 16, 1907, denying the application. A copy of its letter is inclosed.

The Department also concurs in your decision and it is hereby affirmed.

The papers have been sent to the Indian Office for its files, together with a copy hereof.

Respectfully,

Jesse E. Wilson

Assistant Secretary

1 inc. and
2 to Ind. Of.

Refer in reply to the following.   --Copy--

DEPARTMENT OF THE INTERIOR,
Land.   OFFICE OF INDIAN AFFAIRS,
6297-1907.   WASHINGTON. February 18, 1907.
D. C. 11761.

The Honorable,
    The Secretary of the Interior.

Sir:

I have the honor to transmit herewith a communication from the Commissioner to the Five Civilized Tribes, dated January 16, 1907, enclosing record of the proceedings in the matter of the application for the enrollment of applications for the enrollment of Hagar Eckals, Laura Jones, Emanuel Eckals, Andrew Eckals, Nancy Eckals, George Eckals, Elnora Eckals, and Addilina Eckals as Freedmen citizens of either the Seminole or Creek Nations, including the decision of the Commissioner to the Five Civilized Tribes, dated January 16, 1907, denying the application.

It is shown from the record herein that application was filed with the Commission to the Five Civilized Tribes on June 1, 1905, for the enrollment of Hagar Eckals, Laura Jones, Emanuel Eckals, Andrew Eckals, Nancy Eckals, George Eckals, Elnora Eckals, and Addilina Eckals as Seminole Freedmen; that Laura Jones, Emanuel Eckals, Andrew Eckals, Nancy Eckals, George Eckals, Elnora Eckals, and Addilina Eckals are the children of Hagar Eckals; and that Hagar Eckals is the daughter of Hannah Haley, alleged to be a Seminole Freedman, and Sharper Haley, alleged to be a Creek Freedman.

The records in the office of the Commissioner do not show that any of the applicants, or Hannah and Sharper Haley, the parents of the principal applicant, Hagar Eckals, have ever been enrolled as citizens of either the Seminole or the Creek Nation nor

Applications for Enrollment of Seminole Newborn Freedmen
Act of 1905

have they, or any of them, nor Hannah and Sharper Haley, ever been admitted to citizenship in either of these nations by the tribal authorities thereof, the Commission to the Five Civilized Tribes, or the United States Courts in the Indian Territory.

The Office is of the opinion that under the facts shown by the record there is no authority of law for the enrollment of the applicants and that the decision of the Commissioner to the Five Civilized Tribes denying their enrollment as Freedmen citizens of either the Seminole or Creek Nation is correct; and it is therefore recommended that it be affirmed.

Very respectfully,

C. F. Larrabee,

Acting Commissioner.

EWE-D

Sem NB FR 47
BIRTH AFFIDAVIT.
DEPARTMENT OF THE INTERIOR.
COMMISSION TO THE FIVE CIVILIZED TRIBES.

IN RE APPLICATION FOR ENROLLMENT, as a citizen of the   Seminole   Nation, of
Anderson Garfield   , born on the 3   day of   Aug , 1902

Name of Father: James Garfield   a citizen of the   U. S.   ~~Nation~~.
Name of Mother: Cora Garfield   2318   a citizen of the   Seminole   Nation.
                 nee Pompey
                          Postoffice   Sasakwa IT

(Child present)
AFFIDAVIT OF MOTHER.

UNITED STATES OF AMERICA, Indian Territory,
   Western   DISTRICT.

I,   Cora Garfield nee Pompey   , on oath state that I am 19   years of age
and a citizen by   adoption   , of the   Seminole   Nation; that I am the lawful wife

177

Applications for Enrollment of Seminole Newborn Freedmen
Act of 1905

of   James Garfield   , who is a citizen, by   of the   U. S.   Nation; that a
male   child was born to me on 3   day of   Aug   , 1902; that said child has been
named   Anderson Garfield   , and was living March 4, 1905.

Cora Garfield

Witnesses To Mark: nee Pompey
   ⎰ Chas E Webster
   ⎱ Frank C. Sabourin

     Subscribed and sworn to before me this 8 day of   May   , 1905.

Chas E Webster
Notary Public.

AFFIDAVIT OF ATTENDING PHYSICIAN OR MID-WIFE.

UNITED STATES OF AMERICA, Indian Territory, ⎱
    Western   **DISTRICT.** ⎰

    I,   Nellie Thomas   , a   midwife   , on oath state that I attended on
Mrs. Cora Garfield   , wife of   James Garfield   on the 3 day of   August   ,
1902; that there was born to her on said date a   male   child; that said child was living
March 4, 1905, and is said to have been named   Anderson Garfield

her
Nellie x Thomas

Witnesses To Mark: mark
   ⎰ Chas E Webster
   ⎱ Frank C. Sabourin

     Subscribed and sworn to before me 8   day of   May   , 1905.

Chas E Webster
Notary Public.

Applications for Enrollment of Seminole Newborn Freedmen
Act of 1905

SemFr. NB 48

Muskogee, Indian Territory, June 29, 1905.

Commission to the
Five Civilized Tribes,
Creek Enrollment Division.

Gentlemen:

On May 31, 1905, there was filed with the Commission application for the enrollment of Joseph Add, born January 3, 1903, as a Seminole Freedman. It is stated in said application that the father of said child is Albert Add a citizen by adoption of the Creek Nation and that the mother of said child is Betsy Cobb a Seminole Freedman.

You are requested to inform the Seminole Enrollment Division as to whether application has been made to the Commission for the enrollment of said Joseph Add as a citizen of the Creek Nation, and if so what disposition, if any, has been made of such application.

Respectfully,

Chairman.

———————

HGH

DEPARTMENT OF THE INTERIOR.
COMMISSION TO THE FIVE CIVILIZED TRIBES.

Sem.Fr.NB.48.

Muskogee, Indian Territory, July 10, 1905.

Seminole Enrollment Division,
General Office.

Gentlemen:

Receipt is acknowledged of your communication of June 29, 1905, (Sem.Fr.NB.48), in which you ask if application for the enrollment as a citizen of the Creek Nation has been made for Joseph Add, child of Albert Add, a citizen of the Creek Nation, and Betsey Cobb, a Seminole Freedman.

In reply you are advised that the records of this office have been examined and it does not appear that application has been made for the enrollment of said Joseph Add, as a citizen of the Creek Nation.

Respectfully,

Tams Bixby   Commissioner.

———————

179

Applications for Enrollment of Seminole Newborn Freedmen
Act of 1905

Sem NB FR 48
BIRTH AFFIDAVIT.

DEPARTMENT OF THE INTERIOR.
COMMISSION TO THE FIVE CIVILIZED TRIBES.

IN RE APPLICATION FOR ENROLLMENT, as a citizen of the   Seminole   Nation, of
Joseph Add   , born on the 3   day of   Jan , 1903

Name of Father: Albert Add   a citizen of the   Creek   Nation.
Name of Mother: Betsy Cobb   2324   a citizen of the   Seminole   Nation.

Postoffice   Wewoka I.T.

Child present

AFFIDAVIT OF ~~MOTHER~~.
Mother sick.

UNITED STATES OF AMERICA, Indian Territory, ⎫   Father
   Western   DISTRICT. ⎭

    I,   Albert Add   , on oath state that I am   28   years of age and a citizen by
adoption   , of the   Creek   Nation; that I am not the lawful wife of   Betsy Cobb,
who is a citizen, by   adoption   of the   Seminole   Nation; that a   male
child was born to ~~me~~ her on   3   day of   Jan   , 1903, that said child has been named
Joseph Add   , and is now living.   his
                                    Albert   x   Add
Witnesses To Mark: mark
   ⎧ Chas E Webster
   ⎩ John R. McBeth

    Subscribed and sworn to before me this   31 day of   May   , 1905.

                         Chas E Webster
                           Notary Public.

AFFIDAVIT OF ATTENDING PHYSICIAN OR MID-WIFE.

UNITED STATES OF AMERICA, Indian Territory, ⎫
   Western   DISTRICT. ⎭

    I,   Angeline Stepney   , a   midwife   , on oath state that I attended on
M~~rs~~.   Betsy Cobb   , ~~wife of~~   on the   3   day of   Jan , 1903; that there was
born to her on said date a   male   child; that said child is now living and is said to
have been named Joseph Add   her
                           Angeline   x   Stepney
                              mark

Applications for Enrollment of Seminole Newborn Freedmen
Act of 1905

Witnesses To Mark:
   { Chas E Webster
   { John R. McBeth

Subscribed and sworn to before me this   31 day of   May   , 1905.

                         Chas E Webster
                         Notary Public.

W.F.

REFER IN REPLY TO THE FOLLOWING:	DEPARTMENT OF THE INTERIOR,
Sem. Freed.	COMMISSIONER TO THE FIVE CIVILIZED TRIBES.
NB--48	

Muskogee, Indian Territory, July 25, 1905.

Betsy Cobb,
    Wewoka, Indian Territory.

Dear Madam:

On May 31, 1905 Albert Add appeared before the Commission to the Five Civilized Tribes and made application for the enrollment of Joseph Add, born January 3, 1903, as a Seminole freedman. He stated that you were the mother of said child and that he was the father. At that time the affidavits of said Albert Add and Angeline Stepney as to the birth of said child were taken.

You are advised that before the rights of said child as a Seminole freedman can be finally determined it will be necessary for you to furnish this office with your affidavit as to the birth of said child and a blank for that purpose partially filled out is inclosed herewith. Be careful to see that the notary public, before whom the same is sworn to, attaches his name and seal to the affidavit. In case you can not write and your signature is by mark the same must be attested by two disinterested witnesses.

Respectfully,

C D - 1   Tams Bixby   Commissioner.
Env.

181

Applications for Enrollment of Seminole Newborn Freedmen
Act of 1905

Sem NB FR 48
BIRTH AFFIDAVIT.

DEPARTMENT OF THE INTERIOR.
COMMISSION TO THE FIVE CIVILIZED TRIBES.

———————

IN RE APPLICATION FOR ENROLLMENT, as a citizen of the   Seminole   Nation, of
Joseph Add   , born on the 3rd   day of   January   , 1903

Name of Father: Albert Add   a citizen of the   Creek   Nation.
Name of Mother: Betsy Cobb   a citizen of the   Seminole   Nation.

Postoffice   Wewoka, Ind. Ter.

———————

AFFIDAVIT OF MOTHER.

UNITED STATES OF AMERICA, Indian Territory, ⎱
    Western   DISTRICT. ⎰

    I, Betsy Cobb   , on oath state that I am   years of age and a citizen by
adoption   , of the   Seminole   Nation; that I am not the lawful wife of   Albert
Add, who is a citizen, by   adoption   of the   Creek   Nation; that a   male
child was born to me on 3rd   day of   January   , 1903; that said child has been
named   Joseph Add   , and was living March 4, 1905.

                            Betsy Cobb
Witnesses To Mark:
  {

    Subscribed and sworn to before me this 29th   day of   July   , 1905.

                         J C Johnson
                            Notary Public.

———————

Applications for Enrollment of Seminole Newborn Freedmen
Act of 1905

Sem. Freed.
NB-48.

Muskogee, Indian Territory, August 2, 1905.

Betsy Cobb,
Wewoka, Indian Territory.

Dear Madam:

Receipt is acknowledged of your affidavit relative to the birth of your son Joseph Add on January 3, 1903 and the same has been filed with the records of this office in the matter of the application for the enrollment of said child as a Seminole freedman.

Respectfully,

Commissioner.

Sem NB FR 49
BIRTH AFFIDAVIT.
DEPARTMENT OF THE INTERIOR.
COMMISSION TO THE FIVE CIVILIZED TRIBES.

IN RE APPLICATION FOR ENROLLMENT, as a citizen of the   Seminole   Nation, of
Jacob Blanton   , born on the 8th   day of   November , 1904

Name of Father: J.C. Blanton   a citizen of the   U. S.   Nation.
Name of Mother: Rina Davis   (2364)   a citizen of the   Seminole   Nation.

Postoffice   Wewoka IT

Child present
AFFIDAVIT OF MOTHER.

UNITED STATES OF AMERICA, Indian Territory, ⎱
    Western   DISTRICT.   ⎰

I,   Rina Davis   , on oath state that I am   20   years of age and a citizen by adoption   , of the   Seminole   Nation; that I am not the lawful wife of   J.C.

183

Applications for Enrollment of Seminole Newborn Freedmen
Act of 1905

Blanton   , who is a citizen, by   of the   U.S.   Nation; that a   male child was born to me on 8th   day of   November   , 1904; that said child has been named   Jacob Blanton   , and was living March 4, 1905.

her
Rina x Davis
mark

Witnesses To Mark:
{ Frank C. Sabourin
{ Edward Merrick

    Subscribed and sworn to before me this 4th   day of   May   , 1905.

<Seal>

                  Edward Merrick
                  Notary Public.

AFFIDAVIT OF ATTENDING PHYSICIAN OR MID-WIFE.

UNITED STATES OF AMERICA, Indian Territory, ⎫
    Western   DISTRICT.   ⎭

    I,   Sallie Davis   , a midwife   , on oath state that I attended on Mrs.   Rina Davis   my daughter   on the 8th   day of   November   , 1904; that there was born to her on said date a   male   child; that said child was living March 4, 1905, and is said to have been named   Jacob Blanton

her
Sallie x Davis
mark

Witnesses To Mark:
{ Frank C. Sabourin
{ Edward Merrick

    Subscribed and sworn to before me this 4th   day of   May   , 1905.

<Seal>

                  Edward Merrick

                  Notary Public.

Applications for Enrollment of Seminole Newborn Freedmen
Act of 1905

Wewoka, Indian Territory, May 19, 1905.

Rosa Thomas,
    Care Sam Thomas,
        Tidmore, Indian Territory.

Madam:

On May 12, 1905, you appeared before this office and made application for the enrollment of your minor daughter, Matilda Thomas, as a citizen of the Seminole Nation, but no affidavit was made by the attending physician or midwife.

It will be necessary, therefore, to furnish this office with such affidavit, said person either to appear before the Seminole Enrollment Office, at Wewoka, Indian Territory, prior to June 1, 1905, or to have the inclosed blank affidavit filled out and properly executed before a Notary Public, returning same to this office in the inclosed envelope, which requires no postage.

Respectfully,

Enc   Clerk in Charge.

Sem Fr NB 50

Muskogee, Indian Territory, June 29, 1905.

Rosa Thomas
    % Sam Thomas,
        Tidmore, Indian Territory.

Dear Madam:

On May 12, 1905, you appeared before the Commission and made application for the enrollment of your infant child, Matilda Thomas, born June 24, 1904, as a Seminole Freedman and at that time submitted your affidavit only as to the birth of said child.

You are advised that before the rights of said child as a Seminole Freedman can be finally determined it will be necessary for you to furnish the Commission with the affidavit of the attending physician or midwife as to the birth of said child, or in case no physician or midwife attended you when said child was born it will be necessary for o to furnish the Commission with the affidavits of two disinterested persons who know the circumstances attending the birth of said Matilda Thomas, when she was born and whether or not she was living on March 4, 1905.

Respectfully,

Enc-Env.BC.

Chairman.

185

Applications for Enrollment of Seminole Newborn Freedmen
Act of 1905

Sem NB FR 50
BIRTH AFFIDAVIT.

DEPARTMENT OF THE INTERIOR.
COMMISSION TO THE FIVE CIVILIZED TRIBES.

IN RE APPLICATION FOR ENROLLMENT, as a citizen of the   Seminole   Nation, of
Matilda Thomas   , born on the 24   day of   June   , 1904

Name of Father: Sam Thomas   2724   a citizen of the   Seminole   Nation.
Name of Mother: Rosa Thomas   2369   a citizen of the   Seminole   Nation.
                formerly Cudjo
                                  Postoffice   Tidmore IT

AFFIDAVIT OF ATTENDING PHYSICIAN OR MID-WIFE.

UNITED STATES OF AMERICA, Indian Territory, ⎫
        Western   DISTRICT. ⎬

        I,   Deanna Dean   , a midwife   , on oath state that I attended on
Mrs. Rosa Thomas   , wife of Sam Thomas   on the 24   day of June , 1904;
that there was born to her on said date a   female   child; that said child ~~is now living~~
~~and is~~ said to have been named Matilda Thomas   died 13ᵗʰ day of June, 1905
                                                              her
                                          Deanna Dean   x
Witnesses To Mark: mark
    ⎧ John W. Willmott
    ⎩ C. A. Wallace

        Subscribed and sworn to before me this 22   day of   August   , 1905.

                                  John W. Willmott
                                      Notary Public.
Com exp Oct 5-1906

186

Applications for Enrollment of Seminole Newborn Freedmen
Act of 1905

Sem NB FR 50
BIRTH AFFIDAVIT.
DEPARTMENT OF THE INTERIOR.
COMMISSION TO THE FIVE CIVILIZED TRIBES.

IN RE APPLICATION FOR ENROLLMENT, as a citizen of the   Seminole   Nation, of
Matilda Thomas   , born on the   24   day of   June   , 1904

Name of Father: Sam Thomas   (2724)   a citizen of the   Seminole   Nation.
                                (formerly Cudjo, (2369)
Name of Mother: Rosa Thomas   a citizen of the   Seminole   Nation.

Postoffice   Tidmore, IT

Child present

AFFIDAVIT OF MOTHER.

UNITED STATES OF AMERICA, Indian Territory, ⎤
   Western   DISTRICT. ⎦

   I,   Rosa Thomas (formerly Cudjo)   , on oath state that I am   26   years of age
and a citizen by   adoption   , of the   Seminole   Nation; that I am the lawful
wife of   Sam Thomas   , who is a citizen, by   adoption   of the   Seminole
Nation; that a   female   child was born to me on   24   day of   June   , 1904, that
said child has been named   Matilda Thomas   , and is now living.

                                   Rosa Thomas
Witnesses To Mark:
   ⎰
   ⎱

   Subscribed and sworn to before me this 12   day of   May   , 1905.

                         Chas E Webster
                         Notary Public.

187

Applications for Enrollment of Seminole Newborn Freedmen
Act of 1905

Sem NB FR 51
BIRTH AFFIDAVIT.

DEPARTMENT OF THE INTERIOR.
COMMISSION TO THE FIVE CIVILIZED TRIBES.

IN RE APPLICATION FOR ENROLLMENT, as a citizen of the   Seminole   Nation, of
Minnie Cudjo   , born on the   24   day of   February   , 1902

Name of Father: Ned Cudjo   (2368)   a citizen of the   Seminole   Nation.
                                     Cudjo (2369)
Name of Mother: Rosa Thomas (formerly   a citizen of the   Seminole   Nation.

Postoffice   Tidmore, IT

Child present

AFFIDAVIT OF MOTHER.

UNITED STATES OF AMERICA, Indian Territory, ⎫
    Western   DISTRICT.   ⎰

I,   Rosa Thomas (formerly Cudjo)   , on oath state that I am   26   years of age
and a citizen by   adoption   , of the   Seminole   Nation; that I am was the
lawful wife of   Ned Cudjo, deceased   , who is a citizen, by   adoption   of the
Seminole   Nation; that a   female   child was born to me on   24   day of
February   , 1902, that said child has been named   Minnie Cudjo   , and is now living.

Rosa Thomas
Witnesses To Mark:
⎰

Subscribed and sworn to before me this   12   day of   May   , 1905.

Chas E Webster
Notary Public.

AFFIDAVIT OF ATTENDING PHYSICIAN OR MID-WIFE.

UNITED STATES OF AMERICA, Indian Territory, ⎫
    Western   DISTRICT.   ⎰

I,   Sarah Cudjo   , a   midwife   , on oath state that I attended on
Mrs.   Rosa Thomas   then , wife of   Ned Cudjo   on the   24   day of February ,
1902; that there was born to her on said date a   female   child; that said child is now
living and is said to have been named   Minnie Cudjo

Sarah Cudjo

188

Applications for Enrollment of Seminole Newborn Freedmen
Act of 1905

Witnesses To Mark:

{

Subscribed and sworn to before me this 12 day of   May   , 1905.

Chas E Webster
Notary Public.

Sem NB FR 52
BIRTH AFFIDAVIT.
DEPARTMENT OF THE INTERIOR.
COMMISSION TO THE FIVE CIVILIZED TRIBES.

———————

IN RE APPLICATION FOR ENROLLMENT, as a citizen of the   Seminole   Nation, of
Clarence Dosa Hollins   , born on the   20   day of   February   , 1901

Name of Father: John C. Hollins   a citizen of the   U. S.   ~~Nation~~.
Name of Mother: Laura Hollins   (2372)   a citizen of the   Seminole   Nation.

Postoffice   Wewoka, I.T.

———————

Child not present

AFFIDAVIT OF MOTHER.

UNITED STATES OF AMERICA, Indian Territory, ⎤
      Western   **DISTRICT.** ⎦

I,   Laura Hollins   , on oath state that I am   38   years of age and a citizen by
adoption   , of the   Seminole   Nation; that I am the lawful wife of   John P.
Hollins   , who is a citizen, ~~by~~   of the   U.S.   ~~Nation~~; that a   male
child was born to me on   20   day of   February   , 1901; that said child has been
named   Clarence Dosa Hollins   , and was living March 4, 1905.

her
Laura x Hollins
Witnesses To Mark: mark
{ Frank C. Sabourin
⎣ C.E. Webster

189

Applications for Enrollment of Seminole Newborn Freedmen
Act of 1905

Subscribed and sworn to before me this 3$^{\underline{rd}}$ day of   May   , 1905.

Chas E Webster
Notary Public.

AFFIDAVIT OF ATTENDING PHYSICIAN OR MID-WIFE.

UNITED STATES OF AMERICA, Indian Territory, ⎱
  Western   DISTRICT. ⎰

I,   Betsy Winton   , a   midwife   , on oath state that I attended on
Mrs.   Laura Hollins   , wife of   John C. Hollins   on the   20" day of   February ,
1901; that there was born to her on said date a   male   child; that said child was living
March 4, 1905, and is said to have been named   Clarence Dosa Hollins

Betsy Winton

Witnesses To Mark:
{

Subscribed and sworn to before me 3 day of   May   , 1905.

Chas E Webster
Notary Public.

Sem NB FR 53
BIRTH AFFIDAVIT.
DEPARTMENT OF THE INTERIOR.
COMMISSION TO THE FIVE CIVILIZED TRIBES.

Copy

IN RE APPLICATION FOR ENROLLMENT, as a citizen of the   Seminole   Nation, of
John Willis Moore   , born on the   day of   , 1 See Testimony
during the first part of March
Name of Father: Bob Moore   a citizen of the   U.S.   Nation.
Name of Mother: Katie Moore   (2378)   a citizen of the   Seminole   Nation.

190

Applications for Enrollment of Seminole Newborn Freedmen
Act of 1905

Postoffice   Emahaka I.T.

UNITED STATES OF AMERICA, Indian Territory,⎫
Western   DISTRICT. ⎭

I,   Katie Moore   , on oath state that I am   30   years of age and a citizen by adoption   , of the   Seminole   Nation; that I am the lawful wife of   Bob Moore, who is a citizen, by   of the   U. S.   Nation; that a   male   child was born to me ~~on the~~ during the   ~~day of~~ first part of March , 1905, that said child has been named John Willis Moore   , and is now living.   her

                                                    Katie x Moore
Witnesses To Mark: mark
  ⎧ Chas E Webster
  ⎩ Frank C. Sabourin

Subscribed and sworn to before me this 6   day of   May   , 1905.

                              Chas E Webster
                                 Notary Public.

DEPARTMENT OF THE INTERIOR,
COMMISSION TO THE FIVE CIVILIZED TRIBES.

In the matter of the application for the enrollment of John Willis Moore as a freedman of the Seminole Nation.

Bob Moore, being duly sworn, testified as follows:

Q What is your name? A Bob Moore.
Q How old are you? A 41.
Q What is your post office? A Emahaka.
Q Do you desire to make application for the enrollment of your infant child, John Willis Moore as a Seminole Freedman? A Yes sir.
Q Is he a citizen of the Seminole Nation? A Yes sir.
Q Are you a citizen of the Seminole Nation? A No sir.
Q Who is the mother of John Willis Moore? A Katie Moore.
Q Is she a citizen of the Seminole Nation? A Yes sir.

The name of Katie Moore appears on Seminole Freedman Card No. 754; Approved Roll No. 2378.

Q When was John Willis Moore born? A Sometime along the first days of March.
Q Do you know what day of the week it was? A I think it was on Monday.

191

Applications for Enrollment of Seminole Newborn Freedmen
Act of 1905

Q What time in the day, the forenoon or afternoon? A In the afternoon.

Q You don't know whether that child is entitled to enrollment or not? A No sir.

Q Has anybody ever told you anything about it? A Several persons have told me that the the[sic] rolls were stopped on the first day of March.

Q You have been told by several persons that the child was not entitled to enrollment? A Yes sir.

Q How old is the child just before this John Willis? A Three years old, son will be.

Q So then there is nearly three years between the one born just before John Willis and John Willis? A Yes sir.

Q Do you remember whether it was the first or second Monday in March that this child was born? A No sir, I don't but I am pretty sure it was the first Monday. We had the band chief put him on the rolls about the first of April, Quite a little while before we came down here.

Q You don't know how old he was when you had him put on the band chief's roll? A No sir.

Q Was he two weeks old? A He was older than that.

The mother of John Willis Moore appeared before the Commission with the child in her arms. The child seems to be but a few weeks old.

Katie Moore, being duly sworn, testified as follows:

Q What is your name? A Katie Moore.

Q How old are you? A 30.

Q What is your post office? A Emahaka.

Q Are you the mother of John Willis Moore? A Yes sir.

Q When was John Willis born? A I don't know exactly.

Q What month was he born in? A March.

Q Do you know what day of the week? A No sir.

Q You don't know. A No sir.

Q Do you know whether he was born on Sunday of Monday? A He was born on Sunday.

Q He was born the day after Sunday? A Yes sir.

Q There were some people at your house on Sunday before this child was born? A Yes sir.

Q And the next day after these people were at your house, this child was born? A Yes sir.

Q For that reason, you think he was born on Monday? A Yes sir.

Q Do you think he was born about the first of March or the middle of March? A I don't know.

Q You are satisfied he was born on Monday? A Yes sir.

Frank C. Sabourin, being duly sworn states that the above and foregoing is a true and correct transcript of his stenographic notes as taken in said case at Wewoka, Indian Territory, on May 6, 1905.

192

Applications for Enrollment of Seminole Newborn Freedmen
Act of 1905

Frank C. Sabourin

Subscribed and sworn to before me this 6th day of March, 1905.

(SEAL)   Edward Merrick
                                                Notary Public.

I, Lola Mann, a stenographer to the Commissioner to the Five Civilized Tribes, do hereby certify that the above is a true and correct copy of the original now on file in this office in Seminole new born freedman case No. 53.

Lola Mann

Subscribed and sworn to before me this 16th day of February, 1906.

Myron White
Notary Public.

_____

S.F.N.B. 53.
DEPARTMENT OF THE INTERIOR,
COMMISSIONER TO THE FIVE CIVILIZED TRIBES.

In the matter of the application for the enrollment of John Willis Moore as a Seminole citizen.

- D E C I S I O N -

It appears from the record in this case that on May 6, 1905, there was filed with the Commission to the Five Civilized Tribes an application for the enrollment of John Willis Moore as a Seminole citizen.

It further appears from the record herein, and from the records of the Commission to the Five Civilized Tribes, that the applicant was born during the first part of March 1905, (not earlier than March 5, 1905), and is a son of Katie Moore, a recognized and enrolled Seminole citizen, whose name appears as No. 2378 upon the final roll is Seminole citizens approved by the Secretary of the Interior April 2, 1901, and Bob Moore, a non-citizen.

The Act of Congress approved March 3, 1905, (33 Stat., 1060), provides:

"That the Commission to the Five Civilized Tribes is authorized for ninety days after the date of the approval of this act to receive and consider applications for enrollment of infant children born prior to March fourth, nineteen hundred and five, and living on said latter date, to citizens of the Seminole tribe whose enrollment has been approved by the Secretary of the Interior; and to enroll and make allotments to such children."

I am of the opinion that, inasmuch as John Willis Moore was not born prior to March 4, 1905, I am without authority to receive or consider the application for his

193

enrollment as a Seminole citizen, and that, therefore, I should decline to receive or consider the same, and it is so ordered.

Tams Bixby Commissioner.

Muskogee, Indian Territory.
JAN 5- 1906

Seminole F.   **COPY**
N B 53
Muskogee, Indian Territory, June 5, 1906.

Katie Moore,
Emahaka, Indian Territory.

Dear Madam:

Inclosed herewith you will find a copy of the decision of the Commissioner to the Five Civilized Tribes, rendered June 5, 1906, declining to receive or consider the application for the enrollment of John Willis Moore as a Seminole citizen.

The decision, with the record of proceedings in the case, is this day transmitted to the Secretary of the Interior for review. The final decision of the Secretary will be made known to you as soon as this office is informed of the same.

Respectfully,

SIGNED

Tams Bixby

Registered.   Commissioner.
Inc. S F N B 53

Seminole Freedmen   **COPY**
N. B. 53
Muskogee, Indian Territory, June 5, 1906.

Wilmott[sic] & Wilhoit
McKennon & Wilmott,
Attorneys for Seminole Nation,
Wewoka, Indian Territory.

Gentlemen:

Inclosed herewith you will find a copy of the decision of the Commissioner to the Five Civilized Tribes, rendered June 5, 1906, declining to receive or consider the application for the enrollment of John Willis Moore as a Seminole citizen.

194

Applications for Enrollment of Seminole Newborn Freedmen
Act of 1905

The decision, with the record of proceedings in the case, is this day transmitted to the Secretary of the Interior for review. The final decision of the Secretary will be made known to you as soon as this office is informed of the same.

Respectfully,

SIGNED

Tams Bixby
Commissioner.

Incl. S. F. N. B. 53

COPY

Muskogee, Indian Territory, June 5, 1906.

The Honorable,
The Secretary of the Interior.

Sir:

There is transmitted herewith the record of proceedings in the matter of the application for the enrollment of John Willis Moore as a Seminole citizen, including the decision of the Commissioner to the Five Civilized Tribes, dated June 5, 1906, declining to receive or consider said application.

Respectfully,

SIGNED

Tams Bixby

2 Incl. S. F. N. B. 53   Commissioner.

Through the
Commissioner of Indian Affairs.

Applications for Enrollment of Seminole Newborn Freedmen
Act of 1905

J.C. H.

DEPARTMENT OF THE INTERIOR,
WASHINGTON. LLB

D. C. 2914-1907. January 12, 1907.
I.T.D. 154-1907.

LRS

Commissioner to the Five Civilized Tribes,
Muskogee, Indian Territory.

Sir:

June 5, 1906, you transmitted the record in the matter of the application of John Willis Moore, for enrollment as a Seminole freedman, together with your decision of same date, adverse to the applicant.

Reporting January 4, 1907, (Land 49059-1906), the Indian Office recommended that your decision be approved. A copy of its letter is inclosed.

The Department concurs in said recommendation, and your decision is hereby affirmed.

The papers in the matter have been sent to the Indian Office for its files.

Respectfully,

Thos Ryan

Fist Assistant Secretary.

Through the Commissioner
of Indian Affairs.

1 inc. and 2 to Ind. Of.

Applications for Enrollment of Seminole Newborn Freedmen
Act of 1905

Refer in reply to the following:

<table>
<tr><td></td><td>DEPARTMENT OF THE INTERIOR,</td><td></td></tr>
<tr><td>Land</td><td>OFFICE OF INDIAN AFFAIRS,</td><td></td></tr>
<tr><td>49069-1906.</td><td>WASHINGTON.</td><td>January 4, 1907.</td></tr>
<tr><td></td><td>(COPY)</td><td></td></tr>
</table>

The Honorable,
    The Secretary of the Interior.

Sir:

    There is transmitted herewith a report of Commissioner Bixby, dated June 5, 1906, in the matter of the application for the enrollment of John Willis Moore as a Seminole citizen, including the decision of the Commissioner of the same date declining to receive or consider the application.

    The record shows that on May 6, 1905, there was filed with the Commission to the Five Civilized Tribes an application for the enrollment of John Willis Moore, as above. The evidence shows that the applicant was born during the first part of March, 1905 (not earlier than March 5, 1905), and is the son of Katie Moore, a recognized and enrolled Seminole citizen, and Bob Moore, a non-citizen. The Commissioner reports that the records of his office corroborate the evidence as to the date of birth of the applicant. Under the provisions of the Act of March 3, 1905 (33 Stat. L., 1060), providing for the application and enrollment of infant children born prior to March 4, 1905, and living on that date, to citizens of the Seminole tribe, there is no authority in law to receive or consider the application herein, inasmuch as John Willis Moore was not born prior to March 4, 1905. It is therefore recommended that the application be denied.

Very respectfully,

C. F. Larrabee

AJW-SD   Acting Commissioner.

Seminole F.
N B 53

                   Muskogee, Indian Territory, January 23, 1907.

Katie Moore,
    Emahaka, Indian Territory.

Dear Madam:

    You are hereby notified that on January 12, 1907, the Secretary of the Interior affirmed the decision of the Commissioner to the Five Civilized Tribes declining to receive the application for the enrollment of John Willis Moore as a Seminole citizen.

197

Applications for Enrollment of Seminole Newborn Freedmen
Act of 1905

Respectfully,

Commissioner.

Seminole F.
N. B. 53

Muskogee, Indian Territory, January 23, 1907.

Wilmott[sic] & Wilhoit,
Attorneys at Law,
Wewoka, Indian Territory.

Dear Sir:

You are hereby notified that on January 12, 1907, the Secretary of the Interior affirmed the decision of the Commissioner to the Five Civilized Tribes declining to receive the application for the enrollment of John Willis Moore as a Seminole citizen.

Respectfully,

Commissioner.

Sem NB FR 53
BIRTH AFFIDAVIT.

DEPARTMENT OF THE INTERIOR.
COMMISSION TO THE FIVE CIVILIZED TRIBES.

IN RE APPLICATION FOR ENROLLMENT, as a citizen of the   Seminole   Nation, of
Elzora Moore   , born on the   4   day of   Dec   , 1902

Name of Father: Bob Moore   a citizen of the   U S   ~~Nation~~.
Name of Mother: Katie Moore   (2378)   a citizen of the   Seminole   Nation.

Postoffice   Emahaka I.T.

Child present

AFFIDAVIT OF MOTHER.

UNITED STATES OF AMERICA, Indian Territory,⎱
      Western   **DISTRICT.** ⎰

I,   Katie Moore   , on oath state that I am   30   years of age and a citizen by adoption   , of the   Seminole   Nation; that I am the lawful wife of   Bob Moore   , who is a citizen, ~~by~~   of the   U.S.   Nation; that a   Female   child was

198

Applications for Enrollment of Seminole Newborn Freedmen
Act of 1905

born to me on 4 day of Dec , 1902, that said child has been named Elzora
Moore, and is now living.

Katie x Moore
                                                             her
Witnesses To Mark: mark
  ⎰ Chas E Webster
  ⎱ Frank C. Sabourin

Subscribed and sworn to before me this 6 day of May , 1905.

Chas E Webster
Notary Public.

AFFIDAVIT OF ATTENDING PHYSICIAN OR MID-WIFE.

UNITED STATES OF AMERICA, Indian Territory, ⎱
    Western   DISTRICT. ⎰

I, Rhoda Cudjo   , a midwife , on oath state that I attended on
Mrs. Katie Moore , wife of Bob Moore on the 4 day of Dec , 1902; that
there was born to her on said date a Female child; that said child is now living and
is said to have been named Elzora Moore
                                                             her
                                           Rhoda x Cudjo
Witnesses To Mark: mark
  ⎰ Chas E Webster
  ⎱ Frank C. Sabourin

Subscribed and sworn to before me this 6 day of May , 1905.

Chas E Webster
Notary Public.

Sem NB FR 53
BIRTH AFFIDAVIT.
DEPARTMENT OF THE INTERIOR.
COMMISSION TO THE FIVE CIVILIZED TRIBES.

IN RE APPLICATION FOR ENROLLMENT, as a citizen of the   Seminole   Nation, of
Arvey Moore , born on the 15 day of Aug , 1900

Name of Father: Bob Moore   a citizen of the   U S   N̶a̶t̶i̶o̶n̶.
Name of Mother: Katie Moore   a citizen of the Seminole Nation.

Postoffice   Emahaka I.T.

Applications for Enrollment of Seminole Newborn Freedmen
Act of 1905

Child present

UNITED STATES OF AMERICA, Indian Territory,
Western   DISTRICT.

I, Katie Moore , on oath state that I am 30 years of age and a citizen by adoption , of the Seminole Nation; that I am the lawful wife of Bob Moore , who is a citizen, ~~by~~   of the U.S. Nation; that a Male child was born to me on 15 day of Aug , 1900, that said child has been named Arvey Moore, and is now living.

Witnesses To Mark:

{ Chas E Webster
{ Frank C. Sabourin

her
Katie x Moore
mark

Subscribed and sworn to before me this 6 day of May   , 1905.

Chas E Webster
Notary Public.

UNITED STATES OF AMERICA, Indian Territory,
Western   DISTRICT.

I, Rhoda Cudjo   , a midwife   , on oath state that I attended on Mrs. Katie Moore , wife of Bob Moore on the 15 day of Aug , 1900; that there was born to her on said date a male child; that said child is now living and is said to have been named Arvey Moore

Witnesses To Mark:

{ Chas E Webster
{ Frank C. Sabourin

her
Rhoda x Cudjo
mark

Subscribed and sworn to before me this 6 day of May   , 1905.

Chas E Webster
Notary Public.

Applications for Enrollment of Seminole Newborn Freedmen
Act of 1905

Sem NB FR 54
BIRTH AFFIDAVIT.
DEPARTMENT OF THE INTERIOR.
COMMISSION TO THE FIVE CIVILIZED TRIBES.

IN RE APPLICATION FOR ENROLLMENT, as a citizen of the   Seminole   Nation, of
Arvaline Cudjo   , born on the 21st day of   February   , 1900

Name of Father: King Cudjo   (2381)   a citizen of the   Seminole   Nation.
Name of Mother: Dafney Cudjo   (2382)   a citizen of the   Seminole   Nation.

Postoffice   Emahaka IT

Child present
AFFIDAVIT OF MOTHER.

UNITED STATES OF AMERICA, Indian Territory, ⎱
   Western   DISTRICT. ⎰

     I,   Dafney Cudjo   , on oath state that I am   27   years of age and a citizen by
adoption   , of the   Seminole   Nation; that I am the lawful wife of   King Cudjo ,
who is a citizen, by   adoption   of the   Seminole   Nation; that a   female
child was born to me on   21st day of   February   , 1900, that said child has been
named   Arvaline Cudjo   , and is now living.

her
Dafney x Cudjo
mark

Witnesses To Mark:
  ⎰ Frank C. Sabourin
  ⎱ Chas E Webster

    Subscribed and sworn to before me this   8th day of   May   , 1905.

Chas E Webster
Notary Public.

AFFIDAVIT OF ATTENDING PHYSICIAN OR MID-WIFE.

UNITED STATES OF AMERICA, Indian Territory, ⎱
   Western   DISTRICT. ⎰

     I,   Venus Davis   , a   midwife   , on oath state that I attended on
Mrs.   Dafney Cudjo   , wife of   King Cudjo   on the   21st day of February ,
1900; that there was born to her on said date a   female   child; that said child is now
living and is said to have been named Arvaline Cudjo

Applications for Enrollment of Seminole Newborn Freedmen
Act of 1905

Witnesses To Mark:
   ⎰ Frank C. Sabourin
   ⎱ Chas E Webster

her
Venus x Davis
mark

Subscribed and sworn to before me this 8th day of   May   , 1905.

Chas E Webster
Notary Public.

Sem NB FR 54
BIRTH AFFIDAVIT.

DEPARTMENT OF THE INTERIOR.
COMMISSION TO THE FIVE CIVILIZED TRIBES.

IN RE APPLICATION FOR ENROLLMENT, as a citizen of the   Seminole   Nation, of
Clayton Cudjo   , born on the 27 day of July , 1904

Name of Father: King Cudjo	(2381)	a citizen of the Seminole Nation.
Name of Mother: Dafney Cudjo	(2382)	a citizen of the Seminole Nation.

Postoffice   Emahaka IT

Child present

AFFIDAVIT OF MOTHER.

UNITED STATES OF AMERICA, Indian Territory, ⎤
    Western   **DISTRICT.** ⎦

    I, Darney Cudjo   , on oath state that I am 27   years of age and a citizen by adoption , of the   Seminole Nation; that I am the lawful wife of King Cudjo , who is a citizen, by adoption   of the   Seminole   Nation; that a   male child was born to me on 27th   day of July   , 1904; that said child has been named Clayton Cudjo   , and was living March 4, 1905.

her
Dafney x Cudjo
mark

Witnesses To Mark:
   ⎰ Frank C. Sabourin
   ⎱ Chas E Webster

Subscribed and sworn to before me this 8th day of   May   , 1905.

Chas E Webster
Notary Public.

202

Applications for Enrollment of Seminole Newborn Freedmen
Act of 1905

UNITED STATES OF AMERICA, Indian Territory,
 Western   DISTRICT.

I,   Venus Davis   , a   midwife   , on oath state that I attended on
Mrs.   Dafney Cudjo   , wife of   King Cudjo   on the   27ᵗʰ day of   July   ,
1904; that there was born to her on said date a   male   child; that said child was living
March 4, 1905, and is said to have been named Clayton Cudjo

                                                      her
                                          Venus x Davis
Witnesses To Mark: mark
 ⌠ Frank C. Sabourin
 ⌡ Chas E Webster

Subscribed and sworn to before me 8ᵗʰ day of   May   , 1905.

                                  Chas E Webster
                                      Notary Public.

Sem NB FR 54
BIRTH AFFIDAVIT.
DEPARTMENT OF THE INTERIOR.
COMMISSION TO THE FIVE CIVILIZED TRIBES.

IN RE APPLICATION FOR ENROLLMENT, as a citizen of the   Seminole   Nation, of
Perryman Cudjo   , born on the 9ᵗʰ   day of   October   , 1902

Name of Father: King Cudjo   (2381)   a citizen of the   Seminole   Nation.
Name of Mother: Dafney Cudjo   (2382)   a citizen of the   Seminole   Nation.

                   Postoffice   Emahaka IT

Child present
AFFIDAVIT OF MOTHER.

UNITED STATES OF AMERICA, Indian Territory,
 Western   DISTRICT.

I,   Dafney Cudjo , on oath state that I am   27 years of age and a citizen by
adoption   , of the   Seminole   Nation; that I am the lawful wife of   King Cudjo ,
who is a citizen, by   adoption   of the   Seminole   Nation; that a   male
child was born to me on   9ᵗʰ   day of   October   , 1902, that said child has been
named   Perryman Cudjo   , and is now living.

203

Applications for Enrollment of Seminole Newborn Freedmen
Act of 1905

Witnesses To Mark:
    ⎰ Frank C. Sabourin
    ⎱ Chas E Webster

her
Dafney x Cudjo
mark

Subscribed and sworn to before me this   8th   day of   May   , 1905.

Chas E Webster
Notary Public.

AFFIDAVIT OF ATTENDING PHYSICIAN OR MID-WIFE.

UNITED STATES OF AMERICA, Indian Territory, ⎱
      Western   **DISTRICT.** ⎰

    I,   Venus Davis   , a   midwife   , on oath state that I attended on Mrs.   Dafney Cudjo   , wife of   King Cudjo   on the   9th   day of October , 1902; that there was born to her on said date a   male   child; that said child is now living and is said to have been named Perryman Cudjo

her
Venus x Davis
mark

Witnesses To Mark:
    ⎰ Frank C. Sabourin
    ⎱ Chas E Webster

Subscribed and sworn to before me this 8th   day of   May   , 1905.

Chas E Webster
Notary Public.

Applications for Enrollment of Seminole Newborn Freedmen
Act of 1905

Sem NB FR 55
BIRTH AFFIDAVIT.
DEPARTMENT OF THE INTERIOR.
COMMISSION TO THE FIVE CIVILIZED TRIBES.

IN RE APPLICATION FOR ENROLLMENT, as a citizen of the   Seminole   Nation, of Human Carolina   , born on the 8th day of August , 1903

Name of Father: Budman Cudjo   (2314)   a citizen of the   Seminole   Nation.
Name of Mother: Jane Davis   (2398)   a citizen of the   Seminole   Nation.

Postoffice   Sasakwa I.T.

Child not present

AFFIDAVIT OF MOTHER.

UNITED STATES OF AMERICA, Indian Territory,
Western   DISTRICT.

I,   Jane Davis   , on oath state that I am   23   years of age and a citizen by adoption   , of the   Seminole   Nation; that I am not the lawful wife of   Budman Carolina (enrolled as Budman Cudjo) , who is a citizen, by   adoption   of the Seminole   Nation; that a   male   child was born to me on   8th   day of August, 1903; that said child has been named   Human Carolina   , and was living March 4, 1905.

her
Jane x Davis
mark

Witnesses To Mark:
{ Frank C. Sabourin
{ Edward Merrick

Subscribed and sworn to before me this 3rd day of   May   , 1905.

< Seal >

Edward Merrick
Notary Public.

AFFIDAVIT OF ATTENDING PHYSICIAN OR MID-WIFE.

UNITED STATES OF AMERICA, Indian Territory,
Western   DISTRICT.

I,   Charlotte Davis   , a   midwife   , on oath state that I attended on Mrs.   Jane Davis   , wife of   on the 8th day of August   , 1903; that there was born to her on said date a   male   child; that said child was living March 4, 1905, and is said to have been named Human Carolina

Applications for Enrollment of Seminole Newborn Freedmen
Act of 1905

Witnesses To Mark:
    ⎰ Frank C. Sabourin
    ⎱ Edward Merrick

her
Charlotte x Davis
mark

Subscribed and sworn to before me this 3rd day of   May   , 1905.

⟨ Seal ⟩

Edward Merrick
Notary Public.

REFER IN REPLY TO THE FOLLOWING:

Seminole Freedman

NB 56

**DEPARTMENT OF THE INTERIOR,
COMMISSIONER TO THE FIVE CIVILIZED TRIBES.**

Muskogee, Indian Territory, May 7, 1906.

Simon Sandy,
    Sasakwa, Indian Territory.

Dear Sir:

You are hereby advised that it appearing from the records of this office that Passie Sandy died prior to March 4, 1905, the Commissioner to the Five Civilized Tribes, on May 4, 1906, dismissed the application for the enrollment of said child as a Seminole freedman.

Respectfully,

Wm O. Beall
Acting Commissioner.

(Note on following Birth Affidavit)

It appearing from the within affidavits that Passie Sandy born August 21, 1904, for whose enrollment as a citizen of the Seminole Nation, application was made under the Act of Congress approved March 3, 1905 (33 Stat., 1071), died January 6, 1905, it is hereby ordered that the application of said Passie Sandy for enrollment as a citizen of the Seminole Nation be dismissed.

Applications for Enrollment of Seminole Newborn Freedmen
Act of 1905

Muskogee, Indian Territory.
MAY 4- 1906

Tams Bixby Commissioner.

Sem NB FR 56
BIRTH AFFIDAVIT.

DEPARTMENT OF THE INTERIOR.
COMMISSION TO THE FIVE CIVILIZED TRIBES.

IN RE APPLICATION FOR ENROLLMENT, as a citizen of the　　Seminole　　Nation, of
Passie Sandy　　, born on the 21　day of　Aug , 1904

Name of Father: Simon Sandy　　(2396)　a citizen of the　Seminole　Nation.
Name of Mother: Ella Carolina　　(2408)　a citizen of the　Seminole　Nation.

Postoffice　　Sasakwa

AFFIDAVIT OF MOTHER.

UNITED STATES OF AMERICA, Indian Territory, ⎱
　　Western　　　　DISTRICT. ⎰

　　I,　Ella Carolina　　, on oath state that I am　20　years of age and a citizen by
adoption　　, of the　Seminole　Nation; that I am not the lawful wife of　Simon
Sandy　　, who is a citizen, by adoption　of the　　Seminole　　Nation; that a
Female　　child was born to me on 21st　day of　Aug　, 1904; that said child has
been named　Passie Sandy　　, and ~~was living March 4, 1905~~. and died Jan 6-1905

　　　　　　　　　　　　　　　　　　Ella Carolina
Witnesses To Mark:
⎧
⎩

　　Subscribed and sworn to before me this　8 day of　　May　　, 1905.

　　　　　　　　　　　　　　　Chas E Webster
　　　　　　　　　　　　　　　Notary Public.

207

Applications for Enrollment of Seminole Newborn Freedmen
Act of 1905

Sem NB FR 56
BIRTH AFFIDAVIT.

DEPARTMENT OF THE INTERIOR.
COMMISSION TO THE FIVE CIVILIZED TRIBES.

IN RE APPLICATION FOR ENROLLMENT, as a citizen of the   Seminole   Nation, of
Evangeline Sandy   , born on the 11   day of Sept   , 1901

Name of Father: Simon Sandy   2396   a citizen of the   Seminole   Nation.
Name of Mother: Ella Carolina   2408   a citizen of the   Seminole   Nation.

Postoffice   Sasakwa IT

AFFIDAVIT OF ATTENDING PHYSICIAN OR MID-WIFE.

UNITED STATES OF AMERICA, Indian Territory,
    Western   DISTRICT.

I,   Rhoda Cudjoe   , a mid-wife   , on oath state that I attended on
Mrs. Ella Carolina   , wife of   on the 11   day of Sept , 1901; that there was
born to her on said date a   female   child; that said child is now living and is said to
have been named Evangeline Sandy

                                        her
                                Rhoda x Cudjoe
Witnesses To Mark: mark
  ⎰ Dailey D. Davis
  ⎱ Edward Cox

Subscribed and sworn to before me this 7 day of   June   , 1905.

My commission   Edward Cox
expires May 30, 1907.   Notary Public.

Sem NB FR 56
BIRTH AFFIDAVIT.

DEPARTMENT OF THE INTERIOR.
COMMISSION TO THE FIVE CIVILIZED TRIBES.

IN RE APPLICATION FOR ENROLLMENT, as a citizen of the   Seminole   Nation, of
Evangeline Sandy   , born on the 11ᵗʰ   day of September   , 1901

Name of Father: Simon Sandy   (2396)   a citizen of the   Seminole   Nation.
Name of Mother: Ella Carolina   (2408)   a citizen of the   Seminole   Nation.

208

Applications for Enrollment of Seminole Newborn Freedmen
Act of 1905

Postoffice   Sasakwa IT

_____

Child not present

UNITED STATES OF AMERICA, Indian Territory,⎫
Western   **DISTRICT.** ⎭

I, Ella Carolina , on oath state that I am 20 years of age and a citizen by adoption , of the Seminole Nation; that I am not the lawful wife of Simon Sandy , who is a citizen, by adoption of the Seminole Nation; that a female child was born to me on 11th day of September , 1901, that said child has been named Evangeline Sandy , and is now living.

Ella Carolina

Witnesses To Mark:
⎰
⎱

Subscribed and sworn to before me this 5" day of May , 1905.

⟨ Seal ⟩   Edward Merrick
                             Notary Public.

_____

UNITED STATES OF AMERICA, Indian Territory,⎫
Western   **DISTRICT.** ⎭

saw
I, Simon Sandy , a~~~~ , on oath state that I ~~attended on~~
Mrs. Ella Carolina , ~~wife of~~ my former wife ~~on~~ the day after the 11 day of Sept , 1901; that there was born to her on said date a female child; that said child is now living and is said to have been named Evangeline Sandy

his
Simon x Sandy
Witnesses To Mark: mark
⎰ Chas E Webster
⎱ John R. McBeth

Subscribed and sworn to before me this 31 day of May , 1905.

Chas E Webster
Notary Public.

209

Applications for Enrollment of Seminole Newborn Freedmen
Act of 1905

Sem NB FR 57
BIRTH AFFIDAVIT.

DEPARTMENT OF THE INTERIOR.
COMMISSION TO THE FIVE CIVILIZED TRIBES.

IN RE APPLICATION FOR ENROLLMENT, as a citizen of the   Seminole   Nation, of
Herbert Williams   , born on the 25   day of March   , 1903

Name of Father: Coley Williams   a citizen of the   U.S.   ~~Nation~~.
Name of Mother: Milly Ann Thomas   2414   a citizen of the   Seminole   Nation.

Postoffice   Wewoka I.T.

(Child present)

AFFIDAVIT OF MOTHER.

UNITED STATES OF AMERICA, Indian Territory, ⎱
      Western   DISTRICT.   ⎰

I,   Milly Ann Thomas   , on oath state that I am about 28 years of age and a
citizen by   adoption   , of the   Seminole   Nation; that I am not the lawful wife
of   Coley Williams   , who is a citizen, ~~by~~   of the   U. S.   Nation; that a
male   child was born to me on   25   day of   March   , 1903, that said child has
been named   Herbert Williams   , and is now living.
                                                     her
                                     Milly Ann x Thomas
Witnesses To Mark: mark
  ⎰ Chas E Webster
  ⎱ Frank C. Sabourin

Subscribed and sworn to before me this 15   day of   May   , 1905.

Chas E Webster
Notary Public.

AFFIDAVIT OF ATTENDING PHYSICIAN OR MID-WIFE.

UNITED STATES OF AMERICA, Indian Territory, ⎱
      Western   DISTRICT.   ⎰

I,   Eliza Thomas   , a   midwife   , on oath state that I attended on
~~Mrs~~. Milly Ann Thomas   , ~~wife of~~   on the   25   day of   March , 1903; that
there was born to her on said date a   male   child; that said child is now living and is
said to have been named Herbert Williams   her
                                          Eliza x Thomas
                                               mark

210

Applications for Enrollment of Seminole Newborn Freedmen
Act of 1905

Witnesses To Mark:
    { Chas E Webster
    { Frank C. Sabourin

Subscribed and sworn to before me this 15 day of   May   , 1905.

Chas E Webster
Notary Public.

Sem NB FR 58
BIRTH AFFIDAVIT.
DEPARTMENT OF THE INTERIOR.
COMMISSION TO THE FIVE CIVILIZED TRIBES.

IN RE APPLICATION FOR ENROLLMENT, as a citizen of the   Seminole   Nation, of
Leona Pompey   , born on the 30   day of   July , 1904

Name of Father: Passy Pompey   2307   a citizen of the   Seminole   Nation.
Name of Mother: Silvey Pompey   2422   a citizen of the   Seminole   Nation.
    formerly Barkus
    Postoffice   Sasakwa, I.T.

(Child present)

AFFIDAVIT OF MOTHER.

UNITED STATES OF AMERICA, Indian Territory,
    Western   DISTRICT.

I,   Silvey Pompey formerly Barkus   , on oath state that I am 25   years of age and a citizen by   adoption   , of the   Seminole   Nation; that I am the lawful wife of Passy Pompey   , who is a citizen, by adoption   of the   Seminole Nation; that a   Female   child was born to me on 30   day of   July   , 1904; that said child has been named   Leona Pompey   , and was living March 4, 1905.

    her
    Silvey x Pompey
Witnesses To Mark: mark
    { Chas E Webster
    { Frank C. Sabourin

211

Applications for Enrollment of Seminole Newborn Freedmen
Act of 1905

Subscribed and sworn to before me this 8 day of   May   , 1905.

Chas E Webster
Notary Public.

AFFIDAVIT OF ATTENDING PHYSICIAN OR MID-WIFE.

UNITED STATES OF AMERICA, Indian Territory,
Western   DISTRICT.

I,   Nellie Thomas   , a   midwife   , on oath state that I attended on
Mrs.   Silvey Pompey   , wife of   Passy Pompey   on the 30 day of   July   ,
1904; that there was born to her on said date a   Female   child; that said child was
living March 4, 1905, and is said to have been named   Leona Pompey

her
Nellie x Thomas
Witnesses To Mark: mark
⎰ Chas E Webster
⎱ Frank C. Sabourin

Subscribed and sworn to before me 8 day of   May   , 1905.

Chas E Webster
Notary Public.

Sem NB FR 59   Roll 2440
BIRTH AFFIDAVIT.   F-Cord 765
DEPARTMENT OF THE INTERIOR.
COMMISSION TO THE FIVE CIVILIZED TRIBES.

IN RE APPLICATION FOR ENROLLMENT, as a citizen of the   Seminole   Nation, of
Leah Sango   , born on the 12   day of   March , 1904
not adopted
Name of Father: Peter Sango   a citizen of the   Creek   Nation.
Name of Mother: Mary Sango   2440   a citizen of the   Seminole   Nation.
nee Bruner
Postoffice   Earlsboro, O.T.

212

Applications for Enrollment of Seminole Newborn Freedmen
Act of 1905

UNITED STATES OF AMERICA, Indian Territory, ⎱
Western   DISTRICT. ⎰

      I,   Mary Sango   , on oath state that I am   28   years of age and a citizen by Blood   , of the   Seminole   Nation; that I am the lawful wife of   Peter Sango   , who is a citizen, by   Marriage   of the   Seminole   Nation; that a   Female child was born to me on   the 12   day of   March   , 1904, that said child has been named   Leah Sango   , and is now living.

her
Mary   x   Sango
mark

Witnesses To Mark:
   ⎰ Hagar Bruner
   ⎱ Peter Sango

      Subscribed and sworn to before me this   30   day of   May   , 1905.

R. N. Bruner
Notary Public.

UNITED STATES OF AMERICA, Indian Territory, ⎱
Western   DISTRICT. ⎰

      I,   Peter Sango   , a ———————   , on oath state that I attended on Mrs.   Mary Sango   , wife of   Peter Sango   on the   12   day of March ; 1904; that there was born to her on said date a   Female   child; that said child is now living and is said to have been named Leah Sango

his
Peter   x   Sango
mark

Witnesses To Mark:
   ⎰ Hagar Bruner
   ⎱ Peter Sango

      Subscribed and sworn to before me this   30   day of   May   , 1905.
My commission expires Oct
          10th 1906   R. N. Bruner
                                 Notary Public.

Applications for Enrollment of Seminole Newborn Freedmen
Act of 1905

Sem NB FR 59   Roll 2440
BIRTH AFFIDAVIT.   F-Cord 765
DEPARTMENT OF THE INTERIOR.
COMMISSION TO THE FIVE CIVILIZED TRIBES.

IN RE APPLICATION FOR ENROLLMENT, as a citizen of the   Seminole   Nation, of
Albert Sango   , born on the 15   day of   February , 1902
                                                            not adopted
Name of Father: Peter Sango   a citizen of the   Creek   Nation.
Name of Mother: Mary Sango   2440   a citizen of the   Seminole   Nation.
                        nee Bruner
                        Postoffice   Earlsboro, O.T.

AFFIDAVIT OF MOTHER.

UNITED STATES OF AMERICA, Indian Territory,
   Western   DISTRICT.

I,   Mary Sango   , on oath state that I am 28 years of age and a citizen by
Blood   , of the   Seminole   Nation; that I am the lawful wife of   Peter Sango   ,
who is a citizen, by   Marriage   of the   Seminole   Nation; that a mail male
child was born to me on   the 15   day of   February , 1902, that said child has been
named   Albert Sango   , and is now living.
                                          her
                                      Mary x Sango
Witnesses To Mark: mark
   Hagar Bruner
   Peter Sango

Subscribed and sworn to before me this 30 day of   May   , 1905.

                        R. N. Bruner
                              Notary Public.

AFFIDAVIT OF ATTENDING PHYSICIAN OR MID-WIFE.

UNITED STATES OF AMERICA, Indian Territory,
   Western   DISTRICT.

I,   Dinah Walker   , a Mid Woman   , on oath state that I attended on
Mrs. Mary Sango   , wife of   Peter Sango   on the 15   day of February , 1902;
that there was born to her on said date a   male   child; that said child is now living
and is said to have been named Albert Sango
                                          her
                                   Dinah x Walker
                                          mark
                        214

Applications for Enrollment of Seminole Newborn Freedmen
Act of 1905

Witnesses To Mark:
⎧ Hagar Bruner
⎩ Peter Sango

Subscribed and sworn to before me this 30 day of   May   , 1905.
My commission expires
      October 10, 1906   R. N. Bruner
                                       Notary Public.

_____

Sem Fr NB 59

Muskogee, Indian Territory, June 29, 1905.

Commission to the
    Five Civilized Tribes,
        Creek Enrollment Division.

Gentlemen:

On May 31, 1905, there were filed with the Commission applications for the enrollment of Albert Sango, born February 15, 1902 and Leah Sango, born March 12, 1904, as Seminole Freedmen. It is stated in said applications that the father of said children is Peter Sango, a citizen of the Creek Nation, and that their mother is Mary Sango, who is identified as Mary Bruner, upon the approved roll of Seminole Freedmen.

You are requested to inform the Seminole Enrollment Division as to whether applications have been made to the Commission for the enrollment of Albert and Leah Sango as citizens of the Creek Nation and what disposition has been made of said applications, if any.

                                    Respectfully,

                                          Chairman.

_____

215

Applications for Enrollment of Seminole Newborn Freedmen
Act of 1905

HGH

DEPARTMENT OF THE INTERIOR.
COMMISSION TO THE FIVE CIVILIZED TRIBES.

Muskogee, Indian Territory, July 13, 1905.

Commissioner to the Five Civilized Tribes,
    Seminole Enrollment Division,
        Muskogee, Indian Territory.

Gentlemen:

Receipt is acknowledged of your communication of June 29, 1905 (Sem.NB.59), in which you ask if application for the enrollment as citizens of the Creek Nation has been made for Albert and Leah Sango, children of Peter Sango, a citizen of the Creek Nation, and Mary Sango, a Seminole Freedman.

In reply you are advised that the records of this office have been examined and it does not appear that application has been made for them, or either of them, as citizens of the Creek Nation.

                 Respectfully,

                        Tams Bixby
                        Commissioner.

Sem. Freed.
NB-59.

                 Muskogee, Indian Territory, July 25, 1905.

Mary Sango,
    Earlsboro, Oklahoma Territory.

Dear Madam:

On May 31, 1905 there were filed with the Commission to the Five Civilized Tribes applications for the enrollment of your children Albert Sango and Leah Sango as Seminole freedmen. The proof of birth in the matter of the application for the enrollment of said children, now on file with the records of this office, is insufficient from which to finally determine their right to enrollment and you are therefore requested to furnish this office with properly verified affidavits as to the birth of said children and two blanks for that purpose are inclosed herewith.

You will notice there is a blank for the affidavit of the mother of of[sic] the child and one for the attending physician or midwife at its birth. In having these affidavits executed be careful to see that all blank spaces are properly filled, all names written in full and that the notary public before whom the affidavits are sworn to attaches his name

216

Applications for Enrollment of Seminole Newborn Freedmen
Act of 1905

and seal to each affidavit. In case any signature is by mark it must be attested by two disinterested witnesses who can write.

In case there was no physician or midwife attending you at the birth of said child it will be necessary for you to furnish this office, in lieu of the affidavit of said attending physician or midwife, with the affidavits of two disinterested persons who are acquainted with said children, know when they were born and whether or not they were living on March 4, 1905.

You should give this matter you[sic] immediate attention.

Respectfully,

Commissioner.

2 B C
Env.

REFER IN REPLY TO THE FOLLOWING:

DEPARTMENT OF THE INTERIOR,
COMMISSIONER TO THE FIVE CIVILIZED TRIBES.

Muskogee, Indian Territory, December 24, 1906.

Chief Clerk,
   Seminole Enrollment Division.

Dear Sir:

Receipt is hereby acknowledged of your letter under date of December 15, 1906, requesting information as to whether application has been made for the enrollment of Albert and Leah Sango, children of Peter Sango, a citizen of the Creek Nation, and Mary Sango, a citizen of the Seminole Nation, as citizens of the Creek Nation under the Act of Congress approved April 26, 1906.

In reply you are advised that it does not appear from the records of this office that application has been made for the enrollment of Albert and Leah Sango as citizens of the Creek Nation.

Respectfully,

Tams Bixby Acting Commissioner.

Applications for Enrollment of Seminole Newborn Freedmen
Act of 1905

Department of the Interior.
Commissioner to the Five Civilized Tribes,
MUSKOGEE, IND. TER,

Peter Sango,
Earlsboro, Oklahoma.

AP

REFER IN REPLY TO THE FOLLOWING:

Sem-Fr-NB-59.

DEPARTMENT OF THE INTERIOR,
COMMISSIONER TO THE FIVE CIVILIZED TRIBES.

Muskogee, Indian Territory, April 15, 1907.

Peter Sango,
Earlsboro, Oklahoma.

Dear Sir:

You are hereby advised that on February 12, 1907, the Secretary of the Interior approved the enrollment of your minor children, Albert and Leah Sango, as new born Seminole freedmen, and their names appear on the final roll of such citizens of the Seminole Nation opposite Nos. 125 and 126, respectively.

Respectfully,

Tams Bixby Commissioner.

Applications for Enrollment of Seminole Newborn Freedmen
Act of 1905

Wewoka, Indian Territory, May 19, 1905.

Winnie Brown,
Wewoka, Indian Territory.

Madam:

On May 13, 1905, you appeared before this office and made application for the enrollment of your minor son, Leroy Brown, as a citizen of the Seminole Nation, but no affidavit was made by the attending physician or midwife.

It will be necessary, therefore, to furnish this office with such affidavit, said person either to appear before the Seminole Enrollment Office at Wewoka, Indian Territory, prior to June 1, 1905, or to have the inclosed blank affidavit filled out and properly executed before a Notary Public, returning same to this office in the inclosed envelope, which requires no postage.

Respectfully,

Enc   Clerk in Charge.

Sem.Fr.NB.60.

Muskogee, Indian Territory, June 29, 1905.

Commission to the Five Civilized Tribes,
Creek Enrollment Division.

Gentlemen:

On May 13, 1905, there was filed with the Commission application for the enrollment of Leroy Brown, born September 10, 1900, as a Seminole freedman. It is stated in said application that said child is the son of Bill Brown, a citizen by adoption of the Creek Nation; and Winnie Brown, who is identified as Winnie Johnson, upon the approved roll of Seminole freedmen.

You are requested to inform the Seminole Enrollment Division as to whether application has been made to the Commission for the enrollment of said Leroy Brown as a citizen of the Creek Nation, and if so what disposition, if any, has been made of said application.

Respectfully,

Chairman.

219

Applications for Enrollment of Seminole Newborn Freedmen
Act of 1905

DEPARTMENT OF THE INTERIOR.
COMMISSION TO THE FIVE CIVILIZED TRIBES.

Muskogee, Indian Territory, July 11, 1905.

Seminole Enrollment Division,
General Office.

Gentlemen:

Receipt is acknowledged of your communication of June 29, 1905 (Sem.Fr.NB.60), in which you ask if application for the enrollment as a citizen of the Creek Nation has been made for Leroy Brown, child of Bill Brown, a citizen of the Creek Nation, and Winnie Brown, a Seminole Freedman.

In reply you are advised that the records of this office have been examined and it does not appear that application has been made for the enrollment of said Leroy Brown, as a citizen of the Creek Nation.

Respectfully,

Tams Bixby   Commissioner.

Sem NB FR 60   B 283
BIRTH AFFIDAVIT.
DEPARTMENT OF THE INTERIOR.
COMMISSION TO THE FIVE CIVILIZED TRIBES.

IN RE APPLICATION FOR ENROLLMENT, as a citizen of the   Seminole   Nation, of
Leroy Brown   , born on the 10   day of   Sept   , 1900

Name of Father: Bill Brown   a citizen of the   Creek   Nation.
Name of Mother: Winnie Brown   a citizen of the   Seminole   Nation.
                        formerly Johnson
                        Postoffice   Wewoka I.T.

AFFIDAVIT OF ATTENDING PHYSICIAN OR MID-WIFE.

UNITED STATES OF AMERICA, Indian Territory, ⎱
        Western   **DISTRICT.** ⎰

    I,   Polly Perry   , a   Female   , on oath state that I attended on
Mrs. Winnie Brown   , wife of   Bill Brown   on the   10   day of   Sept , 1900;

220

Applications for Enrollment of Seminole Newborn Freedmen
Act of 1905

that there was born to her on said date a   male   child; that said child is now living and is said to have been named Leroy Brown

Her
Polly x Perry

Witnesses To Mark: mark
{ CE Guthrie
{ Nora Guthrie

Subscribed and sworn to before me this 8 day of   June   , 1905.

C.E. Guthrie
Notary Public.
My commission expires Feb. 13th, 1909.

Sem NB FR 60
BIRTH AFFIDAVIT.

DEPARTMENT OF THE INTERIOR.

COMMISSION TO THE FIVE CIVILIZED TRIBES.

IN RE APPLICATION FOR ENROLLMENT, as a citizen of the   Seminole   Nation, of Leroy Brown   , born on the about 10   day of Sept , 1900

Name of Father: Bill Brown   a citizen of the   Creek   Nation.
Name of Mother: Winnie Brown   2542   a citizen of the   Seminole   Nation.
                     formerly Johnson
                     Postoffice   Wewoka IT

(Child present)

AFFIDAVIT OF MOTHER.

UNITED STATES OF AMERICA, Indian Territory, ⎤
    Western   **DISTRICT.** ⎦

    I,   Winnie Brown   , on oath state that I am 46 years of age and a citizen by adoption   , of the   Seminole   Nation; that I am the lawful wife of Bill Brown , who is a citizen, by   adoption   of the   Creek   Nation; that a   male   child was born to me on   about the 10   day of   Sept   , 1900, that said child has been named   Leroy Brown   , and is now living.

her
Winnie x Brown

Witnesses To Mark: mark   formerly Johnson
{ Chas E Webster
{ Frank C. Sabourin

221

Applications for Enrollment of Seminole Newborn Freedmen
Act of 1905

Subscribed and sworn to before me this   13   day of   May   , 1905.

Chas E Webster
Notary Public.

Sem NB FR 61
BIRTH AFFIDAVIT.
DEPARTMENT OF THE INTERIOR.
COMMISSION TO THE FIVE CIVILIZED TRIBES.

IN RE APPLICATION FOR ENROLLMENT, as a citizen of the   Seminole   Nation, of
Patsy Davis   , born on the 7th   day of   April   , 1902

Name of Father: Monday Davis   (2444)   a citizen of the   Seminole   Nation.
Name of Mother: Dilsey Davis   (2445)   a citizen of the   Seminole   Nation.

Postoffice   Wewoka I.T.

Child present

AFFIDAVIT OF MOTHER.

UNITED STATES OF AMERICA, Indian Territory,
   Western   **DISTRICT.**

I,   Dilsey Davis   , on oath state that I am   47   years of age and a citizen by
adoption   , of the   Seminole   Nation; that I am the lawful wife of   Monday Davis,
who is a citizen, by adoption   of the   Seminole   Nation; that a   female
child was born to me on   7th   day of   April   , 1902; that said child has been named
Patsy Davis   , and was living March 4, 1905.

Dilsey Davis
Witnesses To Mark:

222

Applications for Enrollment of Seminole Newborn Freedmen
Act of 1905

Subscribed and sworn to before me this 9th day of   May   , 1905.

Chas E Webster
Notary Public.

UNITED STATES OF AMERICA, Indian Territory, ⎫
    Western   DISTRICT. ⎰

I,   Dinah Ishmael   , a   midwife   , on oath state that I attended on
Mrs.   Dilsey Davis   , wife of   Monday Davis   on the 7th   day of April   , 1902;
that there was born to her on said date a   female   child; that said child was living
March 4, 1905, and is said to have been named Patsy Davis
                                                                    her
                                                   Dinah x Ishmael
Witnesses To Mark: mark
⎰ Frank C. Sabourin
⎱ Chas E Webster

Subscribed and sworn to before me 9th day of   May   , 1905.

Chas E Webster
Notary Public.

Sem NB FR 62
BIRTH AFFIDAVIT.
DEPARTMENT OF THE INTERIOR.
COMMISSION TO THE FIVE CIVILIZED TRIBES.

IN RE APPLICATION FOR ENROLLMENT, as a citizen of the   Seminole   Nation, of
Johnny McIntosh   , born on the 30   day of   March   , 1900

Name of Father: Dave McIntosh   (2608)   a citizen of the   Seminole   Nation.
                                                          No. 2467
Name of Mother: Edna McIntosh (nee Dennis)   a citizen of the   Seminole   Nation.

Postoffice   Emahaka IT

223

Applications for Enrollment of Seminole Newborn Freedmen
Act of 1905

Johnny present

UNITED STATES OF AMERICA, Indian Territory, ⎤
Western   DISTRICT. ⎦

     I,   Edna McIntosh   , on oath state that I am   23   years of age and a citizen by adoption   , of the   Seminole   Nation; that I am the lawful wife of   Dave McIntosh   , who is a citizen, by   adoption   of the   Seminole   Nation; that a male   child was born to me on   30th day of   March   , 1900, that said child has been named   Johnny McIntosh   , and is now living.

Edna McIntosh

Witnesses To Mark:

{

     Subscribed and sworn to before me this 8th day of   May   , 1905.

Chas E Webster
Notary Public.

UNITED STATES OF AMERICA, Indian Territory, ⎤
Western   DISTRICT. ⎦

     I,   Ti Lewis   , a   midwife   , on oath state that I attended on Mrs.   Edna McIntosh   , wife of   Dave McIntosh   on the   30th day of March , 1900; that there was born to her on said date a   male   child; that said child is now living and is said to have been named Johnny McIntosh

her
Ti   x   Lewis

Witnesses To Mark: mark
⎧ Frank C. Sabourin
⎩ Chas E Webster

     Subscribed and sworn to before me this 8th day of   May   , 1905.

Chas E Webster
Notary Public.

Applications for Enrollment of Seminole Newborn Freedmen
Act of 1905

Sem NB FR 63
BIRTH AFFIDAVIT.

DEPARTMENT OF THE INTERIOR.
COMMISSION TO THE FIVE CIVILIZED TRIBES.

_____

IN RE APPLICATION FOR ENROLLMENT, as a citizen of the   Seminole   Nation, of
John Davis   , born on the 12"   day of   Jan   , 1900

Name of Father: Jim Davis (Jas A)   a citizen of the   Seminole   Nation.
Name of Mother: Jennie Davis   a citizen of the   "   Nation.

Postoffice   Emahaka I.T.

_____

(Child present)

AFFIDAVIT OF MOTHER.

UNITED STATES OF AMERICA, Indian Territory, ⎫
    Western   DISTRICT. ⎭

    I,   Jennie Davis   , on oath state that I am   28   years of age and a citizen by
Adoption   , of the   Seminole   Nation; that I am the lawful wife of   James A
Davis   , who is a citizen, by Adoption   of the   Seminole   Nation; that a
male   child was born to me on   12th day of   January   , 1900; that said child has
been named   John Davis   , and was living March 4, 1905.
                     her
                  Jennie x Davis
Witnesses To Mark: mark
   ⎰ FC Sabourin
   ⎱ Edward Merrick

    Subscribed and sworn to before me this   1"   day of   May   , 1905.

⟨ Seal ⟩   Edward Merrick
                         Notary Public.

_____

AFFIDAVIT OF ATTENDING PHYSICIAN OR MID-WIFE.

UNITED STATES OF AMERICA, Indian Territory, ⎫
    Western   DISTRICT. ⎭

    I,   Harriett Dennis   , a   midwife   , on oath state that I attended on
Mrs.   Jennie Davis   , wife of   James A Davis   on the   12th day of   Jany   ,
1900; that there was born to her on said date a   male   child; that said child was living
March 4, 1905, and is said to have been named   John Davis

225

Applications for Enrollment of Seminole Newborn Freedmen
Act of 1905

Witnesses To Mark:
{ FC Sabourin
{ Edward Merrick

her
Harriett x Dennis
mark

Subscribed and sworn to before me this 1" day of   May   , 1905.

⟨Seal⟩   Edward Merrick

                                          Notary Public.

Sem NB FR 64
BIRTH AFFIDAVIT.
DEPARTMENT OF THE INTERIOR.
COMMISSION TO THE FIVE CIVILIZED TRIBES.

IN RE APPLICATION FOR ENROLLMENT, as a citizen of the   Seminole   Nation, of
Kerfort Cudjo   , born on the 13 day of Feb , 1904

Name of Father: Carolina Cudjo   2494   a citizen of the Seminole Nation.
Name of Mother: Julia Cudjo   2495   a citizen of the Seminole Nation.

Postoffice   Sasakwa

(Child present)
AFFIDAVIT OF MOTHER.

UNITED STATES OF AMERICA, Indian Territory, ⎫
    Western   **DISTRICT.** ⎭

        I,   Julia Cudjo   , on oath state that I am 23   years of age and a citizen by
adoption   , of the   Seminole   Nation; that I am the lawful wife of   Carolina
Cudjo   , who is a citizen, by adoption   of the   Seminole   Nation; that a
male   child was born to me on 13   day of   Feb   , 1904; that said child has been
named   Kerfort Cudjo   , and was living March 4, 1905.

226

Applications for Enrollment of Seminole Newborn Freedmen
Act of 1905

                                        her
                                   Julia x Cudjo
Witnesses To Mark: mark
⎰ Chas E Webster
⎱ Frank C. Sabourin

Subscribed and sworn to before me this 8 day of   May   , 1905.

                              Chas E Webster
                                   Notary Public.

AFFIDAVIT OF ATTENDING PHYSICIAN OR MID-WIFE.

UNITED STATES OF AMERICA, Indian Territory, ⎤
   Western   DISTRICT.   ⎦

   I,   Nellie Thomas   , a   midwife   , on oath state that I attended on
Mrs. Julia Cudjo   , wife of   Carolina Cudjo   on the 13 day of   Feb , 1904;
that there was born to her on said date a   male   child; that said child was living
March 4, 1905, and is said to have been named Kerfort Cudjo
                                        her
                                   Nellie x Thomas
Witnesses To Mark: mark
⎰ Chas E Webster
⎱ Frank C. Sabourin

Subscribed and sworn to before me 8 day of   May   , 1905.

                              Chas E Webster
                                   Notary Public.

Sem NB FR 64
BIRTH AFFIDAVIT.
DEPARTMENT OF THE INTERIOR.
COMMISSION TO THE FIVE CIVILIZED TRIBES.

   IN RE APPLICATION FOR ENROLLMENT, as a citizen of the   Seminole   Nation, of
Helen Cudjo   , born on the 19 day of Jan , 1902

Name of Father: Carolina Cudjo   2494   a citizen of the   Seminole   Nation.
Name of Mother: Julia Cudjo   2495   a citizen of the   Seminole   Nation.

                    Postoffice   Sasakwa, I.T.

227

Applications for Enrollment of Seminole Newborn Freedmen
Act of 1905

(Child present)

UNITED STATES OF AMERICA, Indian Territory, ⎱
Western   DISTRICT. ⎰

I,   Julia Cudjo   , on oath state that I am   23   years of age and a citizen by adoption   , of the   Seminole   Nation; that I am the lawful wife of   Carolina Cudjo   , who is a citizen, by   adoption   of the   Seminole   Nation; that a Female   child was born to me on   19   day of   Jan   , 1902; that said child has been named   Helen Cudjo   , and was living March 4, 1905.

her
Julia   x   Cudjo
mark

Witnesses To Mark:
⎰ Chas E Webster
⎱ Frank C. Sabourin

Subscribed and sworn to before me this 8   day of   May   , 1905.

Chas E Webster
Notary Public.

UNITED STATES OF AMERICA, Indian Territory, ⎱
Western   DISTRICT. ⎰

I,   Nellie Thomas   , a   midwife   , on oath state that I attended on Mrs.   Julia Cudjo   , wife of   Carolina Cudjo   on the   19   day of   Jan   , 1902; that there was born to her on said date a   Female   child; that said child was living March 4, 1905, and is said to have been named   Helen Cudjo

her
Nellie   x   Thomas
mark

Witnesses To Mark:
⎰ Chas E Webster
⎱ Frank C. Sabourin

Subscribed and sworn to before me 8   day of   May   , 1905.

Chas E Webster
Notary Public.

Applications for Enrollment of Seminole Newborn Freedmen
Act of 1905

Sem NB FR 64
BIRTH AFFIDAVIT.
DEPARTMENT OF THE INTERIOR.
COMMISSION TO THE FIVE CIVILIZED TRIBES.

IN RE APPLICATION FOR ENROLLMENT, as a citizen of the   Seminole   Nation, of
Mitchell Cudjo   , born on the   8   day of   April   , 1900

Name of Father: Carolina Cudjo   2494   a citizen of the   Seminole   Nation.
Name of Mother: Julia Cudjo   2495   a citizen of the   Seminole   Nation.

Postoffice   Sasakwa

(Child present)
AFFIDAVIT OF MOTHER.

UNITED STATES OF AMERICA, Indian Territory,⎱
   Western   DISTRICT. ⎰

     I,   Julia Cudjo   , on oath state that I am   23   years of age and a citizen by
adoption   , of the   Seminole   Nation; that I am the lawful wife of   Carolina
Cudjo   , who is a citizen, by   adoption   of the   Seminole   Nation; that a
male   child was born to me on   8   day of   April   , 1900; that said child has been
named   Mitchell Cudjo   , and was living March 4, 1905.

                          her
                  Julia x Cudjo
Witnesses To Mark: mark
    ⎰ Chas E Webster
    ⎱ Frank C. Sabourin

     Subscribed and sworn to before me this 8 day of   May   , 1905.

                        Chas E Webster
                        Notary Public.

AFFIDAVIT OF ATTENDING PHYSICIAN OR MID-WIFE.

UNITED STATES OF AMERICA, Indian Territory,⎱
   Western   DISTRICT. ⎰

     I,   Nellie Thomas   , a   midwife   , on oath state that I attended on
Mrs.   Julia Cudjo   , wife of   Carolina Cudjo   on the   8   day of   April   ,
1900; that there was born to her on said date a   male   child; that said child was living
March 4, 1905, and is said to have been named   Mitchell Cudjo

Applications for Enrollment of Seminole Newborn Freedmen
Act of 1905

Witnesses To Mark:
    ⎰ Chas E Webster
    ⎱ Frank C. Sabourin

                      her
          Nellie x Thomas
              mark

Subscribed and sworn to before me 8 day of May , 1905.

                    Chas E Webster
                    Notary Public.

                    Sem.Fr.NB.65.

        Muskogee, Indian Territory, June 29, 1905.

Mrs. Alice B. Davis,
    Wewoka, Indian Territory.

Dear Madam:

There is enclosed herewith application and proof of birth of Elene Billy. Said application was sworn to before Mr. Charles E. Webster, and he informs the Commission that you were present when said application was received.

You will notice that there is but one witness to the signature of Harriett Dennis, the attending midwife at the birth of said child. Inasmuch as you were present and witnessed the signature of the said Harriett Dennis, you are requested to sign your name as a witness to said signature upon the blank line provided for that purpose, and return the application to the Commission in the enclosed envelope.

                  Respectfully,

DeB--7/29.   Chairman.
Env.

Applications for Enrollment of Seminole Newborn Freedmen
Act of 1905

Sem NB FR 65
BIRTH AFFIDAVIT.
DEPARTMENT OF THE INTERIOR.
COMMISSION TO THE FIVE CIVILIZED TRIBES.

IN RE APPLICATION FOR ENROLLMENT, as a citizen of the   Seminole   Nation, of
Elene Billy   , born on the 18 day of Jan , 1902

Name of Father: Sam Carolina   (2548)   a citizen of the   Seminole   Nation.
Name of Mother: Georgie Carolina   2503   a citizen of the   Seminole   Nation.

Postoffice   Emahaka, I.T.

(Child present)

AFFIDAVIT OF MOTHER.

UNITED STATES OF AMERICA, Indian Territory,
   Western   DISTRICT.

    I,   Georgie Carolina   , on oath state that I am 20 years of age and a citizen by
adoption   , of the   Seminole   Nation; that I am not the lawful wife of   Sam
Carolina   , who is a citizen, by   adoption   of the   Seminole   Nation; that a
Female   child was born to me on   18   day of   Jan   , 1902, that said child has
been named   Elene Billy   , and is now living.

her
Georgie x Carolina
mark

Witnesses To Mark:
    Chas E Webster
    A. B. Davis

    Subscribed and sworn to before me this 24 day of   May   , 1905.

Chas E Webster
Notary Public.

AFFIDAVIT OF ATTENDING PHYSICIAN OR MID-WIFE.

UNITED STATES OF AMERICA, Indian Territory,
   Western   DISTRICT.

    I,   Harriett Dennis   , a   midwife   , on oath state that I attended on
~~Mrs.~~ Georgie Carolina   , ~~wife of~~   on the   18 day of Jan , 1902; that there
was born to her on said date a   female   child; that said child is now living and is said
to have been named Elene Billy

231

Applications for Enrollment of Seminole Newborn Freedmen
Act of 1905

Witnesses To Mark:
{ Chas E Webster
{ A. B. Davis

her
Harriett x Dennis
mark

Subscribed and sworn to before me this   31   day of   May   , 1905.

Chas E Webster
Notary Public.

Sem NB FR 66

BIRTH AFFIDAVIT.

DEPARTMENT OF THE INTERIOR,
COMMISSION TO THE FIVE CIVILIZED TRIBES.

IN RE Application for Enrollment, as a citizen of the   Seminole   Nation,
of Lou Charles   , born on the   about 10th   day of   March   , 1902

Name of Father: Mike Charles   a citizen of the Seminole   Nation.
Name of Mother: Rhina King   (2509)   a citizen of the Seminole   Nation.

Post-office: Wewoka Ind Ter

AFFIDAVIT OF MOTHER.   Father not a citizen of
Seminole Nation
UNITED STATES OF AMERICA, ⎫   a state man
INDIAN TERRITORY.   ⎬
Western   District. ⎭

I, Rhina Henderson   , on oath state that I am about 26   years of age and a
citizen by Adoption , of the Seminole   Nation; that I am the lawful wife of   David
Henderson , who is a citizen, by   of the United States ~~Nation~~; that a Female child
was born to me on   about 10th   day of   March , 1902 , that said child has been named
Lou Charles   , and is now living.

232

Applications for Enrollment of Seminole Newborn Freedmen
Act of 1905

her
Rhina x Henderson
mark

{ John R McBeth
{ David Henderson

Subscribed and sworn to before me this 17 *day of* April 1905.

JC Johnson

AFFIDAVIT OF ATTENDING PHYSICIAN OR MID-WIFE.

UNITED STATES OF AMERICA,
INDIAN TERRITORY.
Western   District.

A witness to the services performed by

I,   Julia Larry   , a   Mid Wife; now deceased , on oath state that I attended on Mrs. Rhina King , wife of David Henderson on the about 10th day of March , 1902; that there was born to her on said date a   Female   child; that said child is now living and is said to have been named Lou Charles

Julia Lowry [sic]

{

Subscribed and sworn to before me this 8 *day of* April , 1905.

R Brownbridge

My Com. expires Nov. 14 1908

233

Applications for Enrollment of Seminole Newborn Freedmen
Act of 1905

Sem NB FR 67
BIRTH AFFIDAVIT.

DEPARTMENT OF THE INTERIOR.
COMMISSION TO THE FIVE CIVILIZED TRIBES.

IN RE APPLICATION FOR ENROLLMENT, as a citizen of the   Seminole   Nation, of
Royal Barkus   , born on the 26   day of   Nov , 1902

Name of Father: Pilot Barkus   2520   a citizen of the   Seminole   Nation.
Name of Mother: Lucy Barkus   2521   a citizen of the   Seminole   Nation.

Postoffice   Sasakwa I.T.

(Child present)

AFFIDAVIT OF MOTHER.

UNITED STATES OF AMERICA, Indian Territory, ⎱
      Western   DISTRICT. ⎰

I,   Lucy Barkus   , on oath state that I am   30   years of age and a citizen by
adoption   , of the   Seminole   Nation; that I am the lawful wife of Pilot Barkus   ,
who is a citizen, by adoption   of the   Seminole   Nation; that a   male
child was born to me on 26   day of   Nov   , 1902; that said child has been named
Royal Barkus   , and was living March 4, 1905.

                                          her
                                Lucy x Barkus
Witnesses To Mark: mark
⎰ Chas E Webster
⎱ Frank C. Sabourin

Subscribed and sworn to before me this 9 day of   May   , 1905.

                                Chas E Webster
                                Notary Public.

AFFIDAVIT OF ATTENDING PHYSICIAN OR MID-WIFE.

UNITED STATES OF AMERICA, Indian Territory, ⎱
      Western   DISTRICT. ⎰

I,   Rhoda Cudjo   , a midwife   , on oath state that I attended on
Mrs. Lucy Barkus   , wife of   Pilot Barkus   on the 26 day of   November   ,
1902; that there was born to her on said date a   male   child; that said child was living
March 4, 1905, and is said to have been named Royal Barkus

234

Applications for Enrollment of Seminole Newborn Freedmen
Act of 1905

Witnesses To Mark:
⎧ Frank C. Sabourin
⎩ Chas E Webster

he⁻
Rhoda x Cudjo
ma⁻k

Subscribed and sworn to before me 15 day of   May   , 1905.

Chas E Webster
Notary Public.

Midwife appeared at this office 5/15/05.

Sem NB FR 68   Fr 2530
BIRTH AFFIDAVIT.
DEPARTMENT OF THE INTERIOR.
COMMISSION TO THE FIVE CIVILIZED TRIBES.

IN RE APPLICATION FOR ENROLLMENT, as a citizen of the   Seminole   Nation, of
Glass Marshal   , born on the 5"   day of   Mch , 1902

Name of Father: John Marshal   a citizen of the   U.S.   Nation.
Name of Mother: Maggie C. Marshal #2530   a citizen of the   Seminole   Nation.

Postoffice   Emahaka I.T.

(Child present)   Grand
AFFIDAVIT OF ^MOTHER.

UNITED STATES OF AMERICA, Indian Territory, ⎱
    Western   **DISTRICT.** ⎰

I,   Rose Cudjo   (1897-Card 800) , on oath state that I am ~~90~~ 71 years of age
and a citizen by   Adoption   , of the   Seminole   Nation; that I am the ~~lawful~~
~~wife of~~ mother of Maggie C. Marshall[sic]   , who is a citizen, by   Adoption   of
the   Seminole   Nation; that a   male   child was born to ~~me~~ her on   5"   day of
Mch   , 1902, that said child has been named Glass Marshal   , and is now living.

235

Applications for Enrollment of Seminole Newborn Freedmen
Act of 1905

Witnesses To Mark:
    { Edward Merrick
    { Frank C. Sabourin

her
Rose   x   Cudjo
mark

Subscribed and sworn to before me this 5th day of   May   , 1905.

< Seal >

Edward Merrick
Notary Public.

AFFIDAVIT OF ATTENDING PHYSICIAN OR MID-WIFE.

UNITED STATES OF AMERICA, Indian Territory, }
     Western   DISTRICT.

I,   Rhoda Cudjo   , a   midwife   , on oath state that I attended on Mrs.   Maggie C. Marshall   , wife of   John Marshall   on the   5   day of   March , 1902; that there was born to her on said date a   male   child; that said child is now living and is said to have been named Glass Marshall

Witnesses To Mark:
    { Frank C. Sabourin
    { Chas E Webster

her
Rhoda   x   Cudjo
mark

Subscribed and sworn to before me this 15 day of   May   , 1905.

Chas E Webster
Notary Public.

Midwife appeared at this office 5/15/05.

Sem NB FR 69

BIRTH AFFIDAVIT.

DEPARTMENT OF THE INTERIOR,
COMMISSION TO THE FIVE CIVILIZED TRIBES.

IN RE *Application for Enrollment,* as a citizen of the ~~Creek~~   Seminole   Nation, of Jenetta Thompson , born on the   11th   day of   August   , 1901

Name of Father: John Thompson   a citizen of the   Creek   Nation.
Name of Mother: Hattie Thompson   (2537)   a citizen of the   Seminole   Nation.

Post-office: Okemah, Ind Ter

AFFIDAVIT OF MOTHER.

UNITED STATES OF AMERICA,
  INDIAN TERRITORY.
  Western   District.

I, Hattie Thompson   , on oath state that I am 25 years of age and a citizen by Freedman , of the Seminole Nation; that I am the lawful wife of   John Thompson , who is a citizen, by Freedman of the Creek   Nation; that a Female   child was born to me on 11th   day of August , 1901 , that said child has been named   Jenetta Thompson , and is now living.

Hattie Thompson

WITNESSES TO MARK:
  John R. McBeth
  Silas Lovett

Subscribed and sworn to before me this 2nd *day of* March , *1905.*

O T McConnell
NOTARY PUBLIC.

AFFIDAVIT OF ATTENDING PHYSICIAN OR MID-WIFE.

UNITED STATES OF AMERICA,
  INDIAN TERRITORY.
  Western   District.

I, Mary Grayson , a Mid Wife , on oath state that I attended on Mrs. Hattie Thompson , wife of John Thompson on the 11th day of August , 1901 ; that there was born to her on said date a   Female   child; that said child is now living and is said to have been named Jenetta Thompson

237

Applications for Enrollment of Seminole Newborn Freedmen
Act of 1905

WITNESSES TO MARK:
{ John R. McBeth
  Silas Lovett

her
Mary x Grayson
mark

Subscribed and sworn to before me this 2nd *day of* March , 1905.

O T McConnell
NOTARY PUBLIC.

_____

Wewoka, Indian Territory, May 17, 1905.

Hattie Thompson,
    Care John Thompson,
        Okemah, Indian Territory.

Madam:

On March 13, 1905, there was filed with the Commission an application for the enrollment of Jenetta Thompson, minor daughter of John Thompson, a citizen of the Creek Nation, and Hattie Thompson, a citizen of the Seminole Nation.

The Commission is unable to identify you on the approved Seminole Roll, and it will be necessary, therefore, for you to appear before the Seminole Enrollment Office, at Wewoka, Indian Territory, prior to June 1, 1905, in order that such identification may be made.

Respectfully,

Clerk in Charge.

_____

Sem.Fr.NB.-69.

Muskogee, Indian Territory, June 30, 1905.

Commission to the Five Civilized Tribes,
    Creek Enrollment Division.

Gentlemen:

Applications have been made to the Commission for the enrollment of Jenetta Thompson, born August 11, 1901, and Tennessee Thompson, born July 21, 1904, as Seminole freemen. It appears that the father of said children is Mark (or John) Thompson, a citizen by adoption of the Creek Nation, and that their mother is Hettie

238

Applications for Enrollment of Seminole Newborn Freedmen
Act of 1905

Thompson, who is identified as Hettie Lovett upon the approved roll of Seminole freedmen.

You are requested to inform the Seminole Enrollment Division as to whether or not an application has been made to the Commission for the enrollment of said Jenetta Thompson and Tennessee Thompson as citizens of the Creek Nation, and if so what disposition, if any, has been made of said application.

Respectfully,

Chairman.

Sem.Fr.N.B.69.

Muskogee, Indian Territory, June 30, 1905.

Hettie Thompson,
    Care of Mark Thompson,
        Okemah, Indian Territory.

Dear Madam:

In the matter of the application for the enrollment of your daughter, Jenetta Thompson, as a Seminole freedman, there is on file your affidavit and the affidavit of Mary Grayson as to the birth of said child on August 11, 1901. Said affidavits further show that the said Jenetta Thompson was living on March 2, 1905.

Before the rights of said child as a Seminole freedman can be finally determined, evidence must be furnished the Commission showing whether or not said child was living on March 4, 1905. There is, therefore, enclosed herewith a blank for proof of birth, which you are requested to have properly executed and returned to this office in the enclosed envelope.

Respectfully,

DeB-8/29.   Chairman.
Env.

Applications for Enrollment of Seminole Newborn Freedmen
Act of 1905

HGH

DEPARTMENT OF THE INTERIOR.
COMMISSION TO THE FIVE CIVILIZED TRIBES.

Muskogee, Indian Territory, July 11, 1905.

Seminole Enrollment Division,
General Office.

Gentlemen:

Receipt is acknowledged of your communication of June 30, 1905 (Sem.Fr.NB.69), in which you ask if application for enrollment as citizens of the Creek Nation has been made for Jennetta and Tennessee Thompson, children of Mark (or John) Thompson, a citizen of the Creek Nation, and Hettie Lovett, a Seminole Freedman.

In reply you are advised that the records of this office have been examined and it does not appear that application has been made for the enrollment of said Jennetta and Tennessee Thompson, or either of them as citizens of the Creek Nation.

Respectfully,

Tams Bixby   Commissioner.

_____

Sem.Freed.
NB--69

Muskogee, Indian Territory July 26, 1905.

Hettie Thompson,
Okemah, Indian Territory.

Dear Madam:

Receipt is hereby acknowledged of your affidavit and the affidavit of Mary Grayson, midwife, as to the birth of your daughter Jenetta Thompson on August 11, 1901, and the same have been filed with the records of this office in the matter of the application for the enrollment of said child as a Seminole freedman.

Respectfully,

Commissioner.

_____

Applications for Enrollment of Seminole Newborn Freedmen
Act of 1905

Sem NB FR 69
BIRTH AFFIDAVIT.

DEPARTMENT OF THE INTERIOR.
COMMISSION TO THE FIVE CIVILIZED TRIBES.

IN RE APPLICATION FOR ENROLLMENT, as a citizen of the   Seminole   Nation, of
Jenetta Thompson   , born on the 11th day of August , 1901

Name of Father: Mark Thompson   a citizen of the   Creek   Nation.
Name of Mother: Hettie Thompson   a citizen of the   Seminole   Nation.

Postoffice   Okemah, Ind. Ter.

AFFIDAVIT OF MOTHER.

UNITED STATES OF AMERICA, Indian Territory, ⎤
    Western   DISTRICT. ⎦

I,   Hettie Thompson   , on oath state that I am   25   years of age and a
~~citizen by~~   freedman   , of the   Seminole   Nation; that I am the lawful wife of
Mark Thompson   , who is a ~~citizen, by~~ Creek   ~~of the~~   freedman   ~~Nation~~;
that a   female   child was born to me on   11th day of   August   , 1901; that
said child has been named   Jenetta Thompson   , and was living March 4, 1905.

Hattie Thompson

Witnesses To Mark:
⎰
⎱

Subscribed and sworn to before me this 20th day of   July   , 1905.

M. B. Casite
Notary Public.

AFFIDAVIT OF ATTENDING PHYSICIAN OR MID-WIFE.

UNITED STATES OF AMERICA, Indian Territory, ⎤
    Western   DISTRICT. ⎦

I,   Mary Grayson   , a midwife   , on oath state that I attended on
Mrs. Hettie Thompson   , wife of   Mark Thompson   on the   11th day of
August   , 1901; that there was born to her on said date a   female   child; that said
child was living March 4, 1905, and is said to have been named   Jenetta Thompson

her
Mary x Grayson
mark

241

Applications for Enrollment of Seminole Newborn Freedmen
Act of 1905

Witnesses To Mark:
    ⌠ A. A. Grayson
    ⌡ Silas D. Lovett

    Subscribed and sworn to before me 20th day of   July   , 1905.

M. B. Casite
Notary Public.

———————

Sem NB FR 69
BIRTH AFFIDAVIT.

DEPARTMENT OF THE INTERIOR.
COMMISSION TO THE FIVE CIVILIZED TRIBES.

———————

IN RE APPLICATION FOR ENROLLMENT, as a citizen of the   Seminole   Nation, of
Tennessee Thompson   , born on the 21 day of July , 1904

Name of Father: Mark Thompson   a citizen of the   Creek   Nation.
Name of Mother: Hettie Thompson   2537   a citizen of the   Seminole   Nation.
    nee Lovett
    Postoffice   Okemah I.T.

———————

(Child present)

AFFIDAVIT OF MOTHER.

UNITED STATES OF AMERICA, Indian Territory, ⌉
    Western   DISTRICT. ⌡

    I, Hettie Thompson , on oath state that I am 25 years of age and a citizen by
adoption   , of the   Seminole   Nation; that I am the lawful wife of   Mark
Thompson   , who is a citizen, by   adoption   of the   Seminole   Nation; that
a   Female   child was born to me on 21 day of July   , 1903, that said child has
been named   Tennessee Thompson   , and is now living.
                    her
            Hettie x Thompson
Witnesses To Mark: mark
    ⌠ Chas E Webster
    ⌡ A. B. Davis

    Subscribed and sworn to before me this 29 day of   May   , 1905.

Chas E Webster
Notary Public.

———————

242

Applications for Enrollment of Seminole Newborn Freedmen
Act of 1905

UNITED STATES OF AMERICA, Indian Territory,
    Western   DISTRICT.

I, Mary Grayson , a midwife , on oath state that I attended on Mrs. Hettie Thompson , wife of Mark Thompson on the 21 day of July , 1904; that there was born to her on said date a female child; that said child is now living and is said to have been named Tennessee Thompson

her
Mary x Grayson
mark

Witnesses To Mark:
    { Chas E Webster
    { A. B. Davis

Subscribed and sworn to before me this 29 day of May , 1905.

Chas E Webster
Notary Public.

Wewoka, Indian Territory, May 17, 1905.

Fred Franklin,
    Okemah, Indian Territory.

Dear Sir:

On March 13, 1905, there was filed with the Commission the affidavit of Mary Grayson, Indian Territory midwife, relative to the birth of Willie Franklin, the minor son of yourself and Tennisee[sic] Franklin, deceased.

It will be necessary for you, or a near relative of Tennessee Franklin having knowledge of the birth of said child, to appear before the Seminole Enrollment Office, at Wewoka, Indian Territory, in order that further testimony may be taken relative to the application for the enrollment of said child.

Respectfully,

Clerk in Charge.

243

Applications for Enrollment of Seminole Newborn Freedmen
Act of 1905

Sem.Fr.N.B.70.

Muskogee, Indian Territory, June 30, 1905.

Commission to the Five Civilized Tribes,
    Creek Enrollment Division.

Gentlemen:

An application has been made to the Commission for the enrollment of Willie Franklin, born July 9, 1901, as a Seminole freedman. It appears from such application that said child is the son of Fred Franklin, a Creek freedman, and Tennessee Franklin, who is identified as Tennessee Lovett, upon the approved roll of Seminole freedmen.

You are requested to inform the Seminole Enrollment Division as to whether an application has been made to the Commission for the enrollment of the said Willie Franklin as a citizen of the Creek Nation, and if so, what disposition, if any, has been made of such application.

Respectfully,

Chairman.

HGH

DEPARTMENT OF THE INTERIOR.
COMMISSION TO THE FIVE CIVILIZED TRIBES.

Muskogee, Indian Territory, July 11, 1905.

Seminole Enrollment Division,
    General Office.

Gentlemen:

Receipt is acknowledged of your communication of June 30, 1905 (Sem.Fr.NB.70), in which you ask if application for the enrollment as a citizen of the Creek Nation has been made for Willie Franklin, child of Fred Franklin, a citizen of the Creek Nation, and Tennessee Franklin (or Tennessee Lovett), a citizen of the Seminole Nation.

In reply you are advised that the records of this office have been examined and it does not appear that application has been made for the enrollment of said Willie Franklin, as a citizen of the Creek Nation.

Respectfully,

Tams Bixby   Commissioner.

Applications for Enrollment of Seminole Newborn Freedmen
Act of 1905

Sem NB FR 70

BIRTH AFFIDAVIT.

DEPARTMENT OF THE INTERIOR,
COMMISSION TO THE FIVE CIVILIZED TRIBES.

IN RE Application for Enrollment, as a citizen of the   Seminole   Nation, of   Willie Franklin   , born on the   9th day of   July   , 1901

Name of Father: Fred Franklin   a citizen of the   Creek   Nation.
Name of Mother: Tennisee Franklin   a citizen of the   Seminole   Nation.

Post-office: Okemah

AFFIDAVIT OF ~~MOTHER~~.

Mother dead
UNITED STATES OF AMERICA,   See proof of death
INDIAN TERRITORY.   Jacket 790
         District.

I,   Deceased   , on oath state that I am   years of age and a citizen by Freedman , of the   Seminole   Nation; that I am the lawful wife of   Fred Franklin , who is a citizen, by   Freedman   of the   Creek   Nation; that a   Boy   child was born to me on day of   July   , 1   , that said child has been named   Willie Franklin , and is now living.

Deceased

WITNESSES TO MARK:

{

Subscribed and sworn to before me this   x   *day of*   x   , 190 .

              x   x
                 NOTARY PUBLIC.

AFFIDAVIT OF ATTENDING PHYSICIAN OR MID-WIFE.

UNITED STATES OF AMERICA,
INDIAN TERRITORY.
Western   District.

I,   Mary Grayson   , a   Mid Wife   , on oath state that I attended on Mrs.   Tennisee Franklin   , wife of   Fred Franklin   on the   9th day of July , 1901 ; that there was born to her on said date a   Boy   child; that said child is now living and is said to have been named   Willie Franklin

245

Applications for Enrollment of Seminole Newborn Freedmen
Act of 1905

    ⌠ John R McBeth
    ⌡ Silas Lovett

her
Mary x Grayson
mark

Subscribed and sworn to before me this 2nd *day of* March , 1905.

O.T. McConnell
NOTARY PUBLIC.

Sem NB FR 70
BIRTH AFFIDAVIT.

DEPARTMENT OF THE INTERIOR.
COMMISSION TO THE FIVE CIVILIZED TRIBES.

IN RE APPLICATION FOR ENROLLMENT, as a citizen of the   Seminole   Nation, of
Willie Franklin   , born on the 9 day of July , 1901

Name of Father: Fred Franklin   a citizen of the   Creek   Nation.
Name of Mother: Tennessee Franklin   2539   a citizen of the   Seminole   Nation.
    nee Lovett
        Postoffice   Okemah I.T.

(Child present)

AFFIDAVIT OF ~~MOTHER~~.
Sister of Tennessee Franklin

UNITED STATES OF AMERICA, Indian Territory,⎰
    Western   DISTRICT.⎱

    I, Hettie Thompson , on oath state that I am 25 years of age and a citizen by
adoption   , of the   Seminole   Nation; that I am the ~~lawful wife of~~   sister
Tennessee Franklin   , who is a citizen, by   adoption   of the   Seminole
Nation; that a   male   child was born to ~~me~~ her on 9th day of July , 1901,
that said child has been named Willie Franklin , and is now living.
            her
            Hettie x Thompson
Witnesses To Mark: mark   nee Lovett
  ⌠ Chas E Webster
  ⌡ A. B. Davis

    Subscribed and sworn to before me this 29 day of May , 1905.

           Chas E Webster
           Notary Public.

Applications for Enrollment of Seminole Newborn Freedmen
Act of 1905

Sem.Fr.N.B.71.

Muskogee, Indian Territory, June 30, 1905.

Commission to the Five Civilized Tribes,
Creek Enrollment Division.

Gentlemen:

On May 31, 1905, there was filed with the Commission application for the enrollment of Jeff Barnett, born July 1, 1903, as a Seminole freedman. It appears from such application that said child is the son of Dock Barnett, a citizen by adoption of the Creek Nation, and Rachael Barnett, a Seminole freedman.

You are requested to inform the Seminole Enrollment Division as to whether or not an application has been made to the Commission for the enrollment of said Jeff Barnett as a citizen of the Creek Nation, and if so what disposition, if any, has been made of such application.

Respectfully,

Chairman.

HGH
DEPARTMENT OF THE INTERIOR.
COMMISSION TO THE FIVE CIVILIZED TRIBES.

Sem.NB.71.

Muskogee, Indian Territory, July 10, 1905.

Seminole Enrollment Division,
General Office.

Gentlemen:

Receipt is acknowledged of your communication of June 30, 1905 (Sem.Fr.NB.71), in which you ask if application for the enrollment as a citizen of the Creek Nation has been made for Jeff Barnett, child of Dock Barnett, a citizen of the Creek Nation and Rachael Barnett, a Seminole Freedman.

In reply you are advised that the records of this office have been examined and it does not appear that application has been made for the enrollment of said Jeff Barnett, as a citizen of the Creek Nation.

Respectfully,

Tams Bixby   Commissioner.

247

Applications for Enrollment of Seminole Newborn Freedmen
Act of 1905

Sem NB FR 71
BIRTH AFFIDAVIT.
DEPARTMENT OF THE INTERIOR.
COMMISSION TO THE FIVE CIVILIZED TRIBES.

IN RE APPLICATION FOR ENROLLMENT, as a citizen of the   Seminole   Nation, of
Jeff Barnett   , born on the 1   day of   July   , 1903

Name of Father: Dock Barnett   a citizen of the   Creek   Nation.
Name of Mother: Rachael Barnett   2551   a citizen of the   Seminole   Nation.

Postoffice   Clareview I.T.

(Child present)
AFFIDAVIT OF MOTHER.

UNITED STATES OF AMERICA, Indian Territory,
     Western   DISTRICT.

     I,   Rachael Barnett   , on oath state that I am   26 years of age and a citizen by
blood   , of the   Seminole   Nation; that I am the lawful wife of Dock Barnett   ,
who is a citizen, by   adoption   of the   Creek   Nation; that a   male   child
was born to me on 1   day of   July   , 1903, that said child has been named   Jeff
Barnett   , and is now living.

                                              Rachael Barnett
Witnesses To Mark:

{

     Subscribed and sworn to before me this 31   day of   May   , 1905.

                                   Chas E Webster
                                   Notary Public.

AFFIDAVIT OF ATTENDING PHYSICIAN OR MID-WIFE.

UNITED STATES OF AMERICA, Indian Territory,
     Western   DISTRICT.

     I,   Lizzie Holmes   , a   midwife   , on oath state that I attended on
Mrs. Rachael Barnett   , wife of   Dock Barnett   on the 1   day of July , 1903;
that there was born to her on said date a   male   child; that said child is now living
and is said to have been named   Jeff Barnett
                                   Lizzie Holmes
Witnesses To Mark:

{

248

Applications for Enrollment of Seminole Newborn Freedmen
Act of 1905

Subscribed and sworn to before me this 31 day of   May   , 1905.

Chas E Webster
Notary Public.

Sem NB FR 72
BIRTH AFFIDAVIT.
DEPARTMENT OF THE INTERIOR.
COMMISSION TO THE FIVE CIVILIZED TRIBES.

IN RE APPLICATION FOR ENROLLMENT, as a citizen of the   Seminole   Nation, of
Andy Lottie   , born on the 7 day of May , 1904

Name of Father: Manuel Lottie   2426   a citizen of the   Seminole   Nation.
Name of Mother: Eliza Lottie   2570   a citizen of the   Seminole   Nation.
                          nee Davis
                                    Postoffice   Emahaka, I.T.

(Child present)
AFFIDAVIT OF MOTHER.

UNITED STATES OF AMERICA, Indian Territory, ⎫
    Western   **DISTRICT.** ⎬

    I,   Eliza Lottie   , on oath state that I am   20   years of age and a citizen by
adoption   , of the   Seminole   Nation; that I am the lawful wife of   Manuel
Lottie, who is a citizen, by adoption   of the   Seminole   Nation; that a   male
child was born to me on   7 day of   May   , 1904; that said child has been named
Andy Lottie   , and was living March 4, 1905.

                                            her
                                    Eliza x Lottie
Witnesses To Mark: mark
  ⎰ Chas E Webster
  ⎱ Frank C. Sabourin

Subscribed and sworn to before me this 3 day of   May   , 1905.

Chas E Webster
Notary Public.

249

Applications for Enrollment of Seminole Newborn Freedmen
Act of 1905

UNITED STATES OF AMERICA, Indian Territory, ⎱
    Western   DISTRICT. ⎰

    I,   Venus Davis   , a midwife   , on oath state that I attended on Mrs.   Eliza Lottie   , wife of Manuel Lottie   on the 7 day of May   , 1904; that there was born to her on said date a   male   child; that said child was living March 4, 1905, and is said to have been named Andy Lottie

her

Venus x Davis

mark

Witnesses To Mark:
    ⎰ Chas E Webster
    ⎱ Frank C. Sabourin

    Subscribed and sworn to before me 3 day of   May   , 1905.

Chas E Webster

Notary Public.

Sem NB FR 72
BIRTH AFFIDAVIT.
DEPARTMENT OF THE INTERIOR.
COMMISSION TO THE FIVE CIVILIZED TRIBES.

    IN RE APPLICATION FOR ENROLLMENT, as a citizen of the   Seminole   Nation, of Bettie Lottie   , born on the 27 day of May , 1902

Name of Father: Manuel Lottie   2426   a citizen of the Seminole   Nation.
Name of Mother: Eliza Lottie   2570   a citizen of the Seminole   Nation.
                nee Davis
                Postoffice   Emahaka, I.T.

UNITED STATES OF AMERICA, Indian Territory, ⎱
    Western   DISTRICT. ⎰

    I,   Eliza Lottie   , on oath state that I am 20 years of age and a citizen by adoption   , of the   Seminole   Nation; that I am the lawful wife of   Manuel Lottie, who is a citizen, by adoption of the   Seminole   Nation; that a   Female child was born to me on 27 day of   May   , 1902; that said child has been named Bettie Lottie   , and was living March 4, 1905.

Applications for Enrollment of Seminole Newborn Freedmen
Act of 1905

	her
	Eliza x Lottie
Witnesses To Mark:	mark
⎧ Chas E Webster	
⎩ Frank C. Sabourin	

Subscribed and sworn to before me this 3 day of   May   , 1905.

Chas E Webster
Notary Public.

_____

AFFIDAVIT OF ATTENDING PHYSICIAN OR MID-WIFE.

UNITED STATES OF AMERICA, Indian Territory, ⎫
    Western   **DISTRICT.** ⎭

    I,   Venus Davis   , a midwife   , on oath state that I attended on Mrs.   Eliza Lottie   , wife of Manuel Lottie   on the 27 day of   May , 1902; that there was born to her on said date a   Female   child; that said child was living March 4, 1905, and is said to have been named Bettie Lottie

	her
	Venus x Davis
Witnesses To Mark:	mark
⎧ Chas E Webster	
⎩ Frank C. Sabourin	

Subscribed and sworn to before me 3 day of   May   , 1905.

Chas E Webster
Notary Public.

_____

Sem NB FR 72
BIRTH AFFIDAVIT.
DEPARTMENT OF THE INTERIOR.
COMMISSION TO THE FIVE CIVILIZED TRIBES.

_____

    IN RE APPLICATION FOR ENROLLMENT, as a citizen of the   Seminole   Nation, of Arthur Lottie   , born on the 12 day of Sept , 1900

Name of Father: Manuel Lottie   F2426   a citizen of the Seminole   Nation.
Name of Mother: Eliza Lottie   F2570   a citizen of the Seminole   Nation.
               nee Davis
               Postoffice   Emahaka, I.T.

_____

Applications for Enrollment of Seminole Newborn Freedmen
Act of 1905

UNITED STATES OF AMERICA, Indian Territory, ⎫
Western　　　　　　DISTRICT.　⎬

　　I,　　Eliza Lottie　　, on oath state that I am　20　years of age and a citizen by adoption　, of the　Seminole　Nation; that I am the lawful wife of　Manuel Lottie, who is a citizen, by adoption　of the　Seminole　Nation; that a　male child was born to me on　12 day of　Sept　, 1900; that said child has been named Arthur Lottie　, and was living March 4, 1905.

her
Eliza x Lottie
mark

Witnesses To Mark:
{ Chas E Webster
{ Frank C. Sabourin

　　Subscribed and sworn to before me this 3　day of　May　, 1905.

Chas E Webster
Notary Public.

AFFIDAVIT OF ATTENDING PHYSICIAN OR MID-WIFE.

UNITED STATES OF AMERICA, Indian Territory, ⎫
Western　　　　　DISTRICT.　⎬

　　I,　Venus Davis　　, a　midwife　　, on oath state that I attended on Mrs.　Eliza Lottie　, wife of　Manuel Lottie　on the　12 day of　Sept　, 1900; that there was born to her on said date a　male　child; that said child was living March 4, 1905, and is said to have been named　Arthur Lottie

her
Venus x Davis
mark

Witnesses To Mark:
{ Chas E Webster
{ Frank C. Sabourin

　　Subscribed and sworn to before me 3rd　day of　May　, 1905.

Chas E Webster
Notary Public.

252

Applications for Enrollment of Seminole Newborn Freedmen
Act of 1905

Sem.Fr.N.B.73.

Muskogee, Indian Territory, June 30, 1905.

Joseph Barkus,
    Emahaka, Indian Territory.

Dear Sir:

On May 3, 1905, you and your wife, Mollie Barkus, appeared before the Commission and made application for the enrollment of your children, Jeff Barkus, born June 16, 1900, and Naman Barkus, born October 20, 1903, as Seminole freedmen, and at that time submitted your affidavits as to the birth of said children.

You are advised that before the rights of said children as Seminole freedmen can be finally determined, it will be necessary for you to file with the Commission the affidavits of two disinterested persons, who know the circumstances attending the birth of said children; when they were born, the names of their parents and whether or not they were living on March 4, 1905.

You should give this matter your prompt attention.

Respectfully,

Chairman.

Sem.Freed.
NB-73.

Muskogee, Indian Territory, July 26, 1905.

McKennon & Wilhoit,
    Attorneys at Law,
        Wewoka, Indian Territory.

Gentlemen:

Receipt is hereby acknowledged of your letter of July 20, 1905 transmitting to this office the affidavits of Lena Barkus and Harriett Dennis relative to the birth of Jeff Barkus and Naman Barkus who are applicants for enrollment as Seminole freedmen.

Said affidavits have been filed with the records of this office in the matter of the application of the enrollment of said children as Seminole freedmen.

Respectfully,

Commissioner.

253

Applications for Enrollment of Seminole Newborn Freedmen
Act of 1905

In re application for enrollment, as a citizen of the Seminole Nation, of Jeff Barkus, born on the 16th day of June, 190o[sic]; Name of father Joseph Barkus; Name of mother Molly Barkus, both citizens of the Seminole Nation.

United States of America, Indian Territory,
    Western Judicial District.

I,   Lena Barkus   , on oath state that I am a citizen of the Seminole Nation, Indian Territory, above the age of   45   years, that I am well acquainted with Joseph Barkus and Molly Barkus, his wife, both citizens of the Seminole Nation that I was present, on or about the 16th day of July, 1900, when there was born to said Molly Barkus, wife of said Joseph Barkus, a male child, which was named, and is now known by the name of Jeff Barkus. Said Jeff Barkus is now living, this 20th day of July, 1905.

her

Witnesses to marks   Lena x Barkus
A S McKennon   mark
William S Webb

Subscribed and sworn to before me, this 20th day of July, A. D. 1905.

John W. Willmott

My commission expires   Notary Public.
   Oct 5-1906

In re application for enrollment, as a citizen of the Seminole Nation, of Jeff Barkus, born on the 16th day of June, 190o; Name of father Joseph Barkus; Name of mother Molly Barkus, both citizens of the Seminole Nation.

United States of America, Indian Territory,
    Western Judicial District.

I,   Harriett Dennis   , on oath state that I am a citizen of the Seminole Nation, Indian Territory, above the age of   70   years, that I am well acquainted with Joseph Barkus and Molly Barkus, his wife, both citizens of the Seminole Nation that I was present, on or about the 16th day of July, 1900, when there was born to said Molly Barkus, wife of said Joseph Barkus, a male child, which was named, and is now known by the name of Jeff Barkus. Said Jeff Barkus is now living, this 20th day of July, 1905.

her
Harriett x Dennis
mark

Applications for Enrollment of Seminole Newborn Freedmen
Act of 1905

Witnesses to marks
A S McKennon
William S Webb

Subscribed and sworn to before me, this 20th day of July, A. D. 1905.

My commission expires
Oct 5-1906

John W. Willmott
Notary Public.

In re application for enrollment, as a citizen of the Seminole Nation, of Naman Barkus, born October 20th, 1903; Name of father Joseph Barkus; Name of mother Molly Barkus, both citizens of the Seminole Nation.

United States of America, Indian Territory,
    Western Judicial District.

I,   Lena Barkus   , on oath state that I am a citizen of the Seminole Nation, Indian Territory, above the age of   45   years, that I am well acquainted with Joseph Barkus and Molly Barkus, his wife, both citizens of the Seminole Nation that I was present, on or about the 20th day of October, 1903, when there was born to said Molly Barkus, wife of said Joseph Barkus, a male child, which was named, and is now known by the name of Naman Barkus. Said Naman Barkus is now living, this 20th day of July, 1905.

Witnesses to marks
A S McKennon
William S Webb

her
Lena x Barkus
mark

Subscribed and sworn to before me, this 20th day of July, A. D. 1905.

My commission expires
Oct 5-1906

John W. Willmott
Notary Public.

In re application for enrollment, as a citizen of the Seminole Nation, of Naman Barkus, born October 20th, 1903; Name of father Joseph Barkus; Name of mother Molly Barkus, both citizens of the Seminole Nation.

United States of America, Indian Territory,
    Western Judicial District.

Applications for Enrollment of Seminole Newborn Freedmen
Act of 1905

I, Harriett Dennis , on oath state that I am a citizen of the Seminole Nation, Indian Territory, above the age of 70 years, that I am well acquainted with Joseph Barkus and Molly Barkus, his wife, both citizens of the Seminole Nation that I was present, on or about the 20th day of October, 1903, when there was born to Molly Barkus, wife of said Joseph Barkus, a male child, which was named, and is now known by the name of Naman Barkus. Said Naman Barkus is now living, this 20th day of July, 1905.

<table>
<tr><td></td><td>her</td></tr>
<tr><td>Witnesses to marks</td><td>Harriett x Dennis</td></tr>
<tr><td>A S McKennon</td><td>mark</td></tr>
<tr><td>William S Webb</td><td></td></tr>
</table>

Subscribed and sworn to before me, this 20th day of July, A. D. 1905.

John W. Willmott

My commission expires   Notary Public.
Oct 5-1906

Sem NB FR 73
BIRTH AFFIDAVIT.
DEPARTMENT OF THE INTERIOR.
COMMISSION TO THE FIVE CIVILIZED TRIBES.

IN RE APPLICATION FOR ENROLLMENT, as a citizen of the Seminole Nation, of Naman Barkus , born on the 20 day of October , 1903

Name of Father: Joseph Barkus   2500   a citizen of the Seminole Nation.
Name of Mother: Molly Barkus   2580   a citizen of the Seminole Nation.

Postoffice   Emahaka I.T.

Child not present

AFFIDAVIT OF MOTHER.

UNITED STATES OF AMERICA, Indian Territory,
Western   **DISTRICT.**

I, Molly Barkus , on oath state that I am 27 years of age and a citizen by adoption , of the Seminole Nation; that I am the lawful wife of Joseph Barkus , who is a citizen, by adoption of the Seminole Nation; that a male child was born to me on 20 day of October , 1903; that said child has been named Naman Barkus , and was living March 4, 1905.

Mollie Barkus

256

Applications for Enrollment of Seminole Newborn Freedmen
Act of 1905

Witnesses To Mark:

{

Subscribed and sworn to before me this 3rd day of   May   , 1905.

Chas E Webster
Notary Public.

_____

AFFIDAVIT OF ATTENDING PHYSICIAN OR MID-WIFE.

UNITED STATES OF AMERICA, Indian Territory,}
      Western   **DISTRICT.**

I,   Joseph Barkus   , ᵃ   , cn oath state that I attended on
Mrs. Molly Barkus   my wife ᵒᶠ   on the 20 day of   October   , 1903;
that there was born to her on said date a   male   child; that said child was living
March 4, 1905, and is said to have been named Naman Barkus

Joseph Barkus

Witnesses To Mark:

{

Subscribed and sworn to before me 3rd day of   May   , 1905.

Chas E Webster
Notary Public.

_____

Sem NB FR 73
BIRTH AFFIDAVIT.

DEPARTMENT OF THE INTERIOR.
COMMISSION TO THE FIVE CIVILIZED TRIBES.

_____

IN RE APPLICATION FOR ENROLLMENT, as a citizen of the   Seminole   Nation, of
Jeff Barkus   , born on the 16   day of June , 1900

Name of Father: Joseph Barkus   (2500)   a citizen of the   Seminole   Nation.
Name of Mother: Molly Barkus   (2580)   a citizen of the   Seminole   Nation.

Postoffice   Emahaka I.T.

_____

257

Applications for Enrollment of Seminole Newborn Freedmen
Act of 1905

Child not present

AFFIDAVIT OF MOTHER.

UNITED STATES OF AMERICA, Indian Territory,
Western   DISTRICT.

    I, Molly Barkus , on oath state that I am 27 years of age and a citizen by adoption , of the Seminole Nation; that I am the lawful wife of Joseph Barkus , who is a citizen, by adoption of the Seminole Nation; that a male child was born to me on 16 day of June , 1900; that said child has been named Jeff Barkus , and was living March 4, 1905.

                                 Mollie Barkus

Witnesses To Mark:
{

    Subscribed and sworn to before me this 3ʳᵈ day of May , 1905.

                         Chas E Webster
                         Notary Public.

AFFIDAVIT OF ATTENDING PHYSICIAN OR MID-WIFE.

UNITED STATES OF AMERICA, Indian Territory,
Western   DISTRICT.

    I, Joseph Barkus   , a   , on oath state that I attended on Mrs. Molly Barkus my wife of   on the 16 day of June , 1900; that there was born to her on said date a male child; that said child was living March 4, 1905, and is said to have been named Jeff Barkus

                         Joseph Barkus

Witnesses To Mark:
{

    Subscribed and sworn to before me 3ʳᵈ day of May , 1905.

                         Chas E Webster
                         Notary Public.

Applications for Enrollment of Seminole Newborn Freedmen
Act of 1905

Sem.Fr.N.B.74.

Muskogee, Indian Territory, June 30, 1905.

Clara Davis,
Care of Thomas Davis,
Emahaka, Indian Territory.

Dear Madam:

On May 2, 1905, you and your husband, Thomas Davis, appeared before the Commission and made application for the enrollment of your daughter, Christiana Davis, born January 23, 1902, as a Seminole freedman, and at that time submitted your affidavits as to the birth of said child.

You are advised that before the rights of said child as a Seminole freedman can be finally determined, it will be necessary for you to file with the Commission the affidavits of two disinterested persons who have the knowledge of the circumstances attending the birth of said child;, when she was born, the names of her parents, and whether or not she was living on March 4, 1905.

You should give this matter your immediate attention.

Respectfully,

Chairman.

Sem.Freed.
NB-74

Muskogee, Indian Territory, July 25, 1905.

McKennon & Willmott,
Attorneys at Law,
Wewoka, Indian Territory.

Gentlemen:

Receipt is hereby acknowledged of your letter of July 19, 1905, inclosing the affidavits of Venus Davis and Fie Lewis as to the birth of Christiana Davis some time prior to March 1, 1902, and the same have been filed with the records of this office in the matter of the application for the enrollment of application for the enrollment of said Christiana Davis as a Seminole freedman.

Respectfully,

Commissioner.

259

Applications for Enrollment of Seminole Newborn Freedmen
Act of 1905

Sem NB FR 74
BIRTH AFFIDAVIT.
DEPARTMENT OF THE INTERIOR.
COMMISSION TO THE FIVE CIVILIZED TRIBES.

IN RE APPLICATION FOR ENROLLMENT, as a citizen of the   Seminole   Nation, of
Lina Davis   , born on the 19th day of October   , 1904

Name of Father: Thomas Davis   (F$^{\#}$2582) a citizen of the   Seminole   Nation.
Name of Mother: Clara Davis   (F$^{\#}$2583) a citizen of the   Seminole   Nation.

Postoffice   Emahaka, IT

Child present

AFFIDAVIT OF MOTHER.

UNITED STATES OF AMERICA, Indian Territory,
Western   DISTRICT.

I,   Clara Davis   , on oath state that I am   38   years of age and a citizen by
adoption   , of the   Seminole   Nation; that I am the lawful wife of   Thomas Davis,
who is a citizen, by adoption   of the   Seminole   Nation; that a   female
child was born to me on   19th day of   October   , 1904; that said child has been
named   Lina Davis   , and was living March 4, 1905.

                                        her
                                Clara x Davis
Witnesses To Mark: mark
  Frank C. Sabourin
  Edward Merrick

Subscribed and sworn to before me this 2nd day of   May   , 1905.

Seal   Edward Merrick
                                    Notary Public.

AFFIDAVIT OF ATTENDING PHYSICIAN OR MID-WIFE.

UNITED STATES OF AMERICA, Indian Territory,
Western   DISTRICT.

I,   Thomas Davis, husband of Clara Davis , on oath state that I attended on Mrs.
Clara Davis   , wife of   on the 19th day of   October   , 1904; that there
was born to her on said date a   female   child; that said child was living March 4,
1905, and is said to have been named Lina Davis

260

Applications for Enrollment of Seminole Newborn Freedmen
Act of 1905

Thomas Davis

Witnesses To Mark:

{

Subscribed and sworn to before me this 2nd day of   May   , 1905.

⟨ Seal ⟩   Edward Merrick
                                            Notary Public.

Sem NB FR 74
BIRTH AFFIDAVIT.

DEPARTMENT OF THE INTERIOR.
COMMISSION TO THE FIVE CIVILIZED TRIBES.

IN RE APPLICATION FOR ENROLLMENT, as a citizen of the   Seminole   Nation, of
Christiana Davis   , born on the 23rd   day of   January   , 1902

Name of Father: Thomas Davis   (F#2582) a citizen of the   Seminole   Nation.
Name of Mother: Clara Davis   (F#2583) a citizen of the   Seminole   Nation.

Postoffice   Emahaka, IT

Child not present

AFFIDAVIT OF MOTHER.

UNITED STATES OF AMERICA, Indian Territory, ⎫
    Western   **DISTRICT.** ⎭

I,   Clara Davis   , on oath state that I am   38   years of age and a citizen by
adoption   , of the   Seminole   Nation; that I am the lawful wife of   Thomas Davis,
who is a citizen, by   adoption   of the   Seminole   Nation; that a   female
child was born to me on   23rd   day of   January   , 1902; that said child has been
named   Christiana Davis   , and was living March 4, 1905.

                                            her
                                    Clara x Davis
Witnesses To Mark: mark
    { Frank C. Sabourin
    { Edward Merrick

Subscribed and sworn to before me this 2nd day of   May   , 1905.

⟨ Seal ⟩   Edward Merrick
                                            Notary Public.

261

Applications for Enrollment of Seminole Newborn Freedmen
Act of 1905

AFFIDAVIT OF ATTENDING PHYSICIAN OR MID-WIFE.

UNITED STATES OF AMERICA, Indian Territory,
   Western   DISTRICT.

I,   Thomas Davis, husband of Clara Davis , on oath state that I attended on Mrs. Clara Davis   , ~~wife of~~   on the 23rd   day of   January   , 1902; that there was born to her on said date a   female   child; that said child was living March 4, 1905, and is said to have been named Christiana Davis

                                        Thomas Davis
Witnesses To Mark:

{

   Subscribed and sworn to before me this 2nd   day of   May   , 1905.

⟨Seal⟩   Edward Merrick
                                         Notary Public.

In re application for enrollment, as a citizen of the Seminole Nation, of Christiana Davis, born on the 23rd day of January, 1902. Name of father, Thomas Davis, Name of mother, Clara Davis, both citizens of the Seminole Nation.   Post office Emahaka, I. T.

United States of America, Indian Territory,
      Western Judicial District.

I,   Fie Lewis   , on oath state that I am a citizen of the Seminole Nation, above the age of   50   years; that I am personally well acquainted with Thomas Davis and Clara Davis, his wife, both citizens of the Seminole Nation, that I was present when there was born to Clara Davis, wife of Thomas Davis, a female child. Said child was born in the year 1902, some time prior to March 1st, of that year' that I am well acquainted with said child, she being known by the name of Christiana Davis, she being still living, this 18th day of July, 1905.   her
                                         Fie Lewis x
Witness to marks: mark
   WS Webb
   M.J. Trott

   Subscribed and sworn to before me, on this the 18th day of July, A. D. 1905.

                                         DW Jenning
My Commission expires 2/6/07   Notary Public.

262

Applications for Enrollment of Seminole Newborn Freedmen
Act of 1905

In re application for enrollment, as a citizen of the Seminole Nation, of Christiana Davis, born on the 23rd day of January, 1902. Name of father, Thomas Davis, Name of mother, Clara Davis, both citizens of the Seminole Nation. Post office Emahaka, I. T.

United States of America, Indian Territory,
    Western Judicial District.

    I,   Venus Davis   , on oath state that I am a citizen of the Seminole Nation, above the age of 35 years; that I am personally well acquainted with Thomas Davis and Clara Davis, his wife, both citizens of the Seminole Nation, that I was present when there was born to Clara Davis, wife of Thomas Davis, a female child. Said child was born in the year 1902, some time prior to March 1st, of that year' that I am well acquainted with said child, she being known by the name of Christiana Davis, she being still living, this 18th day of July, 1905.

her
Venus x Davis
mark

Witness to marks:
  WS Webb
  M.J. Trott

    Subscribed and sworn to before me, on this the 18th day of July, A. D. 1905.

                    DW Jenning
My Commission expires 2/6/07   Notary Public.

263

Applications for Enrollment of Seminole Newborn Freedmen
Act of 1905

Sem NB FR 75
BIRTH AFFIDAVIT.

DEPARTMENT OF THE INTERIOR.
COMMISSION TO THE FIVE CIVILIZED TRIBES.

IN RE APPLICATION FOR ENROLLMENT, as a citizen of the   Seminole   Nation, of
Ben Williams   , born on the   14   day of   Octo   , 1903
by adoption
Name of Father: Thomas Williams   a citizen of the   Cherokee   Nation.
by adoption
Name of Mother: Emma Williams   2584   a citizen of the   Seminole   Nation.
nee Davis
Postoffice   Emahaka I.T.

Child present

AFFIDAVIT OF MOTHER.

UNITED STATES OF AMERICA, Indian Territory,
Western   DISTRICT.

I,   Emma Williams   , on oath state that I am   19   years of age and a citizen by
adoption   , of the   Seminole   Nation; that I am the lawful wife of   Thomas
Williams   , who is a citizen, by   adoption   of the   Cherokee   Nation; that a
male   child was born to me on   14   day of   Octo   , 1903, that said child has been
named   Ben Williams   , and is now living.

Emma Williams
Witnesses To Mark:

Subscribed and sworn to before me this   26   day of   May   , 1905.

Chas E Webster
Notary Public.

AFFIDAVIT OF ATTENDING PHYSICIAN OR MID-WIFE.

UNITED STATES OF AMERICA, Indian Territory,
Western   DISTRICT.

I,   Harriett Dennis   , a   midwife   , on oath state that I attended on
Mrs.   Emma Williams   , wife of   Thomas Williams   on the   14   day of Octo ,
1903; that there was born to her on said date a   male   child; that said child is now
living and is said to have been named   Ben Williams

264

Applications for Enrollment of Seminole Newborn Freedmen
Act of 1905

Witnesses To Mark:
{ Chas E Webster
{ *(No signature given)*

her
Harriett x Dennis
mark

Subscribed and sworn to before me this 31 day of   May   , 1905.

Chas E Webster
Notary Public.

Sem NB FR 76
BIRTH AFFIDAVIT.
DEPARTMENT OF THE INTERIOR.
COMMISSION TO THE FIVE CIVILIZED TRIBES.

IN RE APPLICATION FOR ENROLLMENT, as a citizen of the   Seminole   Nation, of
Dollie Sandridge   , born on the 18 day of April , 1902

Name of Father: Arvey Sandridge   a citizen of the   U. S.   ~~Nation.~~
Name of Mother: Kate Sandridge   2624   a citizen of the   Seminole   Nation.

Postoffice   Wewoka I.T.

(Child present)
AFFIDAVIT OF MOTHER.

UNITED STATES OF AMERICA, Indian Territory, ⎤
    Western   **DISTRICT.** ⎦

I,   Kate Sandridge   , on oath state that I am 44   years of age and a citizen
by   adoption   , of the   Seminole   Nation; that I am the lawful wife of   Arvey
Sandridge   , who is a citizen, ~~by~~   of the   U. S.   Nation; that a   Female
child was born to me on 18   day of April   , 1902; that said child has been named
Dollie Sandridge   , and was living March 4, 1905.

Witnesses To Mark:
{ Chas E Webster
{ Frank C. Sabourin

her
Kate x Sandridge
mark

265

Applications for Enrollment of Seminole Newborn Freedmen
Act of 1905

Subscribed and sworn to before me this 10 day of   May   , 1905.

Chas E Webster
Notary Public.

AFFIDAVIT OF ATTENDING PHYSICIAN OR MID-WIFE.

UNITED STATES OF AMERICA, Indian Territory, ⎫
Western   DISTRICT.   ⎭

I,   Agnes Cyrus   , a   midwife   , on oath state that I attended on
Mrs.   Kate Sandridge   , wife of   Arvey Sandridge   on the 18 day of   April ,
1902; that there was born to her on said date a   Female   child; that said child was
living March 4, 1905, and is said to have been named   Dollie Sandridge

her
Agnes x Cyrus
mark

Witnesses To Mark:
⎧ Chas E Webster
⎩ Frank C. Sabourin

Subscribed and sworn to before me 10 day of   May   , 1905.

Chas E Webster
Notary Public.

Sem NB FR 77
BIRTH AFFIDAVIT.

DEPARTMENT OF THE INTERIOR.
COMMISSION TO THE FIVE CIVILIZED TRIBES.

IN RE APPLICATION FOR ENROLLMENT, as a citizen of the   Seminole   Nation, of
Lee Sandridge   , born on the 11 day of   Sept , 1904
not
Name of Father: Bud Sandridge   a citizen of the   U. S.   ~~Nation~~.
Name of Mother: Minerva Sandridge   a citizen of the   Seminole   Nation.

Postoffice   Wewoka I.T.

266

Applications for Enrollment of Seminole Newborn Freedmen
Act of 1905

(Child present)

UNITED STATES OF AMERICA, Indian Territory, ⎫
Western   DISTRICT.   ⎭

I,   Minerva Sandridge   , on oath state that I am   23   years of age and a citizen by   adoption   , of the   Seminole   Nation; that I am the lawful wife of Bud Sandridge   , who is a citizen, ~~by~~   of the   U. S.   Nation; that a male   child was born to me on   11   day of   Sept   , 1904; that said child has been named   Lee Sandridge   , and was living March 4, 1905.

her
Minerva x Sandridge
mark

Witnesses To Mark:
⎰ Chas E Webster
⎱ Frank C. Sabourin

Subscribed and sworn to before me this   10 day of   May   , 1905.

Chas E Webster
Notary Public.

UNITED STATES OF AMERICA, Indian Territory, ⎫
Western   DISTRICT.   ⎭

I,   Agnes Cyrus   , a   midwife   , on oath state that I attended on Mrs.   Minerva Sandridge   , wife of   Bud Sandridge   on the 11   day of   Sept , 1904; that there was born to her on said date a   male   child; that said child was living March 4, 1905, and is said to have been named   Lee Sandridge

her
Agnes x Cyrus
mark

Witnesses To Mark:
⎰ Chas E Webster
⎱ Frank C. Sabourin

Subscribed and sworn to before me   10 day of   May   , 1905.

Chas E Webster
Notary Public.

Applications for Enrollment of Seminole Newborn Freedmen
Act of 1905

Sem NB FR 77

BIRTH AFFIDAVIT.

DEPARTMENT OF THE INTERIOR.

COMMISSION TO THE FIVE CIVILIZED TRIBES.

IN RE APPLICATION FOR ENROLLMENT, as a citizen of the   Seminole   Nation, of
Allen Sandridge   , born on the   10   day of   March   , 1902

not

Name of Father: Bud Sandridge   a citizen of the   U. S.   ~~Nation.~~
Name of Mother: Minerva Sandridge   2625   a citizen of the   Seminole   Nation.

Postoffice   Wewoka I.T.

Child present

AFFIDAVIT OF MOTHER.

UNITED STATES OF AMERICA, Indian Territory, ⎱
     Western   DISTRICT.   ⎰

I,   Minerva Sandridge   , on oath state that I am   23   years of age and a
citizen by   adoption   , of the   Seminole   Nation; that I am the lawful wife of
Bud Sandridge   , who is a citizen, ~~by~~   of the   U. S.   Nation; that a
male   child was born to me on   10   day of   March   , 1902; that said child has
been named   Allen Sandridge   , and was living March 4, 1905.

                                    her
                            Minerva x Sandridge
Witnesses To Mark: mark
    ⎰ Chas E Webster
    ⎱ Frank C. Sabourin

Subscribed and sworn to before me this   10 day of   May   , 1905.

                        Chas E Webster
                        Notary Public.

AFFIDAVIT OF ATTENDING PHYSICIAN OR MID-WIFE.

UNITED STATES OF AMERICA, Indian Territory, ⎱
     Western   DISTRICT.   ⎰

I,   Kate Sandridge   , a   midwife   , on oath state that I attended on
Mrs. Minerva Sandridge , wife of   Bud Sandridge   on the 10 day of   March ,
1902; that there was born to her on said date a   male   child; that said child was living
March 4, 1905, and is said to have been named   Allen Sandridge

268

Applications for Enrollment of Seminole Newborn Freedmen
Act of 1905

Witnesses To Mark:
{ Chas E Webster
{ Frank C. Sabourin

her
Kate x Sandridge
mark

Subscribed and sworn to before me 10 day of   May   , 1905.

Chas E Webster
Notary Public.

Sem NB FR 78
BIRTH AFFIDAVIT.
DEPARTMENT OF THE INTERIOR.
COMMISSION TO THE FIVE CIVILIZED TRIBES.

IN RE APPLICATION FOR ENROLLMENT, as a citizen of the   Seminole   Nation, of
Sherman Payne   , born on the 28   day of Dec , 1903

Name of Father: Tom Payne   2630   a citizen of the Seminole   Nation.
Name of Mother: Annie Payne   2631   a citizen of the Seminole   Nation.

Postoffice   Little, I.T.

(Child present)

AFFIDAVIT OF MOTHER.

UNITED STATES OF AMERICA, Indian Territory, ⎱
     Western   DISTRICT. ⎰

I,   Annie Payne   , on oath state that I am 38 years of age and a citizen by
adoption   , of the   Seminole   Nation; that I am the lawful wife of   , who is
a citizen, by   adoption   of the   Seminole   Nation; that a   male   child was
born to me on 28   day of   Dec   , 1903, that said child has been named   Sherman
Payne   , and is now living.

Annie Payne

269

Applications for Enrollment of Seminole Newborn Freedmen
Act of 1905

Witnesses To Mark:

{

Subscribed and sworn to before me this 24   day of   May   , 1905.

Chas E Webster
Notary Public.

AFFIDAVIT OF ATTENDING PHYSICIAN OR MID-WIFE.

UNITED STATES OF AMERICA, Indian Territory,
Western   DISTRICT.

I,   Rosy Fay   , a   midwife   , on oath state that I attended on
Mrs. Annie Payne   , wife of   Tom Payne   on the   28   day of Dec , 1903; that
there was born to her on said date a   male   child; that said child is now living and is
said to have been named   Sherman Payne   her

Rosy x Fay
Witnesses To Mark: mark
{ Chas E Webster
{ A. B. Davis

Subscribed and sworn to before me this 24   day of   May   , 1905.

Chas E Webster
Notary Public.

Sem NB FR 78
BIRTH AFFIDAVIT.
DEPARTMENT OF THE INTERIOR.
COMMISSION TO THE FIVE CIVILIZED TRIBES.

IN RE APPLICATION FOR ENROLLMENT, as a citizen of the   Seminole   Nation, of
Ola Payne   , born on the   17   day of   March   , 1902

Name of Father: Tom Payne   2630   a citizen of the   Seminole   Nation.
Name of Mother: Annie Payne   2631   a citizen of the   Seminole   Nation.

Postoffice   Little, I.T.

Applications for Enrollment of Seminole Newborn Freedmen
Act of 1905

(Child present)

UNITED STATES OF AMERICA, Indian Territory, ⎱
Western   DISTRICT. ⎰

I,   Annie Payne   , on oath state that I am 38 years of age and a citizen by adoption   , of the   Seminole   Nation; that I am the lawful wife of   , who is a citizen, by   adoption   of the   Seminole   Nation; that a   Female   child was born to me on 17   day of   March   , 1902, that said child has been named   Ola Payne   , and is now living.

Annie Payne

Witnesses To Mark:
{

Subscribed and sworn to before me this 24   day of   May   , 1905.

Chas E Webster
Notary Public.

UNITED STATES OF AMERICA, Indian Territory, ⎱
Western   DISTRICT. ⎰

I,   Rosy Fay   , a   midwife   , on oath state that I attended on Mrs. Annie Payne   , wife of   Tom Payne   on the   17 day of March , 1902; that there was born to her on said date a   Female   child; that said child is now living and is said to have been named   Ola Payne

her
Rosy x Fay
mark

Witnesses To Mark:
⎰ Chas E Webster
⎱ A. B. Davis

Subscribed and sworn to before me this 24   day of   May   , 1905.

Chas E Webster
Notary Public.

Applications for Enrollment of Seminole Newborn Freedmen
Act of 1905

Sem NB FR 79

BIRTH AFFIDAVIT.

DEPARTMENT OF THE INTERIOR.
COMMISSION TO THE FIVE CIVILIZED TRIBES.

_____

IN RE APPLICATION FOR ENROLLMENT, as a citizen of the   Seminole   Nation, of
Joe Crawford Peoples   , born on the 21st   day of   May   , 1903

Name of Father: Amos Peoples   a citizen of the United States XXX.
                     (2640)
Name of Mother: Tina Peoples (Nee Sango)   a citizen of the   Seminole   Nation.

Postoffice   Wewoka I.T.

_____

AFFIDAVIT OF MOTHER.

UNITED STATES OF AMERICA, Indian Territory,
     Western   DISTRICT.

     I,   Tina Peoples (nee Sango)   , on oath state that I am   22   years of age and
a citizen by   adoption   , of the   Seminole   Nation; that I am the lawful wife of
Amos Peoples   , who is a citizen, by   XXX   United States   Nation; that
a   male   child was born to me on   21st   day of   May   , 1903; that said child
has been named   Joe Crawford Peoples   , and was living March 4, 1905.

                               Tina Peoples   nee Sango
Witnesses To Mark:
{

     Subscribed and sworn to before me this   24th   day of   April   , 1905.

                           John W. Willmott
                           Notary Public.

_____

AFFIDAVIT OF ATTENDING PHYSICIAN OR MID-WIFE.

UNITED STATES OF AMERICA, Indian Territory,
     Western   DISTRICT.

     I,   Margaret Greenwood   , a   mid-wife   , on oath state that I attended on
Mrs.   Tina Peoples   , wife of   Amos Peoples   on the   21st day of   May   ,
1903; that there was born to her on said date a   male   child; that said child was living
March 4, 1905, and is said to have been named   Joe Crawford Peoples

Applications for Enrollment of Seminole Newborn Freedmen
Act of 1905

her
Margaret Greenwood x
mark

Witnesses To Mark:
{ W.S. Webb
{ John W. Willmott

Subscribed and sworn to before me 24th day of   April   , 1905.

John W. Willmott
Notary Public.

Sem NB FR 80
BIRTH AFFIDAVIT.

DEPARTMENT OF THE INTERIOR.
COMMISSION TO THE FIVE CIVILIZED TRIBES.

IN RE APPLICATION FOR ENROLLMENT, as a citizen of the   Seminole   Nation, of
Carolina Bennett   , born on the 30th day of   March , 1904

Name of Father: Aaron Bennett   a citizen of the United States Nation.
                              (2641)
Name of Mother: Ellen Bennett (nee Sango)   a citizen of the   Seminole   Nation.

Postoffice   Earlsboro, O.T.

AFFIDAVIT OF MOTHER.

UNITED STATES OF AMERICA, Indian Territory, ⎫
    Western   DISTRICT. ⎭

    I, Ellen Bennett (nee Sango)   , on oath state that I am 17   years of age and
a citizen by   adoption   , of the   Seminole   Nation; that I am the lawful wife of
Aaron Bennett   , who is a citizen, ~~by~~   of the   United States   ~~Nation~~;
that a   female   child was born to me on   30th day of   March   , 1904; that
said child has been named   Carolina Bennett   , and was living March 4, 1905.

273

Applications for Enrollment of Seminole Newborn Freedmen
Act of 1905

Witnesses To Mark:
{ John W. Willmott

Ellen Bennett
nee Ellen Sango

Subscribed and sworn to before me this 19 day of   August   , 1905.

Com exp.
Oct 5-1906

John W. Willmott
Notary Public.

AFFIDAVIT OF ATTENDING PHYSICIAN OR MID-WIFE.

UNITED STATES OF AMERICA, Indian Territory, }
   Western   DISTRICT.

I, Margaret Greenwood   , a   midwife , on oath state that I attended on
Mrs. Ellen Bennett   , wife of   Aaron Bennett   on the 30th day of   March ,
1904; that there was born to her on said date a   female   child; that said child was
living March 4, 1905, and is said to have been named   Carolina Bennett

Witnesses To Mark:
{ J J Blanton
{ John W. Willmott

Margaret Greenwood
her
x
mark

Subscribed and sworn to before me 19 day of   August   , 1905.

Com exp Oct 5-1905

John W. Willmott
Notary Public.

Sem NB FR 80
BIRTH AFFIDAVIT.
DEPARTMENT OF THE INTERIOR.
COMMISSION TO THE FIVE CIVILIZED TRIBES.

IN RE APPLICATION FOR ENROLLMENT, as a citizen of the   Seminole   Nation, of
Willie Bennett   , born on the 24th   day of   February , 1905

Name of Father: Aaron Bennett   a citizen of the United States Nation.
                                    2641
Name of Mother: Ellen Bennett nee Sango   a citizen of the   Seminole   Nation.

Postoffice   Earlsboro, O.T.

274

Applications for Enrollment of Seminole Newborn Freedmen
Act of 1905

UNITED STATES OF AMERICA, Indian Territory, ⎱
Western   DISTRICT. ⎰

I, Ellen Bennett (nee Sango)   , on oath state that I am   17   years of age and a citizen by   adoption   , of the   Seminole   Nation; that I am the lawful wife of   Aaron Bennett   , who is a citizen, by   of the   United States Nation; that a   male   child was born to me on   24th day of   February   , 1905; that said child has been named   Willie Bennett   , and was living March 4, 1905.

Witnesses To Mark:
{

Ellen Bennett nee Sango
(Ellen Bennett)

Subscribed and sworn to before me this 24th   day of   April   , 1905.

John W. Willmott
Notary Public.

AFFIDAVIT OF ATTENDING PHYSICIAN OR MID-WIFE.

UNITED STATES OF AMERICA, Indian Territory, ⎱
Western   DISTRICT. ⎰

I, Margaret Greenwood   , a   mid-wife , on oath state that I attended on Mrs. Ellen Bennett   , wife of   Aaron Bennett   on the 24th day of   February , 1905; that there was born to her on said date a   male   child; that said child was living March 4, 1905, and is said to have been named   Willie Bennett

Witnesses To Mark:
{ W S Webb
{ John W. Willmott

her
Margaret x Greenwood
mark

Subscribed and sworn to before me   24th day of   April   , 1905.

John W. Willmott
Notary Public.

Applications for Enrollment of Seminole Newborn Freedmen
Act of 1905

Sem NB FR 80
BIRTH AFFIDAVIT.

DEPARTMENT OF THE INTERIOR.
COMMISSION TO THE FIVE CIVILIZED TRIBES.

IN RE APPLICATION FOR ENROLLMENT, as a citizen of the   Seminole   Nation, of
Carolina Bennett   , born on the   30th   day of   May   , 1904   X See Postal
                                                                              attached
Name of Father: Aaron Bennett   a citizen of the United States   Nation.
                                       (2641)
Name of Mother: Ellen Bennett (nee Sango)   a citizen of the   Seminole   Nation.

Postoffice   Earlsboro, O.T.

AFFIDAVIT OF MOTHER.

UNITED STATES OF AMERICA, Indian Territory,
   Western   DISTRICT.

   I,   Ellen Bennett (nee Sango)   , on oath state that I am   17   years of age and
a citizen by   adoption   , of the   Seminole   Nation; that I am the lawful wife of
Aaron Bennett   , who is a citizen, by   of the   United States   Nation;
that a   female   child was born to me on   30th   day of   May   , 1904; that said
child has been named   Carolina Bennett   , and was living March 4, 1905.

                                                 Ellen Bennett nee Sango
Witnesses To Mark: (Ellen Bennett)

{

   Subscribed and sworn to before me this 24th   day of   April   , 1905.

                                                 John W. Willmott
                                                 Notary Public.

AFFIDAVIT OF ATTENDING PHYSICIAN OR MID-WIFE.

UNITED STATES OF AMERICA, Indian Territory,
   Western   DISTRICT.

   I,   Margaret Greenwood   , a   mid-wife , on oath state that I attended on
Mrs.   Ellen Bennett   , wife of   Aaron Bennett   on the 30th day of   May   ,
1904; that there was born to her on said date a   female   child; that said child was
living March 4, 1905, and is said to have been named   Carolina Bennett

276

Applications for Enrollment of Seminole Newborn Freedmen
Act of 1905

Witnesses To Mark:
{ WS Webb
{ John W. Willmott

her
Margaret x Greenwood
mark

Subscribed and sworn to before me this 24th day of   April   , 1905.

John W. Willmott
Notary Public.

(The below post card typed as given.)

Wewoka I T Apr 25 1905

Mr Tams Bixby Sending in my alfidavit for my children I being in a very big *(illegible)* for the *(illegible)* made a little mistake in Carolina Bennett my living child age which I wish to correct before to late of you pleas I have got correct time it was born. She was born March the 30 instead of May the 30   Mr Bixby pleas chang it for me the other age is correct yours Respectivly

Ellen Bennett
mother of child

Sem.Fr.N.B.80.

Muskogee, Indian Territory, June 30, 1905.

Ellen Bennett,
Wewoka, Indian Territory.

Dear Madam:

Receipt is hereby acknowledged of your postal card of April 25, 1905, stating that you made a mistake when you stated in your affidavit as to the birth of your child, Carolina Bennett that said child was born May 30, 1904, and that you wish to correct said statement and make it to appear that said child was born March 30, 1904.

For that purpose a blank for proof of birth is enclosed herewith which you are requested to execute and return to this office.

There is also a suggestion in your postal card that your son, Willie Bennett, is now dead. For the purpose of making his death a matter of record there is enclosed herewith a blank for proof of death which you are requested to have filled out, executed and returned to this office.

Applications for Enrollment of Seminole Newborn Freedmen
Act of 1905

Respectfully,

Deb--9/29.
D.C.

_____

Sem Fr NB - 80

Muskogee, Indian Territory, August 23, 1905.

McKennon & Willmott,
Attorneys-at-Law,
Wewoka, Indian Territory.

Gentlemen:

Receipt is hereby acknowledged of your letter of August 19, 1905, transmitting the affidavits of Ellen Bennett and Margaret Greenwood, relative to the birth of Carolina Bennett on March 30, 1904, and the affidavits of Aaron Bennett and Margaret Greenwood relative to the death of Willie Bennett about March 24, 1905.

Said affidavits have been filed with the records of this Office in the matter of the application for the enrollment of said children as Seminole Freedmen.

Respectfully,

Commissioner.

═══

Sem NB FR 81
BIRTH AFFIDAVIT.

DEPARTMENT OF THE INTERIOR.
COMMISSION TO THE FIVE CIVILIZED TRIBES.

_____

IN RE APPLICATION FOR ENROLLMENT, as a citizen of the   Seminole   Nation, of
Cyrus Sancho   , born on the   19th day of   February   , 1900

Name of Father: July Sancho   (Fr. 2646)   a citizen of the   Seminole   Nation.
Name of Mother: Bettie Sancho   (Fr. 2647)   a citizen of the   Seminole   Nation.

Postoffice   Wewoka, IT

_____

278

Applications for Enrollment of Seminole Newborn Freedmen
Act of 1905

Child present

UNITED STATES OF AMERICA, Indian Territory,
Western   DISTRICT.

       I,   Bettie Sancho   , on oath state that I am   37   years of age and a citizen by adoption   , of the   Seminole   Nation; that I am the lawful wife of   July Sancho , who is a citizen, by adoption   of the   Seminole   Nation; that a   male child was born to me on   19"   day of   February   , 1900; that said child has been named   Cyrus Sancho   , and was living March 4, 1905.

her
Bettie x Sancho
mark

Witnesses To Mark:
{ Frank C. Sabourin
{ Chas E Webster

Subscribed and sworn to before me this 2nd day of   May   , 1905.

Chas E Webster
Notary Public.

UNITED STATES OF AMERICA, Indian Territory,
Western   DISTRICT.

       I,   Jane Washington   , a   midwife   , on oath state that I attended on Mrs. Bettie Sancho   , wife of   July Sancho   on the 19" day of   February , 1900; that there was born to her on said date a   male   child; that said child was living March 4, 1905, and is said to have been named   Cyrus Sancho

her
Jane x Washington
mark

Witnesses To Mark:
{ Frank C. Sabourin
{ Chas E Webster

Subscribed and sworn to before me 2   day of   May   , 1905.

Chas E Webster
Notary Public.

Applications for Enrollment of Seminole Newborn Freedmen
Act of 1905

Sem NB FR 81
BIRTH AFFIDAVIT.
DEPARTMENT OF THE INTERIOR.
COMMISSION TO THE FIVE CIVILIZED TRIBES.

IN RE APPLICATION FOR ENROLLMENT, as a citizen of the   Seminole   Nation, of
Sipiew Sancho   , born on the 5th day of   March , 1902

Name of Father: July Sancho   (Fr. 2646)   a citizen of the   Seminole   Nation.
Name of Mother: Bettie Sancho (Fr. 2647)   a citizen of the   Seminole   Nation.

Postoffice   Wewoka, IT

Child present

AFFIDAVIT OF MOTHER.

UNITED STATES OF AMERICA, Indian Territory,
Western   DISTRICT.

I,   Bettie Sancho   , on oath state that I am   37   years of age and a citizen by
adoption   , of the   Seminole   Nation; that I am the lawful wife of   July Sancho ,
who is a citizen, by adoption   of the   Seminole   Nation; that a   male
child was born to me on   5th day of   March   , 1902; that said child has been
named   Sipiew Sancho   , and was living March 4, 1905.

her
Bettie x Sancho
mark

Witnesses To Mark:
  Frank C. Sabourin
  Chas E Webster

Subscribed and sworn to before me this 2nd day of   May   , 1905.

Chas E Webster
Notary Public.

AFFIDAVIT OF ATTENDING PHYSICIAN OR MID-WIFE.

UNITED STATES OF AMERICA, Indian Territory,
Western   DISTRICT.

I,   Jane Washington   , a   midwife   , on oath state that I attended on
Mrs. Bettie Sancho   , wife of   July Sancho   on the 5th day of   March , 1902;
that there was born to her on said date a   male   child; that said child was living
March 4, 1905, and is said to have been named   Sipiew Sancho

Applications for Enrollment of Seminole Newborn Freedmen
Act of 1905

her
Jane x Washington
mark

Witnesses To Mark:
⎰ Frank C. Sabourin
⎱ Chas E Webster

Subscribed and sworn to before me 2 day of   May   , 1905.

Chas E Webster
Notary Public.

Sem NB FR 82
BIRTH AFFIDAVIT.
DEPARTMENT OF THE INTERIOR.
COMMISSION TO THE FIVE CIVILIZED TRIBES.

IN RE APPLICATION FOR ENROLLMENT, as a citizen of the   Seminole   Nation, of
Georgie Williams   , born on the 7   day of   March   , 1904

Name of Father: Sie Williams   a citizen of the   Texas   ~~Nation~~.
Name of Mother: Katie Williams   a citizen of the   Seminole   Nation.

Postoffice   Earlsboro, O.T.

AFFIDAVIT OF MOTHER.

UNITED STATES OF AMERICA, Indian Territory, ⎱
    Western   DISTRICT. ⎰

I,   Katie Williams   , on oath state that I am   35   years of age and a citizen
by   Blood   , of the   Seminole Nation   Nation; that I am the lawful wife of   Sie
Williams   , who is a citizen, by marriage   of the   Seminole   Nation; that
a   Female   child was born to me on   Seventh   day of   March   , 1904; that
said child has been named   Georgie Williams   , and was living March 4, 1905.
her
Katie x Williams
Witnesses To Mark: mark
⎰ Sam Norton
⎱ Hagar Bruner

281

Applications for Enrollment of Seminole Newborn Freedmen
Act of 1905

Subscribed and sworn to before me this Third day of   May   , 1905.

R.N. Bruner
Notary Public.

My commission expires October 10 1906

_____

AFFIDAVIT OF ATTENDING PHYSICIAN OR MID-WIFE.

UNITED STATES OF AMERICA, Indian Territory,
Western   DISTRICT.

I, Ann Tiger Alexander   , a   , on oath state that I attended on
Mrs.   Katie Williams   , wife of   Sie Williams   on the Seventh day of March,
1904; that there was born to her on said date a   Female   child; that said child was
living March 4, 1905, and is said to have been named   Georgie Williams

Ann Tiger Alexander

Witnesses To Mark:
{

Subscribed and sworn to before me this Third day of   May   , 1905.

R.N. Bruner
Notary Public.

_____

Sem NB FR 83
BIRTH AFFIDAVIT.
DEPARTMENT OF THE INTERIOR.
COMMISSION TO THE FIVE CIVILIZED TRIBES.

_____

IN RE APPLICATION FOR ENROLLMENT, as a citizen of the   Seminole   Nation, of
Letha Ann Doser   , born on the 5 day of   June , 1904

Name of Father: Hozen Doser   (2026)   a citizen of the   Seminole   Nation.
Name of Mother: Lucy Sancho   (2654)   a citizen of the   Seminole   Nation.

Postoffice of Mother, Wewoka, I.T.
of Father, Tidmore, I.T.

_____

282

Applications for Enrollment of Seminole Newborn Freedmen
Act of 1905

(Child present)

AFFIDAVIT OF MOTHER.

UNITED STATES OF AMERICA, Indian Territory, ⎫
Western   DISTRICT. ⎬⎰

I,   Lucy Sancho   , on oath state that I am   21   years of age and a citizen by adoption   , of the   Seminole   Nation; that I am not the lawful wife of   Hozen Dozer[sic]   , who is a citizen, by adoption   of the   Seminole   Nation; that a   female   child was born to me on   5ᵗʰ   day of   June   , 1904; that said child has been named   Letha Ann Doser   , and was living March 4, 1905.

Lucy Sancho

Witnesses To Mark:
⎰

Subscribed and sworn to before me this 3ʳᵈ   day of   May   , 1905.

⬡ Seal ⬡

Edward Merrick
Notary Public.

Sem NB FR 83
BIRTH AFFIDAVIT.

DEPARTMENT OF THE INTERIOR.
COMMISSION TO THE FIVE CIVILIZED TRIBES.

IN RE APPLICATION FOR ENROLLMENT, as a citizen of the   Seminole   Nation, of Leathia Ann Doser   , born on the   5   day of   June , 1904

Name of Father: Hozen Doser   2026   a citizen of the   Seminole   Nation.
Name of Mother: Lucy Sancho   2654   a citizen of the   Seminole   Nation.

Postoffice   Wewoka

AFFIDAVIT OF MOTHER.

UNITED STATES OF AMERICA, Indian Territory, ⎫
Western   DISTRICT. ⎬⎰

I,   Lucy Sancho   , on oath state that I am   21   years of age and a citizen by adoption   , of the   Seminole   Nation; that I am not the lawful wife of   Hozen Doser   , who is a citizen, by adoption   of the   Seminole   Nation; that a female   child was born to me on   5   day of   June   , 1904; that said child has been named   Leathia Ann Doser   , and was living March 4, 1905.

283

Applications for Enrollment of Seminole Newborn Freedmen
Act of 1905

her
Lucy x Sancho
mark

Witnesses To Mark:
- Chas E Webster
- Frank C. Sabourin

Subscribed and sworn to before me this 10   day of   May   , 1905.

Chas E Webster
Notary Public.

AFFIDAVIT OF ATTENDING PHYSICIAN OR MID-WIFE.

UNITED STATES OF AMERICA, Indian Territory,
    Western   DISTRICT.

I,   Maria Grayson   , a   midwife   , on oath state that I attended on Mrs.   Lucy Sancho   , ~~wife of~~   on the   5 day of   June   , 1904; that there was born to her on said date a   Female   child; that said child was living March 4, 1905, and is said to have been named   Leathia Ann Doser

her
Maria x Grayson
mark

Witnesses To Mark:
- Chas E Webster
- Frank C. Sabourin

Subscribed and sworn to before me 10   day of   May   , 1905.

Chas E Webster
Notary Public.

Applications for Enrollment of Seminole Newborn Freedmen
Act of 1905

Sem.Fr.N.B.84.

Muskogee, Indian Territory, June 30, 1905.

Commission to the Five Civilized Tribes,
Creek Enrollment Division.

Gentlemen:

On May 8, 1905, there was filed with the Commission application for the enrollment of Liddie Grayson, Indian Territory born March 24, 1902, as a Seminole freedman. It appears from said application that said child is the daughter of Sunny Grayson, Indian Territory a citizen by adoption of the Creek Nation, and Ida Grayson, Indian Territory, a Seminole freedman.

You are requested to inform the Seminole Enrollment Division as to whether or not application has been made to the Commission for the enrollment of Liddie Grayson as a citizen of the Creek Nation, and if so what disposition, if any, has been made of such application.

Respectfully,

Chairman.

HGH

DEPARTMENT OF THE INTERIOR.
COMMISSION TO THE FIVE CIVILIZED TRIBES.

Muskogee, Indian Territory, July 11, 1905.

Seminole Enrollment Division,
General Office.

Gentlemen:

Receipt is acknowledged of your communication of May 8[sic], 1905 (Sem.Fr.NB.84), in which you ask if application for the enrollment as a citizen of the Creek Nation has been made for Liddie Grayson, child of Sunny Grayson, a citizen of the Creek Nation, and Ida Grayson, a Seminole Freedman.

In reply you are advised that the records of this office have been examined and it does not appear that application has been made for the enrollment of said Liddie Grayson, as a citizen of the Creek Nation.

Respectfully,
Tams Bixby
Commissioner.

285

Applications for Enrollment of Seminole Newborn Freedmen
Act of 1905

Sem NB FR 84
BIRTH AFFIDAVIT.

DEPARTMENT OF THE INTERIOR.
COMMISSION TO THE FIVE CIVILIZED TRIBES.

IN RE APPLICATION FOR ENROLLMENT, as a citizen of the   Seminole   Nation, of
Liddie Grayson , born on the 24 day of March , 1902

Name of Father: Sunny Grayson   a citizen of the   Creek   Nation.
Name of Mother: Ida Grayson   2667   a citizen of the   Seminole   Nation.

Postoffice   Tidmore IT

(Child present)

AFFIDAVIT OF MOTHER.

UNITED STATES OF AMERICA, Indian Territory, ⎫
    Western   **DISTRICT.** ⎭

    I, Ida Grayson   , on oath state that I am 30 years of age and a citizen by
adoption   , of the   Seminole   Nation; that I am the lawful wife of Sunny
Grayson , who is a citizen, by adoption of the   Creek   Nation; that a
Female   child was born to me on 24 day of March   , 1902, that said child has
been named Liddie Grayson   , and is now living.

her
Ida x Grayson
mark

Witnesses To Mark:
    ⎰ Chas E Webster
    ⎱ Frank C. Sabourin

    Subscribed and sworn to before me this 8ᵗʰ day of May   , 1905.

Chas E Webster
Notary Public.

AFFIDAVIT OF ATTENDING PHYSICIAN OR MID-WIFE.

UNITED STATES OF AMERICA, Indian Territory, ⎫   Husband
    Western   **DISTRICT.** ⎭

    I, Sunny Grayson   , ~~a~~   , on oath state that I attended on
Mrs. Ida Grayson , ~~wife of~~ My wife on the 24 day of March , 1902; that
there was born to her on said date a Female child; that said child is now living and
is said to have been named Liddie Grayson

Applications for Enrollment of Seminole Newborn Freedmen
Act of 1905

Witnesses To Mark:
    ⌠ Chas E Webster
    ⌡ Frank C. Sabourin

his
Sunny x Grayson
mark

Subscribed and sworn to before me this 8th day of   May   , 1905.

Chas E Webster
Notary Public.

Sem.Fr.N.B.85.

Muskogee, Indian Territory, June 30, 1905.

Commission to the Five Civilized Tribes,
    Creek Enrollment Division.

Gentlemen:

An application has been made to the Commission for the enrollment of Ollie Grayson, Indian Territory born August 15, 1903, as a Seminole freedman. It appears that said child is the daughter of Joe Grayson, Indian Territory a citizen by adoption of the Creek Nation, and Evaline Lincoln, who is identified as Evaline Cudjo upon the approved roll of Seminole freedmen.

You are requested to inform the Seminole Enrollment Division as to whether an application has been made to the Commission for the enrollment of said Ollie Grayson as a citizen of the Creek Nation, and if so what disposition, if any, has been made of such application.

Respectfully,

Chairman.

287

Applications for Enrollment of Seminole Newborn Freedmen
Act of 1905

DEPARTMENT OF THE INTERIOR.
COMMISSION TO THE FIVE CIVILIZED TRIBES.

Muskogee, Indian Territory, July 12, 1905.

Seminole Enrollment Division,
    General Office.

Gentlemen:

Receipt is acknowledged of your communication of June 30, 1905 (Sem.NB.85), in which you ask if application for the enrollment as a citizen of the Creek Nation has been made for Ollie Grayson, child of Joe Grayson, a citizen of the Creek Nation, and Evaline Lincoln, a Seminole Freedman.

In reply you are advised that the records of this office have been examined and it does not appear that application has been made for the enrollment of said Ollie Grayson, as a citizen of the Creek Nation.

Respectfully,

Tams Bixby
         Commissioner.

Sem NB FR 85
BIRTH AFFIDAVIT.

DEPARTMENT OF THE INTERIOR.
COMMISSION TO THE FIVE CIVILIZED TRIBES.

IN RE APPLICATION FOR ENROLLMENT, as a citizen of the   Seminole   Nation, of Ollie Grayson   , born on the about 15   day of Aug   , 1903

Name of Father: Joe Grayson   a citizen of the   Creek   Nation.
Name of Mother: Evaline Lincoln   2668   a citizen of the   Seminole   Nation.
                nee Cudjo
                    Postoffice   *(Illegible)*

AFFIDAVIT OF ATTENDING PHYSICIAN OR MID-WIFE.

UNITED STATES OF AMERICA, Indian Territory,
      Western   DISTRICT.

I, Ida Grason[sic]   , a mid-woman   , on oath state that I attended on Mrs. Evaline Lincoln   , wife of Sunnie[sic] Grason   on the 15   day of Aug ,

288

Applications for Enrollment of Seminole Newborn Freedmen
Act of 1905

1903; that there was born to her on said date a   Female   child; that said child is now living and is said to have been named Ollie Grayson

her

Ida x Grayson

mark

Witnesses To Mark:
- { Cate Bowlegs
- { David Cudjo

   Subscribed and sworn to before me this 31   day of   May   , 1905.

R.N. Bruner

Notary Public.

Sem NB FR 85
BIRTH AFFIDAVIT.

DEPARTMENT OF THE INTERIOR.
COMMISSION TO THE FIVE CIVILIZED TRIBES.

   IN RE APPLICATION FOR ENROLLMENT, as a citizen of the   Seminole   Nation, of Ollie Grayson   , born on the about 15   day of July   , 1903

Name of Father: Joe Grayson   a citizen of the   Creek   Nation.
Name of Mother: Evaline Cudjo   2668   a citizen of the   Seminole   Nation.

Postoffice   Tidmore IT

AFFIDAVIT OF ATTENDING PHYSICIAN OR MID-WIFE.

UNITED STATES OF AMERICA, Indian Territory,
   Western   **DISTRICT.**

   I,   Ida Grayson   , a   midwife   , on oath state that I attended on Mrs.   Evaline Cudjo   , ~~wife of~~ my daughter   on the   15 day of July , 1903; that there was born to her on said date a   Female   child; that said child is now living and is said to have been named Ollie Grayson

her

Ida x Grayson

mark

Witnesses To Mark:
- { Chas E Webster
- { Frank C. Sabourin

289

Applications for Enrollment of Seminole Newborn Freedmen
Act of 1905

Subscribed and sworn to before me this 8th day of   May   , 1905.

Chas E Webster
Notary Public.

Sem NB FR 85
BIRTH AFFIDAVIT.

DEPARTMENT OF THE INTERIOR.
COMMISSION TO THE FIVE CIVILIZED TRIBES.

IN RE APPLICATION FOR ENROLLMENT, as a citizen of the   Seminole   Nation, of
Ollie Grayson   , born on the about 15   day of Aug   , 1903

Name of Father: Joe Grayson   a citizen of the   Creek   Nation.
Name of Mother: Evaline Lincoln   2668   a citizen of the   Seminole   Nation.
nee Cudjo
Postoffice   Econtuchka IT

(Child present)

AFFIDAVIT OF MOTHER.

UNITED STATES OF AMERICA, Indian Territory,
      Western   **DISTRICT.**

I, Evaline Lincoln   , on oath state that I am 17 years of age and a citizen by
adoption   , of the   Seminole   Nation; that I am not the lawful wife of   Joe
Grayson   , who is a citizen, by   adoption   of the   Creek   Nation; that a
female   child was born to me on about the 15   day of   Aug   , 1903, that said
child has been named   Ollie Grayson   , and is now living.

her
Evaline x Lincoln
Witnesses To Mark: mark
Chas E Webster
A. B. Davis

Subscribed and sworn to before me this 29   day of   May   , 1905.

Chas E Webster
Notary Public.

Applications for Enrollment of Seminole Newborn Freedmen
Act of 1905

Sem NB FR 86   820
BIRTH AFFIDAVIT.   766

DEPARTMENT OF THE INTERIOR.
COMMISSION TO THE FIVE CIVILIZED TRIBES.

IN RE APPLICATION FOR ENROLLMENT, as a citizen of the   Seminole   Nation, of
Ruthie Davis   , born on the   26th day of   February   , 1901

Name of Father: Isaac Davis   a citizen of the   Seminole   Nation.
Name of Mother: Bettie Davis nee Cudjo   a citizen of the   Seminole   Nation.

Postoffice   Wewoka I.T.

AFFIDAVIT OF MOTHER.

UNITED STATES OF AMERICA, Indian Territory, ⎫
     Western   **DISTRICT.** ⎭

     I,   Bettie Davis   , on oath state that I am   22   years of age and a citizen by
adoption   , of the   Seminole   Nation; that I am the lawful wife of   Isaac Davis   ,
who is a citizen, by   adoption   of the   Seminole   Nation; that a   Female
child was born to me on   26th day of   February   , 1901; that said child has been
named   Ruthie Davis   , and was living March 4, 1905.

Bettie Davis

Witnesses To Mark:
  ⎰

     Subscribed and sworn to before me this   1st day of   April   , 1905.

J.C. Johnson
Notary Public.

AFFIDAVIT OF ATTENDING PHYSICIAN OR MID-WIFE.

UNITED STATES OF AMERICA, Indian Territory, ⎫
     Western   **DISTRICT.** ⎭

     I,   Dinah Esop   , a   midwife   , on oath state that I attended on
Mrs.   Bettie Davis   , wife of   Isaac Davis   on the   26th day of   February   ,
1901; that there was born to her on said date a   Female   child; that said child was
living March 4, 1905, and is said to have been named   Ruthie Davis

her
Dinah [sic] Esop
mark

291

Applications for Enrollment of Seminole Newborn Freedmen
Act of 1905

Witnesses To Mark:
   { John R McBeth
   { J C Johnson

     Subscribed and sworn to before me this 1st day of   April   , 1905.

                              J.C. Johnson
                                  Notary Public.

                                        Sem.Fr.N.B.87.

              Muskogee, Indian Territory, June 30, 1905.

Commission to the Five Civilized Tribes,
     Creek Enrollment Division.

Gentlemen:

     On May 10, 1905, there was filed with the Commission an application for the enrollment of Herbert Brown, born March 5, 1903, as a Seminole freedman. It appears that said child is the son of George Brown, a citizen of the Creek Nation, and Lora Cyrus, a Seminole freedman.

     You are requested to inform the Seminole Enrollment Division as to whether or not application has been made to the Commission for the enrollment of said Herbert Brown as a citizen of the Creek Nation, and if so what disposition, if any, has been made of such application.

                      Respectfully,

                               Chairman.

Applications for Enrollment of Seminole Newborn Freedmen
Act of 1905

HGH

DEPARTMENT OF THE INTERIOR.
COMMISSION TO THE FIVE CIVILIZED TRIBES.

Sem.NB.87.

Muskogee, Indian Territory, July 10, 1905.

Seminole Enrollment Division,
    General Office.

Gentlemen:

Receipt is acknowledged of your communication of June 29, 1905 (Sem.NB.87), in which you ask if application for the enrollment as a citizen of the Creek Nation has been made for Herbert Brown, child of George Brown, a citizen of the Creek Nation, and Lora Cyrus, a Seminole Freedman.

In reply you are advised that the records of this office have been examined and it does not appear that application has been made for the enrollment of said Herbert Brown, as a citizen of the Creek Nation.

Respectfully,

Tams Bixby   Commissioner.

Sem NB FR 87
BIRTH AFFIDAVIT.

DEPARTMENT OF THE INTERIOR.
COMMISSION TO THE FIVE CIVILIZED TRIBES.

IN RE APPLICATION FOR ENROLLMENT, as a citizen of the   Seminole   Nation, of
Herbert Brown   , born on about the 5 day of March , 1903

Name of Father: George Brown   a citizen of the   Creek   Nation.
Name of Mother: Lora Cyrus   2678   a citizen of the   Seminole   Nation.

Postoffice

(Child present)

AFFIDAVIT OF MOTHER.

Mother sick in bed

UNITED STATES OF AMERICA, Indian Territory,
    Western   DISTRICT.

I,   Nancy Davis   , on oath state that I am   53   years of age and a citizen by adoption   , of the   Seminole   Nation; that I am the ~~lawful wife~~ mother of   Lora

293

Applications for Enrollment of Seminole Newborn Freedmen
Act of 1905

Cyrus   , who is a citizen, by adoption   of the   Seminole   Nation; that a
male   child was born to ~~me~~ her on about the 5   day of   March   , 1903; that
said child has been named   Herbert Brown   , and was living March 4, 1905.

her
Nancy x Davis
mark

Witnesses To Mark:
- Chas E Webster
- Frank C. Sabourin

    Subscribed and sworn to before me this   10 day of   May   , 1905.

Chas E Webster
Notary Public.

AFFIDAVIT OF ATTENDING PHYSICIAN OR MID-WIFE.

UNITED STATES OF AMERICA, Indian Territory,
     Western   DISTRICT.

    I,   Jane Washington   , a   midwife   , on oath state that I attended on
~~Mrs.~~   Lora Cyrus   , ~~wife of~~   about on the 5 day of   March   , 1903; that
there was born to her on said date a   male   child; that said child was living March 4,
1905, and is said to have been named   Herbert Brown

her
Jane x Washington
mark

Witnesses To Mark:
- Chas E Webster
- Frank C. Sabourin

    Subscribed and sworn to before me 10   day of   May   , 1905.

Chas E Webster
Notary Public.

Applications for Enrollment of Seminole Newborn Freedmen
Act of 1905

Sem NB FR 88
BIRTH AFFIDAVIT.

DEPARTMENT OF THE INTERIOR.
COMMISSION TO THE FIVE CIVILIZED TRIBES.

IN RE APPLICATION FOR ENROLLMENT, as a citizen of the   Seminole   Nation, of
Lillie Wright   , born on the 6 day of Jan , 1902

Name of Father: William Wright   2459   a citizen of the Seminole Nation.
Name of Mother: Lora Cyrus   2671   a citizen of the Seminole Nation.

Postoffice   Wewoka I.T.

Child present   grand
AFFIDAVIT OF ^ MOTHER.

                                          mother sick

UNITED STATES OF AMERICA, Indian Territory,⎤
    Western   DISTRICT.⎦

      I, Nancy Davis   , on oath state that I am   about 53   years of age and a
citizen by   adoption   , of the   Seminole   Nation; that ~~I am~~ my daughter Lora
Cyrus is not the lawful wife of   William Wright   , who is a citizen, by adoption
of the   Seminole   Nation; that a   Female   child was born to ~~me~~ her on the
6 day of Jan   , 1902; that said child has been named Lillie Wright   , and was
living March 4, 1905.
                                         her
                               Nancy x Davis
Witnesses To Mark: mark
    ⎰ Chas E Webster
    ⎱ Frank C. Sabourin

    Subscribed and sworn to before me this 18 day of   May   , 1905.

                            Chas E Webster
                            Notary Public.

AFFIDAVIT OF ATTENDING PHYSICIAN OR MID-WIFE.

UNITED STATES OF AMERICA, Indian Territory,⎤
    Western   DISTRICT.⎦

      I, Jennie Thompson   , a midwife   , on oath state that I attended on
Mrs. Lora Cyrus   , ~~wife of~~   on the 6 day of Jan   , 1902; that there was
born to her on said date a   Female   child; that said child was living March 4, 1905,
and is said to have been named Lillie Wright   her
                               Jennie x Thompson
                               mark

Applications for Enrollment of Seminole Newborn Freedmen
Act of 1905

Witnesses To Mark:
{ Chas E Webster
{ Frank C. Sabourin

Subscribed and sworn to before me   18   day of   May   , 1905.

Chas E Webster
Notary Public.

Sem NB FR 89
BIRTH AFFIDAVIT.

DEPARTMENT OF THE INTERIOR.
COMMISSION TO THE FIVE CIVILIZED TRIBES.

IN RE APPLICATION FOR ENROLLMENT, as a citizen of the   Seminole   Nation, of
Gracie Davis   , born on the   last Saturday ~~day~~ of   March   , 1901

Name of Father: Charlie Davis   (F. 2074) a citizen of the   Seminole   Nation.
Name of Mother: Nellie Davis deceased (2701)   a citizen of the   Seminole   Nation.

Postoffice   Wewoka I.T.

Child present

AFFIDAVIT OF MOTHER.

UNITED STATES OF AMERICA, Indian Territory, }
     Western   **DISTRICT.** }

I,   Jane Washington (nee Davis)   , on oath state that I am   45   years of age
and a citizen by   adoption   , of the   Seminole   Nation; ~~that I am~~ that I am the
mother of Nellie Davis, deceased, that she was not the lawful wife of   Charlie Davis
, who is a citizen, by   adoption   of the   Seminole   Nation; that a   female
child was born to ~~me~~ her on   the last   ~~day of~~ Saturday in March , 1901; that said child
has been named   Gracie Davis   , and was living March 4, 1905.

her
Jane [sic] Washington
mark

296

Applications for Enrollment of Seminole Newborn Freedmen
Act of 1905

Witnesses To Mark:
   ⎰ Frank C. Sabourin
   ⎱ Ed. Merrick

    Subscribed and sworn to before me this 4th day of   May   , 1905.

⟨ Seal ⟩   Edward Merrick
                               Notary Public.

AFFIDAVIT OF ATTENDING PHYSICIAN OR MID-WIFE.

UNITED STATES OF AMERICA, Indian Territory,
    Western   DISTRICT.

                                      am acquainted
    I,   Sallie Davis   , a   , on oath state that I ~~attended on~~
~~Mrs.~~ with Nellie Davis   , ~~wife of~~   and that on the last   on ~~the~~   Saturday in
~~day of~~ March   , 1901; that there was born to her on said date a   female   child;
that said child was living March 4, 1905, and is said to have been named Gracie Davis

                               her
                       Sallie x Davis
Witnesses To Mark: mark
   ⎰ Frank C. Sabourin
   ⎱ Edward Merrick

    Subscribed and sworn to before me this 4th day of   May   , 1905.

⟨ Seal ⟩   Edward Merrick
                               Notary Public.

Applications for Enrollment of Seminole Newborn Freedmen
Act of 1905

Wewoka, Indian Territory, May 19, 1905.

Mary Wallace,
Wynnwood[sic], Indian Territory

Madam:

On May 10, 1905, your mother, Tena Smith, appeared before this office and made application for the enrollment of your two minor children, Azaline and Florence Wallace, as citizens of the Seminole Nation.

There are inclosed herewith blanks which it will be necessary for you to have filled out and properly executed by yourself and the attending physician or midwife before a Notary Public, returning same to this office in the enclosed envelope, which requires no postage.

Respectfully,

Clerk in Charge.

Env.

Sem.Fr.N.B.90.

Muskogee, Indian Territory June 30, 1905.

Mary Wallace,
Wynnewood, Indian Territory.

Dear Madam:

On May 10, 1905, your mother, Tena Smith, appeared before the Commission and made application for the enrollment of your two minor children, Azaline Wallace and Florence Wallace as Seminole Freedmen. At that time her affidavits were taken as to the birth of said children and it appears therefrom that Azaline Wallace was born February 15, 1902. Subsequently you filed with the Commission your affidavit and the affidavit of Rena Kemp, from which it appears that said child was born February 1, 1902.

For the purpose of correcting this discrepancy as to the date of the birth of said child there is enclosed herewith a blank for proof of birth. In having the same executed be careful to see that all blanks are properly filled, all names written in full and that the Notary Public before whom the affidavits are acknowledged attaches his name and seal to each affidavit. Be careful to give the correct date of birth of this child in these affidavits. Inc case any signature is by mark it must be attested by two disinterested persons, witnesses thereto.

In the matter of the enrollment of your daughter, Florence Wallace, you filed with the Commission your affidavit and the affidavit of Malenia Kemp. Said application is

298

Applications for Enrollment of Seminole Newborn Freedmen
Act of 1905

enclosed herewith and you are requested to take the same before E. N. Nesbitt and have him affix his seal to the affidavit of the attending midwife.

Respectfully,

Chairman.

DeB--10/29.
B.C.
Env.

Muskogee, Indian Territory, October 28, 1905.

Mary Wallace,
Wynnewood, Indian Territory.

Dear Madam:

There is returned to you herewith the affidavits of yourself and Rena Kemp, in the matter of the application for the enrollment of application for the enrollment of Azaline Wallace as a New Born Seminole Freedman.

You will note that there is a discrepancy between the two affidavits, in the matter of the application for the enrollment of date of the birth of said Azaline Wallace.

There is inclosed herewith a blank form of birth affidavit which have filled out and executed before a Notary Public, and return to this office as soon as possible.

Respectfully,

LM 1/28

Commissioner.

S.N.B.F.90

Muskogee, Indian Territory, December 6, 1905.

Mary Wallace,
Wynnewood, Indian Territory.

Dear Madam:

It appears from the records of this office that on June 30, 1905, the affidavits of yourself and Malenia Kemp as to the birth of your minor child, Florence Wallace, were returned to you with the request that you have one E. N. Nesbitt, before whom said affidavits were executed, affix his notarial seal thereto. It does not appear that these affidavits have been returned by you.

Applications for Enrollment of Seminole Newborn Freedmen
Act of 1905

You are advised that before any action can be taken relative to the enrollment of your said minor child as a citizen of the Seminole Nation, it will be necessary that you return to this office the above mentioned affidavits.

This matter should receive your very earliest attention.

Respectfully,

Acting Commissioner.

Sem. N B F 90

Muskogee, Indian Territory, December 29, 1905.

McKennon & Willmott,
　　　Attorneys for the Seminoles,
　　　　　Wewoka, Indian Territory.

Gentlemen:

May 10, 1905, Tena Smith made application to the Commission to the Five Civilized Tribes at Wewoka, Indian Territory, for the enrollment of her grandchild, Florence Wallace as a new born Seminole freedman under the provisions of the act of Congress approved March 3, 1905.

It appears from the statement of Tena Smith that the child Florence Wallace was born March 15, 1904 and is the daughter of Thomas Wallace, a noncitizen negro, and Mary Wallace, whose name appears upon the roll of citizens of the Seminole Nation as Mary Smith, opposite Number 2745.

This office has, on several occasions, endeavored to secure from Mary Wallace, the mother of Florence Wallace, her affidavit as to the birth of her child, and also the affidavit of the attending physician or midwife at the birth of said child. It is desired, if practicable, that you secure this evidence and transmit the same to this office at the earliest practicable date in order that disposition may be made of this pending application.

Respectfully,

B C

Commissioner.

300

Applications for Enrollment of Seminole Newborn Freedmen
Act of 1905

Sem. F. R-NB-90

Muskogee, Indian Territory, July 21, 1906.

W. C. Frost,
    Wynnewood, Indian Territory.

Dear Sir:-

Receipt is hereby acknowledged of your letter of July 12, 1906, transmitting affidavit of Joe Simmons to the death of Florence Wallace, child of Tom and Mary Wallace, June 30, 1905, and the same has been filed with the record in the matter of the application for the enrollment of application of Florence Wallace for enrollment as a new born Seminole freedman under the Act of Congress approved March 3, 1905.

Respectfully,

Commissioner.

Sem NB 90

Muskogee, Indian Territory, November 9, 1906.

Mary Wallace,
    Wynnewood, Indian Territory.

Dear Madam:

Receipt is hereby acknowledged of your letter of October 29, 1906, relative to the enrollment of your children Florence and Azaline Wallace as Seminole freedmen.

In reply to your letter you are advised that the affidavits to the birth of Florence and Azaline Wallace, children of Tom and Mary Wallace, have been received at this office, but their names have not yet been placed upon a schedule of Seminole freedmen prepared for forwarding to the Secretary of the Interior. In event further evidence is necessary to enable this office to determine their right to enrollment you will be duly advised.

Respectfully,

Commissioner.

301

Applications for Enrollment of Seminole Newborn Freedmen
Act of 1905

Sem NB FR 90
BIRTH AFFIDAVIT.

DEPARTMENT OF THE INTERIOR.
COMMISSION TO THE FIVE CIVILIZED TRIBES.

IN RE APPLICATION FOR ENROLLMENT, as a citizen of the   Seminole   Nation, of
Azaline Wallace   , born on the 14 day of   February , 1902

Name of Father: Tom Wallace   a citizen of the   U. S.   Nation.
Name of Mother: Mary Wallace (Smith) 2745 a citizen of the   Seminole   Nation.

Postoffice   Wynnewood, I.T.

AFFIDAVIT OF MOTHER.

UNITED STATES OF AMERICA, Indian Territory, ⎱
     Western   **DISTRICT.** ⎰

    I,   Mary Wallace   , on oath state that I am   21   years of age and a citizen
by   , of the   Seminole   Nation; that I am the lawful wife of   Tom Wallace ,
who is a citizen, by   of the   U. S.   Nation; that a   female   child was
born to me on   14th   day of   February   , 1902; that said child has been named
Azaline Wallace   , and was living March 4, 1905.

Mary Wallace

Witnesses To Mark:
{

    Subscribed and sworn to before me this 29   day of   May   , 1906.

Edward Merrick
Notary Public.

Sem NB FR 90
BIRTH AFFIDAVIT.

DEPARTMENT OF THE INTERIOR.
COMMISSION TO THE FIVE CIVILIZED TRIBES.

IN RE APPLICATION FOR ENROLLMENT, as a citizen of the   Seminole   Nation, of
Florence Wallace   , born on the   15   day of   March , 1904

Name of Father: Tom Wallace   a citizen of the United States Nation.
Name of Mother: Mary Wallace   a citizen of the   Seminole   Nation.

Applications for Enrollment of Seminole Newborn Freedmen
Act of 1905

Postoffice   Wynnewood IT

AFFIDAVIT OF MOTHER.

UNITED STATES OF AMERICA, Indian Territory,
   Southern (17)   DISTRICT.

I,   Mary Wallace   , on oath state that I am   22   years of age and a citizen by   Blood   , of the   Seminole   Nation; that I am the lawful wife of   Tom Wallace   , ~~who is a citizen, by~~   of the   ~~Nation~~; that a   female child was born to me on   15   day of   March   , 1904; that said child has been named Florence Wallace   , and was living March 4, 1905.

                                          Mary Wallace

Witnesses To Mark:
   { WH Frost
     W.J. Courtney

    Subscribed and sworn to before me this 18 day of   June   , 1906.

                        W C Frost
                           Notary Public.

AFFIDAVIT OF ATTENDING PHYSICIAN OR MID-WIFE.

UNITED STATES OF AMERICA, Indian Territory,
    Southern   DISTRICT.

                                     we are acquainted with
   We,   Melinia and Rena Kemp   , a   , on oath state that ~~I attended on~~ Mrs.   Mary Wallace   , wife of   Tom Wallace   on the   15 day of   March   , 1904; that there was born to her on said date a   female   child; that said child was living March 4, 1905, and is said to have been named   Florence Wallace

                              her
                        Melina x Kemp
                        mark
Witnesses To Mark: Rena Kemp
   { Mrs M.E. Burton
     Miss Rose Burton

    Subscribed and sworn to before me this 18 day of   June   , 1906.

                        W C Frost
                         Notary Public.

Applications for Enrollment of Seminole Newborn Freedmen
Act of 1905

Sem NB FR 90
BIRTH AFFIDAVIT.

DEPARTMENT OF THE INTERIOR.
COMMISSION TO THE FIVE CIVILIZED TRIBES.

IN RE APPLICATION FOR ENROLLMENT, as a citizen of the   Seminole   Nation, of
Florence Wallace   , born on the   15   day of   March   , 1904

Name of Father: Tom Wallace   a citizen of the   U.S.   Nation.
                           2745
Name of Mother: Mary Wallace (nee Smith)   a citizen of the   Seminole   Nation.

           Postoffice   Wynnewood, I.T.

Child home with sick mother

AFFIDAVIT OF MOTHER.

UNITED STATES OF AMERICA, Indian Territory,
      Western   **DISTRICT.**

     I,   Tena Smith   , on oath state that I am   56   years of age and a citizen by
adoption   , of the   Seminole   Nation; that I am the ~~lawful wife~~ mother of   Mary
Wallace (nee Smith)   , who is a citizen, by   adoption   of the   Seminole
Nation; that a   female   child was born to me on   15   day of   March   , 1904;
that said child has been named   Florence Wallace   , and was living March 4, 1905.

                          her
                 Tena x Smith
Witnesses To Mark: mark
     Frank C. Sabourin
     Chas E Webster

     Subscribed and sworn to before me this   10   day of   May   , 1905.

                         Chas E Webster
                         Notary Public.

Applications for Enrollment of Seminole Newborn Freedmen
Act of 1905

DEPARTMENT OF THE INTERIOR.
COMMISSION TO THE FIVE CIVILIZED TRIBES.

In the matter of the death of   Florence Wallace   a citizen of the Seminole   Nation, who formerly resided at or near   Wynnewood   , Ind. Ter., and died on the   30   day of   June , 1905

AFFIDAVIT OF RELATIVE.

UNITED STATES OF AMERICA, Indian Territory, ⎫
Southern (17)   DISTRICT. ⎰

I,   William Harper , on oath state that I am   22   years of age and a citizen by Blood , of the Seminole   Nation; that my postoffice address is   Wynnewood   , Ind. Ter.; that I am   first cousin   of   Florence Wallace   who was a citizen, by Blood, of the Seminole   Nation and that said   Florence Wallace   died on the   30   day of   June   , 1905

his
William x Harper
mark

Witnesses To Mark:
 { Jeff Melton
  Joe Simmons

Subscribed and sworn to before me this   18   day of   June   , 1906.

W C Frost
Notary Public.

AFFIDAVIT OF ACQUAINTANCE.

UNITED STATES OF AMERICA, Indian Territory, ⎫
Southern (17)   DISTRICT. ⎰

WE,   Joe Simmons   , on oath state that I am   22   years of age, and a citizen by Blood   of the Seminole   Nation; that my postoffice address is   Wynnewood , Ind. Ter.; that I was personally acquainted with   Florence Wallace   who was a citizen, by Blood   , of the   Seminole   Nation; and that said   Florence Wallace   died on the   30   day of   June   , 1905

Joe Simmons

Witnesses To Mark:
 { Jeff Melton
  Sophie Cates

305

Applications for Enrollment of Seminole Newborn Freedmen
Act of 1905

Subscribed and sworn to before me this   18   day of   June   , 1906.

W C Frost
Notary Public.

Application No. 251
BIRTH AFFIDAVIT.

DEPARTMENT OF THE INTERIOR.
COMMISSION TO THE FIVE CIVILIZED TRIBES.

Seminole

IN RE APPLICATION FOR ENROLLMENT, as a citizen of the   ~~Chickasaw~~   Nation,
of   Azaline Wallace   , born on the   15[sic]   day of   Feb   , 1902

Name of Father: Tom Wallace   a citizen of the   Nation.
Name of Mother: Mary Wallace   a citizen of the   Seminole   Nation.

Postoffice   Wynnewood, I.T.

AFFIDAVIT OF MOTHER.

UNITED STATES OF AMERICA, Indian Territory,
    Southern   **DISTRICT.**
         Mary Wallace
    I,   ~~Rena Kemp~~   , on oath state that I am   21   years of age and a citizen by
Blood   , of the   ~~Chickasaw~~ Seminole   Nation; that I am the lawful wife of
Tom Wallace , who is a citizen, by Blood[sic]   of the   Seminole[sic]   Nation;
that a   Female   child was born to me on 1   day of   Feby   , 1902; that said
child has been named   Azaline Wallace   , and was living March 4, 1905.

Mary Wallace

Witnesses To Mark:
    ⎰ Tena Smith
    ⎱ Mallinia Kemp

Subscribed and sworn to before me this 23   day of   May   , 1905.

E N Nesbitt
Notary Public.

306

Applications for Enrollment of Seminole Newborn Freedmen
Act of 1905

UNITED STATES OF AMERICA, Indian Territory,
   Southern   DISTRICT.

I, Rena Kemp   , a   , on oath state that I attended on Mrs. Mary Wallace , wife of Thos Wallace   on the 1 day of   Feby , 1902; that there was born to her on said date a   Female   child; that said child was living March 4, 1905, and is said to have been named Azaline Wallace

her

Rena x Kemp

Witnesses To Mark: mark
     W A Frost
     W C Frost

Subscribed and sworn to before me 23 day of   May   , 1905.

N E Nesbitt

Notary Public.

Sem NB FR 90
BIRTH AFFIDAVIT.

DEPARTMENT OF THE INTERIOR.
COMMISSION TO THE FIVE CIVILIZED TRIBES.

IN RE APPLICATION FOR ENROLLMENT, as a citizen of the   Seminole   Nation, of Azaline Wallace   , born on the 15 day of February , 1902

Name of Father: Tom Wallace   a citizen of the   U. S.   Nation.
2745
Name of Mother: Mary Wallace (nee Smith)   a citizen of the Seminole   Nation.

Postoffice   Wynnewood IT

Child at home with sick mother

grand

AFFIDAVIT OF ^ MOTHER.

UNITED STATES OF AMERICA, Indian Territory,
   Western   DISTRICT.

I, Tena Smith   , on oath state that I am 56   years of age and a citizen by adoption   , of the   Seminole   Nation; that I am the ~~lawful wife~~ mother of   Mary Wallace (nee Smith)   , who is a citizen, by adoption   of the   Seminole Nation; that a   female   child was born to me on 15 day of February   , 1902; that said child has been named Azaline Wallace   , and was living March 4, 1905.

307

Applications for Enrollment of Seminole Newborn Freedmen
Act of 1905

her

Tena x Smith

mark

Witnesses To Mark:
   ⎰ Frank C. Sabourin
   ⎱ Chas E Webster

Subscribed and sworn to before me this   10   day of   May   , 1905.

Chas E Webster
        Notary Public.

DEPARTMENT OF THE INTERIOR.
COMMISSION TO THE FIVE CIVILIZED TRIBES.

In the matter of the death of   Florence Wallace   a citizen of the Seminole   Nation, who formerly resided at or near   Wynnewood   , Ind. Ter., and died on the   30"   day of   June   , 1905

AFFIDAVIT OF RELATIVE.

UNITED STATES OF AMERICA, Indian Territory,
     Western   **DISTRICT.**

I,   Mary Wallace   , on oath state that I am   21   years of age and a citizen by   , of the Seminole   Nation; that my postoffice address is   Wynnewood   , Ind. Ter.; that I am   mother   of   Florence Wallace   who was a citizen, by   , of the Seminole   Nation and that said   Florence Wallace   died on the   30   day of   June   , 1905

Mary Wallace

Witnesses To Mark:

Subscribed and sworn to before me this   29"   day of   May   , 1906.

Edward Merrick
        Notary Public.

308

Applications for Enrollment of Seminole Newborn Freedmen
Act of 1905

Sem NB FR 90
BIRTH AFFIDAVIT.

DEPARTMENT OF THE INTERIOR.
COMMISSION TO THE FIVE CIVILIZED TRIBES.

IN RE APPLICATION FOR ENROLLMENT, as a citizen of the   Seminole   Nation, of
Azaline Wallace   , born on the 14   day of Feb   , 1902

Name of Father: Tom Wallace   a citizen of the UnitedSates[sic]Nation.
Name of Mother: Mary Wallace   a citizen of the   Seminole   Nation.

Postoffice   Wynnewood

AFFIDAVIT OF MOTHER.

UNITED STATES OF AMERICA, Indian Territory,
      Southern (17)   DISTRICT.

   I,   Mary Wallace   , on oath state that I am   22   years of age and a citizen
by   Blood , of the   Seminole   Nation; that I am the lawful wife of Tom Wallace ,
who is a United States citizen, by   of the   Nation; that a   female
child was born to me on   14   day of   Feb   , 1902; that said child has been named
Azaline Wallace   , and was living March 4, 1905.

                                                  Mary Wallace

Witnesses To Mark:
   Jeff Melton
   Joe Simmons

   Subscribed and sworn to before me this 18   day of   June   , 1906.

                                        W. C. Frost
                                             Notary Public.

AFFIDAVIT OF ATTENDING PHYSICIAN OR MID-WIFE.

UNITED STATES OF AMERICA, Indian Territory,
      Southern (17)   DISTRICT.

                                        we are acquainted with
      We,   and, a   , on oath state that I attended on
Mrs.   Mary Wallace   , wife of   Tom Wallace   that   on the 14 day of Feb.   ,
1902; that there was born to her on said date a   female   child; that said child was
living March 4, 1905, and is said to have been named   Azaline Wallace

Applications for Enrollment of Seminole Newborn Freedmen
Act of 1905

(Signature whited out)
her

Witnesses To Mark: Rena x Kemp
    ⌠ Mrs. M.E. Burton   mark
    ⌡ Miss Rose Burton

Subscribed and sworn to before me 18   day of   June   , 1906.

W C Frost
Notary Public.

Sem NB FR 90
BIRTH AFFIDAVIT.

DEPARTMENT OF THE INTERIOR.
COMMISSION TO THE FIVE CIVILIZED TRIBES.

IN RE APPLICATION FOR ENROLLMENT, as a citizen of the Seminole (Freedman)
Nation, of   Azaline Wallace   , born on the 14   day of Feby , 1902

Name of Father: Tom Wallace   a citizen of the United States Nation.
Name of Mother: Mary Wallace   a citizen of the   Seminole   Nation.

Postoffice   Wynnewood Ind. Terry

AFFIDAVIT OF MOTHER.

UNITED STATES OF AMERICA, Indian Territory, ⎫
      Southern   **DISTRICT.** ⎬

    I,   Mary Wallace   , on oath state that I am   21   years of age and a citizen
by   being a freedman , of the   Seminole   Nation; that I am the lawful wife of
Tom Wallace , who is a citizen, by   of the   United States   ~~Nation~~; that a
Female   child was born to me on   14   day of   Feby   , 1902; that said child has
been named   Azaline Wallace   , and was living March 4, 1905.

Mary Wallace

Witnesses To Mark:
  ⌠

Subscribed and sworn to before me this 1ˢᵗ day of   December   , 1905.

R.M. Jarratt
Notary Public.
Southern District Ind Terry

310

Applications for Enrollment of Seminole Newborn Freedmen
Act of 1905

UNITED STATES OF AMERICA, Indian Territory,
Southern   DISTRICT.

I,   Rena Kemp   , a   mid wife   , on oath state that I attended on
Mrs.   Mary Wallace   , wife of   Tom Wallace   on the 14 day of Feby   ,
1902; that there was born to her on said date a   female   child; that said child was
living March 4, 1905, and is said to have been named Azaline Wallace

                                                    her
                                          Rena x Kemp
Witnesses To Mark: mark
  { R M Jarratt
  { John Reider

Subscribed and sworn to before me this 1ˢᵗ day of   December   , 1905.

                              R.M. Jarratt
                                    Notary Public.
                              Southern District I T

Sem NB FR 90
BIRTH AFFIDAVIT.

DEPARTMENT OF THE INTERIOR.
COMMISSION TO THE FIVE CIVILIZED TRIBES.

IN RE APPLICATION FOR ENROLLMENT, as a citizen of the   Seminole   Nation, of
Florence Wallace   , born on the 15 day of March , 1904

Name of Father: Tom Wallace   a citizen of the   U. S.   Nation.
Name of Mother: Mary Wallace (Smith) 2745 a citizen of the   Seminole   Nation.

                    Postoffice   Wynnewood, I.T.

UNITED STATES OF AMERICA, Indian Territory,
Western   DISTRICT.

I,   Mary Wallace   , on oath state that I am   21   years of age and a citizen
by   , of the   Seminole   Nation; that I am the lawful wife of   Tom Wallace ,
who is a citizen, by   of the   Seminole   Nation; that a   female   child was

311

Applications for Enrollment of Seminole Newborn Freedmen
Act of 1905

born to me on   15th   day of   March   , 1904; that said child has been named
Florence Wallace   , and was living March 4, 1905.

Mary Wallace

Witnesses To Mark:

{

Subscribed and sworn to before me this 29" day of   May   , 1906.

Edward Merrick
Notary Public.

Sem NB FR 91
BIRTH AFFIDAVIT.

DEPARTMENT OF THE INTERIOR.
COMMISSION TO THE FIVE CIVILIZED TRIBES.

Copy

IN RE APPLICATION FOR ENROLLMENT, as a citizen of the   Seminole   Nation, of
Josephine Cudjoe   , born on the   day of   , 1

Name of Father: Stephenson Cudjoe   (1998) a citizen of the   Nation.
(nee Stewart)
Name of Mother: Lousanna Cudjoe   (2136)   a citizen of the   Seminole   Nation.

Postoffice   Tidmore I.T.

Child present

AFFIDAVIT OF MOTHER.

UNITED STATES OF AMERICA, Indian Territory, ⎫
Western   DISTRICT. ⎭

I,   Lousanna Cudjoe (nee Stewart)   , on oath state that I am   21   years of
age and a citizen by   adoption   , of the   Seminole   Nation; that I am the lawful
wife of   Stephenson Cudjoe   , who is a citizen, by   adoption   of the
Seminole   Nation; that a   female   child was born to me on   20   day of

312

Applications for Enrollment of Seminole Newborn Freedmen
Act of 1905

March   , 1905; that said child has been named   Josephine Cudjoe   , and ~~was living March 4, 1905~~. is now living

                              (signed) Lousanna Cudjoe

Witnesses To Mark:

{

        Subscribed and sworn to before me this 12 day of   May   , 1905.

(Seal)   (signed) Chas E Webster
                                        Notary Public.

_____

AFFIDAVIT OF ATTENDING PHYSICIAN OR MID-WIFE.

No Good

UNITED STATES OF AMERICA, Indian Territory,
.... **DISTRICT.**

        I, ..., a ...., on oath state that I attended on
Mrs. ...., wife of .... on the .... day of ...., 1......; that there
was born to her on said date a .... child; that said child was living March 4, 1905,
and is said to have been named ....

                              ....

Witnesses To Mark:

{ ....
   ....

        Subscribed and sworn to before me this .... day of ...., 1.......

                              ....
                                        Notary Public.

_____

                                                          EM

S.F.N.B.91.

DEPARTMENT OF THE INTERIOR,
COMMISSIONER TO THE FIVE CIVILIZED TRIBES.

        In the matter of the application for the enrollment of Josephine Cudjoe as a
Seminole citizen.

- D E C I S I O N -

        It appears from the record in this case that on May 12, 1905, there was filed with
the Commission to the Five Civilized Tribes an application for the enrollment of
Josephine Cudjoe as a Seminole citizen.

Applications for Enrollment of Seminole Newborn Freedmen
Act of 1905

It further appears from the record herein, and from the records of the Commission to the Five Civilized Tribes, that the applicant was born on March 20, 1905, and is a daughter of Stephenson Cudjoe, a recognized and enrolled citizen of the Seminole Nation, whose name appears as No. 1998 upon the final roll of Seminole citizens approved by the Secretary of the Interior April 2, 1901, and Lousanna Cudjoe, a recognized and enrolled citizen of the Seminole Nation, whose name (as Lousanna Stewart) appears as No. 2136 upon the final roll of Seminole citizens approved by the Secretary of the Interior, April 2, 1901.

The act of Congress approved March 3, 1905 (33 Stat., 1060), provides:

"That the Commission to the Five Civilized Tribes is authorized for ninety days after the date of the approval of this act to receive and consider applications for enrollment of infant children born prior to March fourth, nineteen hundred and five, and living on said latter date, to citizens of the Seminole tribe whose enrollment has been approved by the Secretary of the Interior; and to enroll and make allotments to such children, giving to each an equal number of acres of land, and such children shall also share equally with other citizens of the Seminole tribe in the distribution of all other tribal property and funds."

I am of the opinion that, inasmuch as Josephine Cudjoe was not born prior to March 4, 1905, I am without authority to receive or consider the application for her enrollment as a Seminole citizen, and that, therefore, I should decline to receive or consider the same, and it is so ordered.

Tams Bixby Commissioner.

Muskogee, Indian Territory.
JUL 28 1906

S.F.N.B.91

Muskogee, Indian Territory, July 28, 1906.

Lousanna Cudjoe,
    Tidmore, Indian Territory.   **COPY**

Dear Madam:

Inclosed herewith you will find a copy of the decision of the Commissioner to the Five Civilized Tribes, rendered July 28, 1906, declining to receive or consider the application for the enrollment of your child, Josephine Cudjoe as a Seminole citizen.

The decision, with the record of proceedings in the case is this day transmitted to the Secretary of the Interior for review. The final decision of the Secretary will be made known to you as soon as this office is informed of the same.

Respectfully,

SIGNED Tams Bixby
Commissioner.

Applications for Enrollment of Seminole Newborn Freedmen
Act of 1905

Registered.
Incl. S.F.N.B.-91

S.F.N.B.-91

Muskogee, Indian Territory, July 28, 1906.

McKennon & Wilmot[sic],
      Attorneys for Seminole Nation,
            Wewoka, Indian Territory.   **COPY**

Gentlemen:

    Inclosed herewith you will find a copy of the decision of the Commissioner to the Five Civilized Tribes, rendered July 28, 1906, declining to receive or consider the application for the enrollment of Josephine Cudjoe as a Seminole citizen.

    The decision, with the record of proceedings in the case, is this day transmitted to the Secretary of the Interior for review. The final decision of the Secretary will be made known to you as soon as this office is informed of the same.

                Respectfully,

                        SIGNED   *Tams Bixby*
                                  Commissioner.
Incl. S.F.N.B.-91.

Muskogee, Indian Territory, July 28, 1906.
                                COPY

The Honorable,
      The Secretary of the Interior.

Sir:
    There is herewith transmitted the record of proceedings in the matter of the application for the enrollment of Josephine Cudjoe as a Seminole citizen, including the decision of the Commissioner to the Five Civilized Tribes, dated July 28, 1906, declining to receive or consider said application.
                  Respectfully,
                    SIGNED   *Tams Bixby*
                          Commissioner.
2 Incl. S.F.N.B.-91

Through the
      Commissioner of Indian Affairs.

Applications for Enrollment of Seminole Newborn Freedmen
Act of 1905

JF

D.C. 32113
I.T.D. 23366-1906.

LRS

DEPARTMENT OF THE INTERIOR, LLB
WASHINGTON,   November 26, 1906.

Commissioner to the Five Civilized Tribes,
     Muskogee, Indian Territory.

Sir:

     July 28, 1906, you transmitted the record in the matter of the application for the enrollment of Josephine Cudjoe as a Sominole[sic] citizen, including your decision of the same date, declining to receive or consider said application.

     Reporting November 21, 1906 (Land 65698), the Indian Office recommended that your decision be approved. A copy of its letter is inclosed.

     The Department concurs in said recommendation, and your decision is hereby affirmed.

     The papers in the matter have been sent to the Indian Office for its files.

Respectfully,

Thos. Ryan,

First Assistant Secretary.

Through the Commissioner
     of Indian Affairs.

1 incl. and 2 to Ind. Of.

Applications for Enrollment of Seminole Newborn Freedmen
Act of 1905

Land.
65698-1906.   DEPARTMENT OF THE INTERIOR,
                                OFFICE OF INDIAN AFFAIRS,
                                WASHINGTON.   November 21, 1906.

The Honorable,
     The Secretary of the Interior.

Sir:

     There is enclosed herewith, for departmental consideration, report of Commissioner Bixby, dated July 28, 1906, together with the record in the matter of the application of Josephine Cudjoe, for enrollment as a citizen of the Seminole Nation.

     It appears from the record that the applicant is a daughter of Stephenson Cudjoe, a recognized and enrolled citizen of the Seminole Nation, whose name appears as No. 1998 on the final roll of Seminole citizens approved by the Department, April 2, 1901, and Louisa Cudjoe, a recognized and enrolled Seminole citizen whose name appears as No. 2136 on the final roll above mentioned, and that the applicant was born on March 20, 1905.

     On this state of the record this Office recommends the approval of Commissioner Bixby's report denying the application for the reason that there is no authority in law, under the Act of Congress approved March 3, 1905, (32 Stats., L., 1071) for her enrollment, it being shown that she was born after March 4, 1905.

                              Very respectfully,

                                   C. F. Larrabee,

A.J.W.- NL   Acting Commissioner.

                         _____

S.F.N.B.91

                    Muskogee, Indian Territory, December 10, 1906.

Lousanna Cudjoe,
     Tidmore, Indian Territory.

Dear Madam:

     You are hereby advised that on November 26, 1906, the Secretary of the Interior affirmed the decision of this office of July 28, 1906, declining to receive or consider the application for the enrollment of your child, Josephine Cudjoe as a Seminole citizen.

                         Respectfully,

                              Commissioner.

317

Applications for Enrollment of Seminole Newborn Freedmen
Act of 1905

S.F.N.B. 91

Muskogee, Indian Territory, December 10, 1906.

McKennon & Wilmot[sic],
     Attorneys for Seminole Nation,
         Wewoka, Indian Territory.

Gentlemen:

     You are hereby advised that on November 26, 1906, the Secretary of the Interior affirmed the decision of this office of July 28, 1906, declining to receive or consider the application for the enrollment of Josephine Cudjoe as a Seminole citizen.

               Respectfully,

                    Commissioner.

United States of America, Indian Territory)
      Western Judicial District   )

     Affiant Hazen Dosar, being of lawful age and first duly sworn, on his oath deposes and says: I am a freedman citizen of the Seminole Nation, above the age of twenty-one years, my wife's name is Viola Dosar; there was born to me and my wife, on the 16th day of September, A.D., 1902, a female child, which has been named Dollie Dosar; that said child is still living; that the reason why no application was made for the enrollment of said child while the land office was located at Wewoka, I. T., for the enrollment of new born Seminole children, is that the mother of said child was dangerously ill, and I was informed that applications could not be made by the father if the mother was living.

                    Hazen Dosar

Subscribed and sworn to before me, this the 28th day of August, A.D., 1905.

                    John W. Willmott
                    Notary Public.

Applications for Enrollment of Seminole Newborn Freedmen
Act of 1905

United States of America, Indian Territory,
    Western Judicial District.

Affiant, Viola Dosar, being of lawful age and first duly sworn, on her oath deposes and says: I am a freedman citizen of the Seminole Nation; my husband's name is Hazen Dosar; there was born to me and my said husband, on the 16th day of September, A.D., 1902, a female child, which we have named Dollie Dosar; that said child is still living; that I was unable to make application before the Dawes Commission for the enrollment of said child as a new born citizen of the Seminole Nation while the office was open at Wewoka, I.T., on account of dangerous illness; and my husband made no application, being under the impression that I alone could make the application.

Viola Dosar

Subscribed and sworn to before me, this the 28th day of August, A.D., 1905.

John W. Willmott
Notary Public.

United States of America, Indian Territory   )
    Western Judicial District   )

Affiant, Dinah Johnson, states on oath, as follows: I am a freedman citizen of the Seminole Nation, above the age of forty-five years; that I well know Hazen Dosar and his wife Viola Dosar, freedmen citizens of the Seminole Nation; that I was present on at their house on the 16th day of September, A.D., 1902, when a female child was born to said Viola and Hazen Dosar; that I acted as mid-wife at the birth of said child; that I am well acquainted with said child, which has been mamed[sic] Dollie Dosar; that said child is still living.   her
Attest   Dinah Johnson x
Jno. W. Willmott   mark

Subscribed and sworn to before me, this the 28th day of August, A.D., 1905.

John W. Willmott
Notary Public.

319

Applications for Enrollment of Seminole Newborn Freedmen
Act of 1905

Sem-Fr-NB-92

DEPARTMENT OF THE INTERIOR,
COMMISSIONER TO THE FIVE CIVILIZED TRIBES.

In the matter of the application for the enrollment of Dollie Dosar as a citizen of the Seminole Nation.

DECISION.

It appears from the record herein that on August 30, 1905, application was made to the Commissioner to the Five Civilized Tribes for the enrollment of Dollie Dosar as a citizen of the Seminole Nation.

It further appears from the record herein that said applicant was born on September 16, 1902, and is the child of Hazen Dosar, whose name appears as number 2026 upon the final roll of citizens of the Seminole Nation approved by the Secretary of the Interior April 2, 1901, and Viola Dosar, who is not identified as a citizen of the Seminole Nation, or an applicant for rights therein; and that said applicant was living on March 4, 1905.

Section One of the Act of Congress approved April 26, 1906 (34 Stats., 137), provides:

"That after the approval of this Act no person shall be enrolled as a citizen or freedman of the Choctaw, Chickasaw, Cherokee, Creek, or Seminole tribes of Indians in the Indian Territory, except as herein otherwise provided, unless application for enrollment was made prior to December first, nineteen hundred and five, and the records in charge of the Commissioner to the Five Civilized Tribes shall be conclusive evidence as to the fact of such application."

I am, therefore, of the opinion that Dollie Dosar should be enrolled as a citizen of the Seminole Nation under the provisions of the Act of Congress approved March 3, 1905 (33 Stats., 1070), and it is so ordered.

Tams Bixby Commissioner.

Muskogee, Indian Territory.
JAN 12 1907

Applications for Enrollment of Seminole Newborn Freedmen
Act of 1905

Sem-Fr-NB-92.   DCL

DEPARTMENT OF THE INTERIOR,
COMMISSIONER TO THE FIVE CIVILIZED TRIBES.

In the matter of the application for the enrollment of Dollie Doser[sic] as a citizen of the Seminole Nation.

ORDER

It appears from the record herein that on January 12, 1907, the Commissioner to the Five Civilized Tribes rendered his decision enrolling Dollie Dosar as a citizen of the Seminole Nation under the provisions of the Act of Congress approved March 3, 1905 (33 Stats., 1070).

It further appears from the record herein and from the records of this office that said Dollie Dosar is the child of Hazen Dosar, whose name appears upon the final roll of citizens of the Seminole Nation approved by the Secretary of the Interior as Hazen Doser.

Inasmuch as the surname of the mother of Dollie Dosar appears upon the final roll as Doser, it is hereby ordered that the name of the applicant shall be placed upon the final roll of citizens of the Seminole Nation as Dollie Doser to conform to the name of her mother and that the decision of January 12, 1907, be, and the same is hereby amended to conform herewith.

Tams Bixby Commissioner.

Muskogee, Indian Territory.
February 26, 1907.

Sem. Freed.
NB-92.

Muskogee, Indian Territory, August 31, 1905.

McKennon & Willmott,
Attorneys at Law,
Wewoka, Indian Territory.

Gentlemen:

Receipt is hereby acknowledged of your letter of August 29, 1905, inclosing an application for the enrollment of Dollie Dosar, born September 16, 1902, daughter of Hazen Dosar and Viola Dosar, as a Seminole freedman and requesting to be advised as to whether application has been made for the enrollment of said child as a citizen of the Seminole Nation. whether there is any way by which this child may yet be enrolled and permitted to share in the division of the surplus lands of the Seminoles.

It does not appear from the records of this office that there was ever filed with the Commission to the Five Civilized Tribes, within the time prescribed by the Act of

321

Applications for Enrollment of Seminole Newborn Freedmen
Act of 1905

Congress approved March 3, 1905 (Public No. 212), any application for the enrollment of said child as a Seminole freedman.

You are advised that this office is now without authority to receive or consider original applications for enrollment as citizens of the Seminole Nation.

Respectfully,

Commissioner.

Sem-Fr-NB-92

Muskogee, Indian Territory, January 12, 1907.

Wilmott[sic] & Wilhoit,
      Wewoka, Indian Territory.

Dear Sir:

You are hereby notified that the Commissioner to the Five Civilized Tribes, on January 12, 1907, rendered his decision granting the application for the enrollment of Dollie Dosar as a citizen of the Seminole Nation.

The name of Dollie Dosar will not be placed upon the next schedule of citizens of the Seminole Nation to be prepared for forwarding to the Secretary of the Interior for his approval.

Respectfully,

Registered.   Commissioner.
Incl. Sem-Fr-NB-92.

Applications for Enrollment of Seminole Newborn Freedmen
Act of 1905

Sem Fr. NB 92

Muskogee, Indian Territory, January 12, 1907.

Hazen Dosar,
   Mekusukey, Indian Territory.

Dear Madam:

Inclosed herewith you will find a copy of the decision of the Commissioner to the Five Civilized Tribes, rendered January 12, 1907, granting the application for the enrollment of Dollie Dosar, as a citizen of the Seminole Nation.

The name of Dollie Dosar will now be placed upon the next schedule of citizens of the Seminole Nation to be prepared for forwarding the Secretary of the Interior for his approval.

Respectfully,

Registered.   Commissioner.
Incl. Sem. Fr. NB 92